ARGUMENTATION AND CRITICAL THOUGHT

AN INTRODUCTION TO ADVOCACY, REASONING, AND DEBATE

First Edition

By Kevin Kuswa and Cameron Sublett
University of South Carolina and Santa Barbara City College

 cognella® | ACADEMIC PUBLISHING

Bassim Hamadeh, CEO and Publisher
Kassie Graves, Vice President of Acquisitions
Jamie Giganti, Senior Managing Editor
Miguel Macias, Senior Graphic Designer
Marissa Applegate, Senior Field Acquisitions Editor
Gem Rabanera, Project Editor
Elizabeth Rowe, Licensing Coordinator
Chelsey Schmid, Associate Editor

Cover image copyright © Depositphotos/venimo.
Interior image copyright © 2014 Depositphotos/halfpoint.

Printed in the United States of America

ISBN: 978-1-5165-0016-1 (pbk) / 978-1-5165-0017-8 (br)

cognella' | ACADEMIC PUBLISHING

CONTENTS

Chapter 4: Proving Your Claims: Conducting Research in the Digital Age **69**

Chapter 5: Case Construction and Flowing **85**

Chapter 6: Argumentation and the Self **127**

Chapter 7: Argumentation, Race, and Identity   155

Chapter 8: Argumentation, Social Movements, and the Public Sphere   169

This textbook covers the theory, background, practice, and judgment of argumentation by position-ing it within Communication Studies, Rhetoric, and academic debate. By clearly explaining the key concepts of argumentation, this book also becomes a guide for critical thinking, debate, and advocacy. In short, this book is a must for any course involving the study or use of argumentation in any way. This is the first textbook to merge theory and practice, fundamentals and critical thinking, and all of the intricacies of argumentation and advocacy. Targeted toward the introductory course in argumentation or critical thinking, this textbook also provides supporting readings for a high school or college-level course in debate, a course centered on advocacy and change in communication, or an advanced argumentation course.

CHAPTER 1

The Nature of Argumentation

Welcome! This textbook on argumentation is designed to offer an accessible yet comprehensive entrance into argumentation and debate. While you may not yet consider yourself an experienced debater, you likely already are. As you will soon see, argumentation is all around. So, to study argumentation and debate is to discover a vibrant set of ideas and practices at the intersection of individuality and community, advocacy and performance, and policy and value. It is not possible to talk about sweeping concepts like the law, social movements, persuasion, government, or even cognition without talking about argumentation. In many ways, argumentation is the fluid or motion between language and communication, a hefty responsibility indeed! So, why wait? Let's begin.

Argumentation is All Around

There is no better place to start than the deep South a few years into the Second Millennium. On June 11, 2008, the Louisiana state legislature passed the Louisiana Science Education Act (LSEA) to promote "students' critical thinking skills" and to "open discussion of scientific theories."[1] More specifically, the law allowed

> teachers, principals, and other school administrators to create and foster an environment within public elementary and secondary schools that promotes critical thinking skills, logical analysis, and open and objective discussion of scientific theories being studied including, but not limited to, evolution, the origins of life, global warming, and human cloning.[2]

The idea, poorly disguised behind the language of "critical inquiry," was to advance the argument that theories of creationism should be taught in the classroom as a way to challenge the mainstream viewpoint defending scientific theories of evolution. In short, the LSEA gave Louisiana teachers permission to use "supplemental materials" such as books and

---

[1] *Louisiana Science Education Act* (2008). Senators Nevers, Crowe, Riser and Thompson, Regular Session, Senate Bill NO. 733, http://ncse.com/files/08_la_sb733-amend.pdf, accessed 11/24/14.

[2] LSEA, ibid. http://ncse.com/files/08_la_sb733-amend.pdf

films to challenge prevailing, scientific theories like evolution discussed in mainstream textbooks. Importantly, though the LSEA was not to be "construed to promote any religious doctrine,"[3] many critics of the law argued that the LSEA would allow teachers in Louisiana to teach creationism and other faith-based alternatives in their science classrooms. An interesting argument, indeed—deploying the rhetoric of "free inquiry" to give religious explanations of the creation of the world a backdoor into the classroom. Arguments operated in multiple ways and directions, however, as the intent of this law was exposed and challenged.

It is not a cut-and-dried argument, however, where the liberal ideal neatly undercuts the more reactionary conservatives. There is a free speech claim to be able to teach unsupported viewpoints, regardless of scientific consensus. Who determines consensus, let alone the assumption that science should always trump alternative viewpoints? Of course, what we want to highlight here is how single-minded actions that close off debate like the LSEA will need to be challenged, and reasoned argumentation provides the best platform for such challenges. The passage of the LSEA was met with instant criticism from many high-profile political figures and proponents of secular science education. Yet, it was a 14-year old student at Baton Rouge Magnet High School who, after writing a paper for his English class on why the LSEA should be repealed, became the face and voice of the opposition to the law. One thing you will realize as you become an expert in argumentation is that not only can one person change the world, one person with a good argument usually does.

In addition to speaking out against the inclusion of religious teachings in science education, Zack Kopplin, with the assistance of his parents, rallied supporters in his hometown and abroad. As a high school senior he created a website, posted his mission statement, and launched a campaign to overturn the LSEA. Since then, he has been featured in *The New York Times, Vogue,* and *The Washington Post* and has appeared on HBO, MSNBC, and NPR. Seventy-Eight Nobel Prize winning scientists have endorsed his campaign and have written on his behalf.[4] There have been several legislative attempts to overturn the LSEA as a direct result of Kopplin's advocacy, and, even though the LSEA is still law in Louisiana, Kopplin has drawn national attention towards the sensitive debate surrounding the intersection of first amendment rights, education, and intellectual freedom. The National Center for Science Education recognized his staunch activism in the name of justice, and called Zach "the new kid who throws himself into the battle for truth, beauty, and the sheer joy of challenging the status quo."[5] Perhaps not as powerful as the

TELESCOPE IN EXHIBITION, 1851.

Figure 1.1 Science Takes Many Shapes Throughout History

---

[3] LSEA, ibid. http://ncse.com/files/08_la_sb733-amend.pdf

[4] "77 Nobel Laureates Call for a Repeal of the LSEA," (April 19, 2011). *Repealing the Louisiana Science Education Act,* http://www.repealcreationism.com/endorsements/, acsd 11/24/14.

[5] National Center for Science Education (2012, March, 5). Master Educator, Young Activist, Honored By NCSE. *National Center for Science Education.* Retrieved from http://ncse.com/evolution/master-educator-young-activist-honored-by-ncse

example of the Buddhist Monk, Thich Quang Duc, who lit himself on fire on June 11, 1963, to protest the oppressive regime of Diem in South Vietnam; perhaps not as dramatic as the Tiananmen Square example where one Chinese citizen blocked an entire military mobilization; perhaps not as widespread as the Mohammed Bouzazi example where a Tunisian fruit vendor helped to spark the Arab Spring and the recent surges between democracy and authoritarianism throughout the Middle East; but the way Zack Kopplin stood up and spoke out against what he perceived to be anti-educational policies shows how important it is to be able to advance an argument and defend a position. We know one person can change the world because one person with a powerful argument can change the world.

From Individual Protests to a Political Party of Protest: Arguments Travel

At the same time Zack Kopplin was advocating for the repeal of the Louisiana Science Education Act, disparate groups of American conservatives and libertarians began coalescing in opposition to a number of federal policies implemented after the economic collapse of 2007–2008. These groups eventually converged to form the Tea Party movement. Members of the Tea Party opposed many of the environmental, social, and economic policies of the Obama administration, and though it was originally a grassroots movement, the Tea Party swelled in both size and influence between 2009 and 2011.

Prominent figures and leaders of the Tea Party included influential media personality Glen Beck, vice presidential nominee Sarah Palin, and numerous house and senate politicians, including Rand Paul. The support of the Tea Party heavily influenced the outcomes of the midterm elections of 2010, which saw the Republican Party regain control of the House of Representatives by taking 63 seats, the largest seat change since 1938. Combined with the six seats gained in the U.S. Senate, after the 2010 elections the Republican Party was able to more powerfully oppose Presidential appointments and Democratic legislation. What really defines the Tea Party is a collection of arguments about government and social welfare or "entitlements." These are essentially arguments about national policy, but they became very compelling rallying points on a local level.

While the issues in Louisiana involving free speech and education are national issues, the protest and the initial argument began with one student. It is a story of the power of argumentation on a micro level. The same time period witnessed that same type of story emerge as an argument on a macro level—a collection of people making similar arguments about the proper role of government in order to influence national or international politics. The origin of the Tea Party movement is found in the immediate aftermath of the inauguration of President Barack Obama in 2009. While adopting this collection of broader and long standing issues such as federalism, anti-welfare, constitutional restraint,[6] the size of the U.S. Federal Government,[7] and the size of the U.S. debt, the political platform and opposition to the President both became central to the Tea Party movement, in that these issues did not propel activists to public demonstration until President

---

[6] Liptak, A. (2010, March 13). Tea-ing up the Constitution. *The New York Times*. Retrieved from http://www.nytimes.com/2010/03/14/weekinreview/14liptak.html

[7] Somashekhar, S. (2010, September 12). Tea Party activists march on Capitol Hill. *Washington Post*. Retrieved from http://www.washingtonpost.com/wp-dyn/content/article/2010/09/12/AR2010091201425.html

Figure 1.2 A Tea Party Demonstration in Hartford, Connecticut

Obama assumed office. The centrality of Barack Obama to the Tea Party movement was corroborated by CBS/New York Times polling,[8] which found that Tea Party supporters were more likely to believe Obama was born outside the United States and only 7% approved of the president's policies at the time of the survey, compared to 50% in the general public.[9]

Because the election of the President spurred the formation of the Tea Party movement and Obama represents the ideology and policy the Tea Party movement protests and wishes to change, the Tea Party is inherently tied to electoral politics and the current political system. Moreover, the Tea Party supporters were generally not new to politics; they were by and large the more extremist base of the Republican Party: "the Tea Party movement is more a rebranding of core Republicanism than a new or distinct entity on the American political scene."[10] Kevin Drum noted that the Tea Party had become synonymous with the conservative core of the Republican Party, but, in the same breath, predicted a short-lived 15 minutes in the sun for the political group because of the echo-effect of many of its media supporters:

> Partly it's a reflection of the long-term rightward shift of the Republican Party. Partly it's a product of the modern media environment: The Birchers were limited to mimeograph machines and PTA meetings to get the word out, while the tea partiers can rely on Fox News and Facebook. Beyond that, though, it's also a reflection of the mainstreaming of extremism.... Unlike the Birchers, or even the Clinton conspiracy theorists, the tea partiers aren't a fringe part of the conservative movement. They are the conservative movement. So where's the good news? Part of it is that the movement's 15 minutes could be nearly up. The tea partiers may have expanded faster than the Birchers thanks to Fox News and talk radio, but the same media echo chamber that enabled this has also shortened attention spans and provided 500 channels of competition for the Glenn Becks of the world. The speed of the tea partiers' rise may foreshadow an equally fast decline as their act begins to grow stale.[11]

---

[8] Berman, R. (2010, July 5). Gallup: Tea Party's top concerns are debt, size of government. *The Hill*. Retrieved from http://thehill.com/blogs/blog-briefing-room/news/107193-gallup-tea-partys-top-concerns-are-debt-size-of-government

[9] Many thanks to Flemming Schneider-Rhode for his assistance with this section as part of a 2013 conference paper on social movements, on file with the authors.

[10] Berman, R. (2010).

[11] Drum, K. (September/October, 2010). Tea Party: Old whine in new bottles. *Mother Jones*. Retrieved from http://www.motherjones.com/politics/2010/08/history-of-the-tea-party?page=3

Figure 1.3 Signs Outside a Tea Party Rally in Wisconsin, 2011

This is when the Tea Party began to define itself as a marker of opposition, a road block for or against the status quo. Despite protestations of Tea Party supporters describing the movement as being a genuine grassroots effort by the people, missing from that description were "the sugar daddies ... bankrolling it."[12] The former House majority leader Richard Armey was particularly active in promoting Tea Party events through the FreedomWorks political organization, along with conservative advocacy groups such as "Americans for Prosperity" and "DontGo."[13] The figures surrounding the movement or operating behind the stage for the Tea Party, as with many groups, are an essential part of the group itself, but ultimately it is the arguments being made by its leaders and its members that define the contours of the organization. Pete Bsumek reminds us that the people and organizations associated with a movement, in addition to "the intellectual currents that inform their actions,"[14] make up a movement's character, strength, and capacity to create change.

Contrasted with Zach Kopplin's individual activism, the Tea Party in many ways represents a collective social movement built around a series of public arguments, including the message that the federal government has become too influential and should not be involved in heavy taxation, forms of welfare, or the provision of social services. The strength of the Tea Party is on the wane, but it represented an important coalition of extremely conservative viewpoints that were able to unite around a few right wing arguments to influence national politics.

You might be asking yourself how Zack Kopplin and the Tea Party relate to the study of argumentation, and you might be thinking that you were expecting to learn about argument, not accounts of local and national politics. Those are natural concerns that we will help to allay shortly, but we want to make three main points through these examples that we hope you will carry through the rest of the text:

1. Examples are important and are one of the best ways to talk about and assess competing arguments. The specifics behind documents like the LSEA or the Tea Party platform are the places where arguments reside and shape our decisions, culture, and society.

[12] Rich, F. (2010, August 28). The billionaires bankrolling the Tea Party. *The New York Times*. Retrieved from http://www.nytimes.com/2010/08/29/opinion/29rich.html

[13] Good, C. (2009, April 13). The Tea Party movement: Who's in charge? *The Atlantic*. Retrieved from http://www.theatlantic.com/politics/archive/2009/04/the-tea-party-movement-whos-in-charge/13041/

[14] Bsumek, P. (2009). Debate as Disease: Debate and the Dialogue and Deliberation Movement. *Contemporary Debate and Argumentation*, v30, http://www.cedadebate.org/files/2009CAD.pdf, pp. 1-30; 3. 3.

2. Perspectives are diverse and can change quickly, making argumentation about the flexibility of articulating a position that matters. You may have a good point to make, but there are always counter-points and then counter-counter-points to those positions. An open mind and a passion for critical thinking are the close companions of argumentation.

3. Think about specific arguments, how they might be addressed, and how they clash with one another. Much of argumentation is listening to what the person on the other side of the question is saying in order to understand the terrain of the overall discourse. From there, the key is to respond to the argument being made and to back up an argument with evidence and sound reasoning. Listen, Clash, Defend.

These three points can be seen on the micro level represented by Zack Kopplin and the macro level represented by the Tea Party. Examples are important, perspectives are diverse, and specific arguments require listening, challenging, and defending. From here, we are poised to enter the theory of argumentation itself.

What is Argumentation?

While the issues were different, the skillset required for Zack Kopplin and members of the Tea Party was the same. Both Zack Kopplin and leaders of the Tea Party needed to establish a position contrary to the status quo, conduct research, build a case, rally support, and, ultimately, advance their arguments through both clear written and verbal communication. At its essence, this is the process of argumentation. **Argumentation is the systematic process of using reasons, evidence, and logic to advance a claim or proposition of fact, value, or policy.** For additional clarity, here is how others have discussed or defined argumentation:

Merriam-Webster
   The act or process of giving reasons for or against something; the act or process of making and presenting arguments.

Dictionary.com
   The process of developing or presenting an argument; reasoning

paraphrasing Plato in The Phaedrus[15]
   Socrates: A person will be unable to handle arguments according to rules of art until acquiring the use of dialectic to discover the truth.

Aristotle in The Rhetoric[16]
   Persuasion is effected through the speech itself when we have provided a truth or an apparent truth by means of persuasive arguments suitable to the case in question.

---

[15] Plato. (1952). The Phaedrus (B. Jowett, Trans.). In *Great Books of the Western World: 7. Plato* (pp. 140–). Chicago: Encyclopedia Britannica. Section 277, "The Judgement upon Lysias," in Thamus and Theuth (*Phaedrus* 274b–278d), http://www.john-uebersax.com/plato/myths/phaedrus.htm.

[16] Aristotle. (1952). The Rhetoric (W. Roberts, Trans.). In *Great Books of the Western World: 9. Aristotle II* (pp. 595–), Chicago: Encyclopedia Britannica. Book I, Part 2, paragraph 3.

Henry Johnstone[17]

> *A philosophical position cannot exist apart from the arguments which support the position .*

Daniel J. O'Keefe[18]

> *Crudely put, an argument₁ is something one person makes (or gives or utters), while an argument₂ is something two or more persons have (or engaged in).*

Wayne Brockreide[19]

> *Arguments are not in statements, they are in people.*

Joseph Wenzel[20]

> *I align the categories of rhetoric, dialectical, and logical with notions of argument as process, procedure, and product.*

Dale Hample[21]

> *If we make the modest change of conceptualizing arguments as being about questions, we will see that arguments originate in uncertainty.*

Appropriately, each of these descriptions acknowledges that arguments and argumentation are all about the ways and means of articulating a position. Argumentation broadly refers to the process of assembling a particular position for or against a proposition. Thus, to generate the clash of competing positions, argumentation also relies on contradictory perspectives—advocates and opponents. Opposition does not require conflict, whether verbal or physical, but it does provide the grounds for argumentation, the clash of competing positions often using reason to advance one claim over the other. Argumentation requires one to build a case, utilize research, synthesize ideas, and communicate persuasively and effectively. The process of argumentation, when done appropriately, is often long and tedious. In many cases, there are issues and debates in

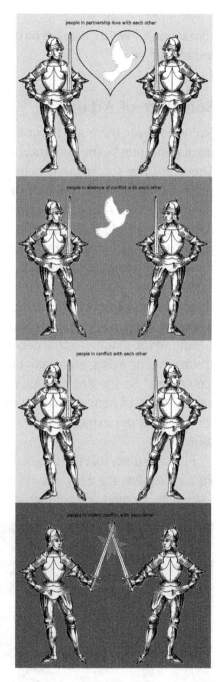

Figure 1.4 People Clash in Many Ways

[17] Johnstone, H. W., Jr. (1959). *Philosophy and Argument.* University Park: the Pennsylvania State University Press.

[18] O'Keefe, D. J. (1977). Two Concepts of Argument. *Journal of the American Forensics Association, 13,* pp. 121–128, p. 121.

[19] Brockreide, W. (1974). Where is Argument? *Journal of the American Forensics Association, 11,* 179–182. Also see Brockriede, W. (1978). Argument as epistemological method. In D. Thomas (Ed.), *Argumentation as a Way of Knowing.* Speech Communication Association.

[20] Wenzel, J.W. (1986). The Rhetorical Perspective on Argument. In F. van Eemeren, R. Grootendorst, J. Blair, & C. Willard (Eds.), *Argumentation: Across the Lines of Discipline. Proceedings of the Conference on Argumentation, 1986* (pp. 101–110). Providence, RI: Foris.

[21] Hample, D. (2010). Argument: Its Origin, Function, and Structure. In Conference Proceedings—National Communication Association/American Forensic Association (Alta Conference on Argumentation)(p. 1–10).

contention for which there are no definitive answers. Patience and commitment are essential in these instances.

Sad State of Affairs

Sadly, however, there are fewer and fewer models of this kind of argumentation in the popular media and press—the very locations where many of us turn for information and deliberation. These are the sources that help us generate the opinions and beliefs that contribute to our personal, professional, and civic decision-making.

Imagine this: An extraterrestrial has left her remote corner of the universe for ours. She discovers a small, blue planet in the Milky Way galaxy. This is our home. This is earth. And we know it well. However, for this life form, it seems very strange. In particular, one species is very unique. They walk on two legs, they cook their food, they cloth their bodies, and, most interestingly, they communicate with one another through abstract sounds and symbols! Importantly, she notices they seem to argue with each other about all sorts of things. This, she thinks to herself, seems like a strange custom—one that is at once combative and cooperative, adversarial and collaborative.

And so the extraterrestrial decides to learn all she can about human argumentation by studying it wherever it exists, especially on the many screens covering the planet called "televisions" or "computers." So she first decides to watch it on television. What better way to discover the ways and customs of humans than by observing them on the box they all seem to worship! But what do you think our extraterrestrial friend would learn about argumentation from watching popular television?

First, it is likely that the extraterrestrial would come across the top-rated TV shows like *the O'Reilly Factor, Crossfire, the Sean Hannity Show, Hardball with Chris Matthews,* and *Countdown with Keith Olbermann.* Second, and not long after, it is likely that she would come to the conclusion that human argumentation mostly involves shouting, cursing, bickering, and petty squabbling absent of research, evidence and, importantly, patience. How sad for our extraterrestrial friend. How sad for us!

The truth is that argumentation on television today is often characterized by strident and hostile communication punctuated by ill-timed commercial breaks. It is a bunch of "talking heads," as the expression goes. The worst part is that the heads are mostly talking *AT* each other as opposed to *WITH* each other. In fact, many times they are speaking *OVER* each other. When a question is asked, the answers are expected to come easily and in dramatic fashion. *Sound bites,* which are short, truncated parts of a larger argument, (often placed in sequence as a

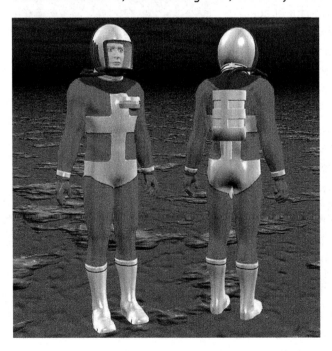

Figure 1.5 Who's the Extraterrestrial?

"ticker" of information) are taken from the shows and replayed—without context—and amplified on the Internet and social media. This can be a good thing when the information is accurate and important for decision-making—let's say in an election. But it is more often than not inaccurate because the "information" is usually incomplete or misrepresented. Exactly how much information can one expect to communicate in a 30-second campaign advertisement, or debate one-liner, or quote taken from an argument and stripped of its context? Exactly how thorough and complete an understanding can we cultivate about an issue from watching a television host scream at his or her guests? The answer is not very much. Our "Twitter reality" may be shorter on substance, but it is still a medium of exchange, a site of communication so all is not lost. The quest is to preserve the weightier and substantive exchanges while seeking out the nuanced wordplay and capability for argumentation in even the most mundane tweets.

So, sad and still curious, our extraterrestrial friend changes her approach and decides to study debate from those who do it for a living: politicians. Surely the people tasked with managing the country's affairs—people who are in large numbers trained as lawyers—would provide our extraterrestrial friend with all of the argumentation instruction she could need. But, as she soon finds out, the quality of debate in the great halls of human government only mirrors that on television (or vice-versa). In fact, the debates occurring in Congress often appear as if they are scripted for television (which they are). And again, sound bites and one-liners are the coin of the realm, if you are lucky—today's political debates are full of exaggeration, invective, personal attacks, grandstanding, and an aversion to discussion of actual policy.

Our extraterrestrial quickly learns that human politicians in many cases are just reciting *talking points*, or scripted and rehearsed agenda items specifically designed to reinforce partisanship. What is labeled a "debate" is actually a line-up of obscure talking points (pre-written briefs) that do not clash with each other and represent competing oratories at best. Where is the deep discussion, our extraterrestrial friend asks? How do humans make the tough decisions with such little and misleading information? The answer, although much harder to discern, is that there are significant and compelling instances of argumentation happening all around us. They are simply harder to locate than they should be, and they are often obscured by the sheer mountain of information we have to grapple with each and every day.

Argumentation in Society

Though argumentation is often confused with bickering, squabbling, and petty fighting, and is something many people actively try to avoid, the reality is that argumentation allows democracy to function. In fact, we make the case in this book that *argumentation is democracy in action*. It is participation is the *sin qua non* of shared governance. In this regard, argumentation can be compared to the chain on a bicycle. Without the chain, one's pedal strokes are unable to move the rear cog, which, as you know, is connected to the rear wheel. And if the rear wheel does not move, the bike does not move. And unless you are a talented circus performer, you know what happens when a bike stands still: It falls over from the lack of forward motion! Without argumentation, democracy would fall flat for lack of deliberation and effective training grounds for citizenship and politics.

The bike in this example is democracy. The chain, again, is argumentation—the exchange of ideas and reasons—the mechanism of circulation. And whether it is a high school senior making

Figure 1.6 Bike

the case that a law in his home state is unjust or a group of passionate voters challenging the policies of their government, argumentation determines the trajectory of a society by determining what is considered true and not true, what is valuable and what is not, and what is to be done as well as what is not to be done. Chain—bicycle. Argumentation—democracy.

Argumentation is not fighting. It is not battle. Argumentation, as previously stated, is the exchange and clash of ideas and reasons. In our experience as teachers and advocates of argumentation—as debate coaches and classroom instructors—fighting only occurs when people do not know how to argue within certain parameters. But when we realize how important the exchange of ideas and reasons is for our society (and relationships), we often can work through deliberation and reasoned decision-making rather than turning toward physical conflict, general violence, or warfare.

Argumentation is everywhere. We argue about education, medical practice, laws, and social policies. We argue with our coworkers and our bosses. We spar with our friends about sports, food, entertainment, and politics. We go back and forth with our parents, our partners, and our children about what is right, what is "just" and "true," and whether or not Kim Kardashian deserves to be famous. As we move into the post-Obama years and a series of acrimonious debates in the context of bitter partisanship clogging up the federal government, a renewed sense of productive argumentation that might even be energizing and enjoyable is necessary. To have fun (yes, argumentation is fun) and productive arguments, we need not always choose topics that are serious and grave. We need not always debate about abortion, stem cell research, the death penalty, and gun-control (though, surprisingly, those debates can be fun too). We can also argue about seemingly trivial things such as who is a better guitar player, Eric Clapton, Jimi Hendrix, or Jimmy Page? (It is Hendrix, of course, given his speed, rhythm, and creativity). The important thing is the process. And when the process of argumentation is respected and engaged with generosity and kindness, argumentation is often fun, challenging, and rewarding. Yes, one might "lose" the argument, but one will gain new knowledge. What is more rewarding than that?

A Brief History of Argumentation from the Greco-Roman Perspective

Should one want to investigate the historical origins of argumentation in great depth, there are many, many great books on the subject, and we have recommended a few in the index. However, for those not wanting to spend a summer's vacation plowing through Plato's *Dialogues*, we will provide an abbreviated history here. It is important for all of us to have at least a superficial awareness of the beginnings of argumentation. Understanding the history will help you appreciate the traditions and personalities of argumentation and even help influence your argumentation abilities.

Surprisingly, little has changed since the foundational theories of argumentation were first proposed. This is mainly because the individuals responsible for much of the argumentation theory we use today were so brilliant and ahead of their time. It is also because, like math, logic is not malleable and vulnerable to whimsical change. Just like 2

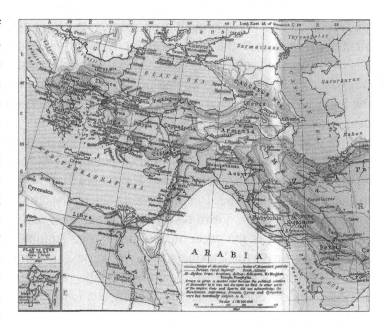

Figure 1.7 Ancient Greece

+ 2 will always equal four, affirming the consequent (a logical fallacy) will always be invalid. To begin, we must reach back to the history of language and Western Philosophy in Greece, although speech and argumentation have a rich history across the globe. Steven Combs reminds us that all commitments to the study of argumentation do not owe their heritage to Greco-Roman understandings of the field. Indeed, "comparative studies of argumentation in different cultures can bring to light literatures that have been overlooked or marginalized and promote new understandings of argumentation processes and practices."[22]

Combs reminds us that many of the characteristics built into Western thought through adversarial notions of dialectic and argumentation coming out of Greco-Roman traditions are not inherent to argumentation. Indeed, the Dao of argumentation allows for contradictions in purpose, goals based on conversation instead of competition, and even a pursuit of the useless. Practicing Daoists would not engage in argumentation where there is a universal perspective or expectation for a particular resolution. Argumentation does not have to rely on "effortful advocacy," dependence on reasoning as a form of proof, or assumptions connecting language to a stable notion of reality. Argumentation from a Daoist perspective, then, would diverge from an emphasis on logic, advocacy, and the structure of arguments, but would join the inquiry into the self, identity, and social movements. We follow the path charted by Aristotle and other Western thinkers, but we follow particular questions until they circle back to the various assumptions implied in knowledge and deliberation. In other words, we take different routes to return to potential roots for transitory awareness, provisional truths, and the articulation of further questioning. Combs (1004, p. 68) notes: "Daoists regularly use argumentation to open up the possibilities for additional conceptions—momentarily foregrounding a provisional claim." We will return to some of the non-Western roots of argumentation later in the textbook, including some exploration into the comparative histories of the area of

---

[22] Combs, S. C. (1994). Challenging Greco-Roman argumentation trajectories: Argument norms and cultural traditions, *Argumentation and Advocacy 41*, 55–57; 55. Also see Combs, S. C. (2004). The useless-/usefulness of argumentation: The Dao of disputation. *Argumentation & Advocacy 41.2*, 58–70.

study throughout the globe, but it is necessary to begin with the roots of argumentation that were planted in Athens with the Sophists and those who followed them.

For the Greeks, the big division between the people we call the Sophists and the post-Sophists was based on how each side viewed "oratory," or what we call "rhetoric." Even though the intent of the Sophists has been debated vigorously (were they concerned with finding ways to manipulate people or were they focused on creating better speakers and better character?), most scholars believe that the Sophists saw oratory as a skill to be mastered in order to trick people—in order to engage in pandering as a means to manipulate or coerce others. Social life, then, was a contest among well-trained speakers making arguments that might or might not have been connected to truth-seeking or virtue. The response to Sophistry, often associated with Plato, was that oratory and rhetoric were not to be trusted and society's real goal should be to seek out the truth as virtue in spite of the deceptions of persuasive argumentation. Although an understandable response, we aim to think through argumentation as a challenge to universal truths and as more than pandering or persuasive manipulation. The resurrection of rhetoric arises from the same setting and a consideration of *ethos*, *pathos*, and *logos*.

The Triad of Ethos, Pathos, Logos

Learning from the Greeks and recognizing that part of their fascination with the "art of rhetoric" included a great deal of dialogue and reflection on argumentation, it should be no surprise that one of the primary moves in rhetoric is to divide up the components of persuasion. What makes a speech compelling? According to the Greeks, primarily Aristotle, we try to persuade one another in three main ways: through content, credibility, and compassion. Content refers to the actual substance of the statement and the actual words themselves. This content element is most heavily represented in transcripts of speeches or written arguments such as legal briefs, position articles, or official documents. When we talk about the content of a particular message, we are talking about the logic and evidence behind the entire message. Does the speech say *something* meaningful that matters? Does it include statistical evidence, reasoned argument, or narrative testimony to make the point? These are all questions that center on *logos*, or the content of the position. Some argue that content, or *logos*, is the most important piece of an argument because it can stand on its own while credibility and compassion cannot. Pure content can constitute an argument by itself, while the other components of persuasion—emotion and credibility—need the content in order to matter.

Through the history of argumentation we can trace the development of these themes and the notion that an argument can be divided up into its forms. In addition to the actual content, or substance of an argument, it is also important to consider the source. Who is making the argument? Where is the source coming from? Does the author or the speaker have a sense of legitimacy or credibility? What some will call *ethos*—the reputation or standing of the speaker—we refer to as the argument's credibility, the reputation and expertise of the author and the source. Credibility refers to how established and trusted the speaker is. A speaker without *ethos* is less likely to make a compelling and reliable statement, while a speaker who is well respected and considered an authority on the subject at hand will add credibility and believability to the argument itself. There is a sense among many scholars that *ethos* is overrated and we should really just analyze the text itself or the actual words being spoken because *logos*, or content, is the most important piece of the argument. The bottom line, though, is that both the credibility of an argument and the compassion behind the argument are connected to its persuasive force—it is not just about the content because we do not have a giant computer in the sky that can assess every argument and provide an objective or neutral answer. Maybe our extra-terrestrial friend could use an algorithm to determine the numerical force of every argument (and that might make her less pessimistic about the state of argumentation in society today), but human beings do not have such a machine, and it is probably important for our uniqueness as individuals that we do not.

Figure 1.8 Aristotle

Emotion matters in argumentation, whether we are talking about a heated dispute, a lovers' quarrel, a stirring halftime speech, or a rousing political oration. Compassion refers to the emotional connection the argument has to the audience or, more generally, the identification of the speech and the speaker with the receivers of the message. Does the argument resonate with the audience? If so, the argument has a greater likelihood of being persuasive and the overall position is more likely to convince the person or group that hears it. *Pathos* is another term for the compassion between the speaker and the audience, and an argument is also considered to have strong *pathos* if there is a relationship—an emotional connection—between the speaker, the content, and the listener. That emotional moment may be sympathy, shared outrage, humor, excitement, anticipation, or any other feeling that is generated, but it is a sense of understanding and common interest between those who hear the argument and those who make it. Together, content, credibility, and compassion make a given instance of rhetoric persuasive and, when applied to argumentation, join together to make an argument compelling. These are all ideas we learn early on through the history of rhetoric and the debates that take place in Plato's dialogues between Socrates and the Sophists.

Aristotle is important to argumentation because he divided up the notion of persuasion—closely tied to the larger concept of rhetoric—into *ethos, pathos,* and *logos.* These appeals are part of the full range of persuasion's ability to succeed. The answer to the question, "What is successful persuasion," is this: Successful persuasion is argumentation that deploys *ethos, pathos,* and *logos.* Again, effective persuasion is based on the message itself, the credibility of the source or the speaker to assert the argument, and the connection to the audience in a passionate and intimate bond of trust. Those three concepts are the most significant portion of Aristotle's description of rhetoric that we need to learn and adapt specifically to argumentation. The context of argumentation has to revolve around the content of an argument, the argument's source, and the argument's audience. The matter, the author, and the audience are another way to break this down.

The three appeals to persuasion that Aristotle discussed were expanded and cataloged in a more practical way by the Romans, Cicero and Quintilian. They were both concerned with speaking as a way to cultivate citizenship. Cicero published a guidebook for speaking, *De inventione,* in which he associated learning to speak well with virtue, and sought to cultivate both. For him, it was a five-part scheme that we can project onto argumentation, a categorization system slightly different from the three-part scheme of *ethos*, *pathos*, and *logos* we just analyzed. There are lots of numbered schemes to be aware of when studying argumentation, the most important being the two we are covering now. A third one will surface in a later section and is based on the idea that every argument has a claim, some evidence, and a warrant (i.e., logic).

The Five Canons of Rhetoric

The five categories outlines by the Greeks and later developed by Cicero are known as the "canons of rhetoric." The categories are designed to be the parts of discourse that an orator should perfect in order to craft the ideal speech: invention (coming up with a topic), arrangement (developing a structure), style (adding flair and distinctiveness), memory (both preparing to deliver the speech and making the speech memorable), and delivery (giving the speech). This five-part arsenal is definitely a list of characteristics that would apply to effective communication as a whole (persuasion or rhetoric as persuasion), but we think it is also possible to meaningfully and accurately discuss this canon through the perspective of argumentation. In other words, let us go further into invention, arrangement, style, memory, and delivery to cap off this chapter and set us up for the next chapter on the study of argumentation.

Invention, in truth, is probably the most important of the five because without a seed—an initial concept—the rest of the elements of a persuasive argument do not matter. Without the creation of an idea or the beginning of a claim, we cannot apply structure or style, let alone delivery or memory. The creative impulse—the "light bulb of the mind"—is the original moment at which the argument is initiated. Generating a purpose or direction is both the "creative thought" and the "creation of thinking." "Pick a topic," "Come up with an idea," or "Defend a position" are all gestures to invention. Invent something to say and then develop it.

Arrangement is the next step in the development of a persuasive argument and involves organizing the overall speech by applying structure. Like an essay, the classic structure consists of an introduction, a main body, and a conclusion. Often the introduction starts broad and funnels into the main claim or thesis. The main body then develops that thesis through a series of major contentions that work together either by building on each other or by independently justifying the larger claim. The main body offers proof, so to speak, of the assertion being advanced at the bottom of the introduction. The matrix making up the main body of a classically arranged speech or essay is followed by the concluding section. Restating the main claim and briefly summarizing the points made in the main body, the conclusion typically postulates on a general level and opens back up to some of the larger questions being raised. Of course, "introduction, body, conclusion" is only one of an infinite number of ways to structure a major argument, but it shows how arrangement takes place and divides the pieces into different stages and divisions.

Stages and divisions—the setting of the argument in many ways—leads perfectly into the category of style. Style is the distinctive tone, flair, or character accompanying the speech or the argument. Much work has taken place listing the various types of style and the distinct approaches that are available, although in many ways the differences are infinite. There are always slight changes in logic, mannerism, accent, emphasis, or wording that can set one style apart from the next. Often the best way to discern the style of an argument is to examine multiple arguments across a wide range of disciplines and pick out the commonalities and repetitive attributes. When applied to rhetoric as a whole, style takes on even deeper dimensions, but it is fair to note that all four of the other canons have stylistic variables. In fact, it makes sense to talk about the creativity behind an argument (invention), the structure of an argument (arrangement), the imprint and durability or an argument (memory), and the writing, presentation, or performance of an argument (delivery) all in terms of style. An argument will often take on striking adjectives through its overall style, including being classified as bold, vicious, brilliant, cunning, tempting, or conclusive. One of the real marks of an effective style is the long-term resonance of a particular argument, its memory.

Memory is the most complicated of the five canons because it has two different functions and modes of operation. Memory works through the arguer's memory of the argument itself, and it works through the audience's reception of the argument in terms of how memorable it is. The form of memory

Figure 1.9 Plato and Aristotle

that works through the arguer's readiness to convey the argument basically deals with the speaker's preparation to recite the argument or the speech in public. This aspect is tied to the ways the Greeks and the Romans conveyed arguments in public by giving impassioned speeches to a live audience. It still has some value as a technique for public speaking, but it has been eclipsed by arguments emanating from screens and various technological devices that pre-package the message. Different techniques for memorizing a sequence would come into play here and allow a speaker to maximize her delivery—the fifth of the canons that we will return to shortly.

The other, more advanced side of the memory canon, concerns the impact or durable force of the argument. Does the argument stand out enough to be repeated, exchanged with others, reproduced, and remembered? In other words, how *memorable* is the argument in question? Does it sink in? Does it have enough of an impact to really matter for a long period of time? A memorable argument is one that really lasts and has durability—a deep and significant imprint. Say we advance three arguments here: 1. Guns should be severely limited in the United States because excess violence has become increasingly fatal and the security of every individual is threatened with such a heavily armed nation; 2. The United Nations should put a much greater level of resources and attention to resolving problems of climate change and fossil fuel consumption. This is necessary because human-induced global warming is the biggest threat to the ability of humans to survive and the United Nations has the ability to facilitate change in that arena; 3. Immigration reform that expands opportunities for legal citizenship should be passed immediately because the crisis is worsening and a hard-line security approach only exacerbates the problem and hurts the economy. Which of these arguments will you remember in a few days and why? What is it about the argument that stays in your mind and makes it more significant? The answer lies in a combination of factors that combine to make an argument memorable.

We will expand these factors as we move through the text, but the essential components of a memorable moment in a speech are that it connects to a certain audience based on its impact, its visual imagery, its context, and its applicability to future situations.

Finally, delivery is all about presentation and performance, the aspects of giving or explaining the argument that enhance the overall process of communication. The essential elements of delivery are treated in more depth in manuals about public speaking, but it is worth noting the primary ways that a speaker or author can augment the actual presentation of the argument in a speech. Movement and gesture are clearly important, for facial gestures and body movement can improve the effectiveness of a speech or the explanation of an argument. The voice itself also opens up a number of delivery variables, including how loud or soft the speech is (volume), how fast or slow the speech is (pace), or how high or low the tone of the speech is (pitch). Manipulating volume, pace, and pitch as well as body and facial gestures gives the speaker a huge array of choices for creating a great delivery.

Overall, the five canons are extremely useful for dividing up the elements of a compelling message or speech (a rhetorical moment), but they are also helpful for thinking through the presentation of an arrangement. Inventing, arranging, and delivering an argument, combined with a stylistic and memorable assembly, is the recipe for a persuasive statement.

Thinking Critically

Congratulations! You now know the difference between *Ethos, Pathos,* and *Logos* and you understand the five canons of rhetoric. Be sure to identify these elements whenever someone or some company tries to convince you of something. Learning how persuasion works is a bit like seeing the "man behind the curtain" from *The Wizard of Oz.* Once you know how it works, it is hard thereafter to fall for the tricks. Before moving on to other concepts, though, it is important to discuss the concept of *logos* just a bit further. In many ways, *logos* is the very heart of argumentation.

It may seem like an easy question, but let's ask it nevertheless. Are human beings logical? Many people would say yes. Many people would say that our logical abilities separate us from other animals on the planet including our closest relatives, the chimpanzee. But is this true? Perhaps it would be helpful to ask a similar question. Are we emotional beings? Many, if not all, would say yes (we cannot all be Spock from *Star Trek,* after all). In *Star Trek,* from the vantage point of Captain Kirk, Spock and McCoy represent logical reasoning and impulsiveness, respectively. The difficulty is determining which one to follow to what degree in a given situation. So, which is it? Are we logical or emotional?

Are we both? And to what degree are we logical over emotional? Or to what degree are we emotional over logical? And how are we supposed to make important political and social decisions that are free from bias if we are even *remotely* vulnerable to emotionality?

It turns out that, indeed, we are both emotional *AND* logical beings (you probably knew this). In fact, we are far from purely logical beings despite our thinking so. Here is a classic example to illustrate this. Imagine two scenarios.

Scenario 1: Suppose you are on a runaway trolley that is racing uncontrollably down a track on which four people are working. All four will die if the trolley continues. However, while you do not know how to stop the trolley, you realize that you can pull a lever that will divert the trolley to a new track on which only one man is working. Moving the trolley to the new track will kill the one man but spare the four. What would you do? Pull the lever and save four lives at the expense of one? Or don't pull the lever and save one life at the expense of four? In short, would you pull the lever if you knew it would save four lives and take one?

Scenario 2: Now, suppose, once again, there is a runaway trolley that is racing uncontrollably toward four men who are working on the track. Like before, all four will die if the trolley continues on its course. However, this time you are not on the trolley; you are standing on a bridge over the tracks. On the bridge with you is a man large enough to stop the trolley if he were pushed from the bridge onto the tracks. If you push this man, he will die, but his heft will stop the trolley and save the four workers. What would you do? Push

Figure 1.10 Mr. Spock: The Embodiment of Logic

the man onto the tracks to save the four workers? Or let the four workers die?

The two scenarios we just described represent what is known as the trolley problem. There is a good chance you have encountered the trolley problem or something similar to it in an introductory philosophy course, where it is often used to discuss ethics and morality. However, we like the trolley problem in communication theory as well because it illustrates the inherent irrationality of human thinking and therefore, argumentation. Let us elaborate.

In scenario 1, if you chose to pull the lever and divert the train onto the other tracks, thereby killing one man to save four, you are like most people. Indeed, many people see scenario one in mathematical terms. Four is more than one. Therefore, four is *better* than one. Let us be clear, killing the one man to save the four would be difficult, but most people feel it is the "right" thing to do given the situation. After all, it is better to lose one life than to lose four. Right?

Now, if you are like most people, you probably found it much more difficult to push the man off the bridge in scenario two. But why? When you think about it carefully, scenario two is no different from scenario one. The end results are the same. In both cases one man is lost for the sake of four. In mathematical terms they are equivalent. But only rarely do we think in purely mathematical terms, especially when human lives are involved. And this is our point. If human beings were purely logical, like a calculator, the trolley problem would not be as popular as it is. A calculator would see the two scenarios as equivalent and would make no distinction. For many people, however, there is a big, big difference. For some, the lever in scenario one is a rational choice in the face of danger, while pushing the man seems much more murderous and immoral. It is a question of the action required in each case—a question that involves a personal calculation between the mathematical reality (is 4 bigger than 1) and the responsibility for certain murder as a result of an explicit decision to act. Indeed, the power of the trolley problem is that it reveals fundamental yet hidden aspects of human decision-making. That positions us well for the last section of the chapter, the mind against the "gut."

Head Versus Gut

In his celebrated book, *Thinking Fast and Slow*, the Nobel-prize winning economist Daniel Kahneman reinforces this idea that the human mind processes information both emotionally and logically (something Aristotle was already hip to). Specifically, Kahneman made the argument that humans today owe a lot of their cognitive processing to their ancient ancestors who, after thousands of years of evolving to their often hostile environments, have given modern humans the ability to make quick, emotional, snap decisions. And this is no insignificant skill. For our ancient ancestors, this was the difference between survival and death in many cases. After all, slow deliberation is not a good thing when you are being hunted by a faster, more adapted predator. Sometimes you need to run quickly and you need to know where to run. Fugivity matters.

While few of us today have to defend against the type of predators our ancestors encountered, it is still crucially important to make snap decisions. If, out of the corner of your eye, you see something slither away, you should immediately act because it could be a snake! If you hear a loud bang, you should rapidly tense up and become alert because it might signal harm. If someone seems suspicious to you, it might behoove you to trust your instincts because he or she might be dangerous. Kahneman refers to this fast acting, rapid decision-making as "system one." It is essentially a form of instinctive reaction, but it is propelled by a capacity to distill large amounts of information and make a decision regarding that information in a very quick period of time. It's instinctual reasoning, and it hints at "argumentation as the self," which we will discuss in Chapter Six In short, system one is ancient and emotional and incredibly effective.

In his book, *The Science of Fear*, Daniel Gardner refers to system one as the "gut"—as in the popular expression "follow your gut." So many of the decisions we make in life we make based on a gut feeling—an intuition that is hard to articulate. We just *feel* it; it is instinct, and we are all told from when we are very little to trust our instincts. And rightly so! Our species owes its existence, in no small part, to the ability to read situations or people and make quick "gut" decisions. Oftentimes we can't explain *why* we made the decision, but it seemed right at the time. That is system one. While we live in a world very different from the one our ancestors inhabited, the way in which we make decisions is very much unchanged. That is unless we *decide* to slow things down and engage "system two," or as Gardner calls it, "head."

Whereas system one relies on emotion, feeling and speed, system two relies on logic, reason, and deliberation. It is sort of like putting your brain into slow motion, where instead of hastily jumping to conclusions, you analyze each thought along the way, breaking down the justifications and implications. Can you see how this "head" (as Gardner calls it) level type of thinking would not be appropriate when, say, a tiger is running at you? Or when you hear a strange rustling in the bushes as you walk home alone late at night? You most likely *do not* want to slow things down in those situations. Speed is good because speed means surviving. But when might a slower approach to reaching conclusions be more attractive? Well, in lots of situations actually.

Engaging system two is useful whenever the stakes are high or when getting the wrong answer could lead to potentially negative consequences. Complex questions also require system two types of thought. Solving a mathematics problem quickly is great and impressive, but not if it means increasing the odds of getting the answer wrong! Especially when the math involves, say, money. Similarly, deciding quickly to vote for a person based on a few misleading arguments or emotional appeals is also not good. A poor reading of the stock market can lead to bad investments; a hasty decision to attend a particular university can affect one for the rest of his or her life.

You should be able to see the temptation behind system one thinking. After all, we live in a fast-paced world. Our news media prides itself on getting the scoop the fastest. Breaking news is a headline itself! We want

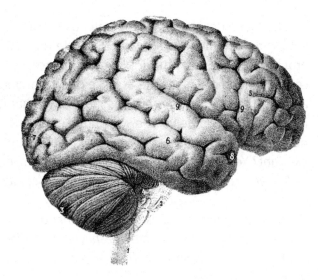

Figure 1.11 Outer Surface of the Human Brain

to be the person to solve the math problem first. And we want to know who we are going to vote for before anybody else as well. But the problem is that reality is complex and easy answers to challenging questions are harmful. As the saying goes, there is much more than meets the eye. Here are a few examples:

A bat and a ball together cost $1.10. The bat costs $1.00 more than the ball. So how much does the ball cost?

If you are like most people, your immediate answer to this question is ten cents. After all, if the bat and ball together cost $1.10 and the bat costs $1.00 dollar *more than the ball*, the difference is just $.10, meaning the ball costs ten cents. But you are wrong! And most depressingly of all, you are *clearly* wrong. Here's proof:

$$\begin{aligned}
\text{Bat} &= \$1.05 \\
+ \text{Ball} &= \$0.05 \\
\hline
&= \$1.10
\end{aligned}$$

If you wish to represent this solution algebraically, you could let y equal the ball and x equal the bat such that:

$$y + x = 1.10$$
$$x = 1.00 + y$$

If you then set about solving the system of equations by substituting equation 2 into equation 1, you come to the following answer:

$$1.00 + 2y = 1.10$$
$$2y = 0.10$$
$$y = 0.05$$

Clearly, you can see that the ball costs just 5 cents and not 10. But how many of you were willing to take the time to prove this little riddle algebraically? Your mind set about solving the problem quickly, and after just a quick glance, it (your mind) was convinced of the answer. Ten cents, it shouted! That is the essence of system one thinking: it is quick and effortless (and a bit arrogant). But, importantly in this case, it was harmful! And after taking the time to thoroughly investigate the riddle, you now see how simple the answer is. It was system two thinking that we needed to find the answer. Was it quick? Not really. Did it require a bit of effort? A little. But were we right? Yes. Let us look at another, more applicable, example.

Say you come across the following advertisement on television:

"Brilliant Smyle Toothpaste is the number one selling toothpaste and is recommended more than any other. Better yet, recent studies show that Brilliant Smyle will whiten your teeth 10 percent more than the leading competitor! Don't waste another minute worrying about your smile: brighten your life with Brilliant Smyle!"

Commercials like this one are a constant nuisance, and often we are able to ignore them and set about the task at hand. However, research indicates that the average American is exposed to hundreds if not thousands of advertisements per day. Think about how many advertisements that is per week, per month, per year! The truth, whether we like to admit it or not, is that advertisements influence our decisions regarding which toothpaste to buy or brands of clothing to wear. Commercials also influence our political views and our electoral decisions. It is inevitable, really. So, where is the harm with that situation? Let us take another look at the *Brilliant Smyle* example.

First, what are the reasons *Brilliant Smyle* says we should buy their toothpaste?
Reason 1. *Brilliant Smyle Toothpaste is the number one selling toothpaste.*
Reason 2. *Brilliant Smyle Toothpaste is recommended more than any other.*
Reason 3. *Recent studies show that Brilliant Smyle will whiten your teeth 10 percent more than the leading competitor!*

To the "gut," this looks like a convincing case. *Brilliant Smyle* is the most popular, most recommended, and most whitening. However, to the "head," *Brilliant Smyle's* case is less compelling. Let us analyze each claim and discover why.

Reason 1. *Brilliant Smyle Toothpaste is the number one selling toothpaste.*

This really does not tell us that much. Being the number one selling toothpaste can be the result of a great marketing strategy or advertising campaign. What if we found out that customers who purchased *Brilliant Smyle* toothpaste once were very unlikely to do it a second time? Is not that a better indicator of quality than number of units sold?

Additionally, is *Brilliant Smyle* the number one selling brand of all time? Or is it the number one selling brand in just the past quarter? Are they compelled to tell the truth in a toothpaste advertisement in the first place? There are so many questions still unanswered.

Reason 2. *Brilliant Smyle Toothpaste is recommended more than any other.*

This really does not tell us that much either. Who is recommending *Brilliant Smyle*? Dentists? And do they work for *Brilliant Smyle* or are they independent? And, again, just because something is the most recommended does not guarantee it is a good product. What criteria are they using for the recommendation? Taste? Price? The ability to bleach your teeth? All of these? None of these? Did *Brilliant Smyle* even conduct a survey to come up with that statement in the first place? There are so many questions still unanswered.

Reason 3. Recent studies show that Brilliant Smyle will whiten your teeth 10 percent more than the leading competitor!

Let us break this reason down as well. When they say "recent studies," exactly what do they mean? How many studies? And were they independently conducted? Were they published in peer-reviewed journals? Who funded the studies? The word "study" sounds authoritative and legitimate to the "gut," but the "head" knows better. Anyone can conduct a study, and as a result not all "studies" are equal. Furthermore, what does it mean to whiten teeth 10 percent more? What is the scale they are using here? What does 10 percent more equate with? In other words, what does 10 percent whiter look like? And is that after one use or a month? Did people in the "study" also not drink coffee? How often did they brush? Following the path of the cynic, we also have to ask if *Brilliant Smyle* is basing its claims on actual, verifiable data, or whether the claims are unsubstantiated and made up. Again, there are so many questions still unanswered.

What we have done here is illustrate how easy it is to critically analyze the often superficial reasons used to advertise products, people, or ideas. Yet, very few of us are willing to take the time to do so, and as a result we make many of the important decisions in our lives based on system one intuitions, snap-decisions or "gut" feelings when, as it should be clear now, using more deliberate and rational decision-making (system two) offers much more insight and perspective. Again, there are some situations where instinctual, system one thinking is the best option, but our argument to you is that in an increasingly complex and nuanced world—a world that is more connected than ever—system two thinking has never been more vital. That is not to say, however, that system two comes easy. Think back to the trolley problem. Exactly why is it that for many of us pulling the lever seems so different from pushing the man off the bridge? The outcome is the same. But one just feels more *evil*. But then again, it is not: The outcome is the same. Rationally it makes sense. But emotionally it does not. The trolley problem is so intriguing because it shows in a very powerful way just how hard it is to disengage and disentangle system one and system two thinking.

In full appreciation of system one, this book is dedicated to teaching you how to develop and exercise your own critical thinking: your system two.

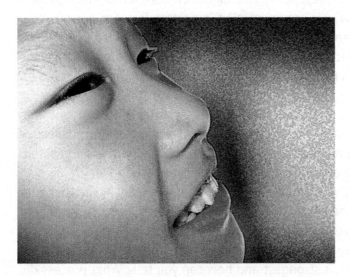

Figure 1.12 A Bright Smile is a Happy Face!

Critical thinking is a skill we all have, but like any muscle in the human body, we need to use it often and correctly in order for it to grow and strengthen. In the chapters that follow we are going to walk you through the process of argumentation, how it is done, and how to evaluate it. We are also going to walk you through the various types of argumentation. We will expose you to the fundamentals of case construction. We will show you just how important argumentation and critical thinking is for society, and we will encourage you to be an active advocate for yourself, your family, and your beliefs. We have made large strides through the terrain of argumentation and are still just introducing the area. There is a lot of ground to cover. By covering a lot of ground here in the introduction, and by engaging with the territory of language and rhetoric, we have collectively begun to map argumentation! You are on your way to becoming an expert, and you are starting to sense the fundamental point that, ultimately, argumentation is simply about detecting and making arguments.

Learning Activities: Chapter One

1. What are your hot-button issues? In other words, which controversial issues and potential debate topics are you likely to become emotional about? How can you strengthen your system two thinking with regard to your hot-button issues?
2. Locate a video of a poorly executed argument or debate. If you struggle to find one, search for things like "Fox News Debate" or "MSNBC argument" on Google. Analyze the argument and determine why it was so poorly executed. Next, determine ways the argument could have been more constructive.
3. Locate an advertisement on the television, radio, or Internet and perform a system-two analysis of the advertisement. Share your analysis with your classmates.
4. Blaise Pascal is often quoted as saying, "The heart has its reasons, which reason knows nothing of." In light of our discussion of system one and system two thinking, what do you think he meant by this quote?
5. Invent five or six characters based on profession—a salesperson, a librarian, a banker, a dentist, and a sports coach, for example. Why is argumentation important for each person? Who encounters argumentation the most and why? What are arguments each person would find her or himself making on the job? Pick new characters with different professions and go through the same inquiries. What does this say about work in general? Do the same thing for characters based on age, race, another identity characteristic.
6. Find the transcript of a speech (there are lots of online sites such as the "Top 100 American Speeches" here: http://www.americanrhetoric.com/top100speechesall.html, accessed 12/1/2014) and analyze its *logos* in terms of effectiveness. How do we fill in *ethos* and *pathos* when reading? In what context would each of the three matter the most and why?
7. Find three examples of each of the five canons of rhetoric from everyday advertisements. Compare them against one another and come up with the aspects that are most prominent in the examples that are most effective. Does that tell us something about persuasion?
8. Write a one minute speech by using the five rhetorical canons. What order did you use them in and why? Give the speech—where is it strongest and how can you tell? What process did you use for the initial invention?

9. Critical thinking cannot be taught in a standard classroom. Discuss. Do you believe that statement? Why or why not? If the entire goal was to teach critical thinking skills, what would be the best way to set up that class? Compare your answer to other answers and create a list of ways to enhance critical thinking.

Figure Credits

Fig. 1.1: "Telescope," https://www.flickr.com/photos/britishlibrary/11237196445/in/album-72157638850077096/. Copyright in the Public Domain.

Fig. 1.2: Copyright © Sage Ross (CC BY-SA 3.0) at http://commons.wikimedia.org/wiki/File:Tea_Party_Protest,_Hartford,_Connecticut,_15_April_2009_-_041.jpg.

Fig. 1.3: Copyright © WisPolitics.com (CC BY-SA 2.0) at https://commons.wikimedia.org/wiki/File:Tea_Party_vs_Reality.jpg.

Fig. 1.4: KVDP, "People in Peace and at War," https://commons.wikimedia.org/wiki/File:People_in_peace_and_at_war.png. Copyright in the Public Domain.

Fig. 1.5: Copyright © Anthony Appleyard (CC BY-SA 3.0) at https://commons.wikimedia.org/wiki/File:2aliens_on_desert_planet.jpg.

Fig. 1.6: Copyright © Lhademmor (CC BY-SA 3.0) at https://commons.wikimedia.org/wiki/File:Cykel.JPG.

Fig. 1.7: William R. Shepherd, "Shepherd-c-018-019 Cropped Middle East," https://commons.wikimedia.org/wiki/File:Shepherd-c-018-019_cropped_Middle_East.JPG. Copyright in the Public Domain.

Fig. 1.8: Jastrow, "Aristotle," http://commons.wikimedia.org/wiki/File:Aristotle_Altemps_Inv8575.jpg. Copyright in the Public Domain.

Fig. 1.9: Raphael, Detail of "The School of Athens," http://commons.wikimedia.org/wiki/File:Plato_and_Aristotle_in_The_School_of_Athens,_by_italian_Rafael.jpg. Copyright in the Public Domain.

Fig. 1.10: "Leonard Nimoy," http://commons.wikimedia.org/wiki/File:Leonard_Nimoy_as_Spock_1967.jpg. Copyright in the Public Domain.

Fig. 1.11: "Brain," https://commons.wikimedia.org/wiki/File:PSM_V46_D167_Outer_surface_of_the_human_brain.jpg. Copyright in the Public Domain.

Fig. 1.12: Copyright © Jan Tik (CC BY-SA 2.0) at https://commons.wikimedia.org/wiki/File:Happy_kid_smile.jpg.

CHAPTER 2

The Study of Argumentation

Success in argumentation requires, among other things, familiarity with the roles and rules of the game. In this way, argumentation is just like any other game you might play. For instance, before you can play chess (and debate is a lot like chess!), you must first learn a few things. First, you need to know how to set up the board. In other words, you need to know which pieces go where. Next, you need to know the pieces themselves—you have to know their names, how they relate to the other pieces, and how they can move. Next, you need to know how the game is played. Finally, you should know a few things about strategy and, most importantly, you should know how to win! You can play the game of chess or engage in the art of argumentation with a limited understanding of the rules, but you will not have much success with either unless you really have a sense of what the respective pieces are, what the pieces do, and how they can be utilized to accomplish the goal.

Can you imagine playing chess *not knowing* these things? You will probably find yourself on the losing end of a very short match. You might even end up playing checkers. Or worse still, you might play your version of the game while your opponent plays her version. What a disaster that would be—you would not get anywhere, and if you did you would have no way of knowing it! Therefore, the point of this Chapter is to acquaint you with the basics so that your arguments with others are productive, efficient, and successful. It is one thing to read about theories of argumentation and the history of argumentation; it is another to make your own arguments and judge other people's arguments. Both sides—the academic side and the practical side—are important to the study of argumentation.

What is an Argument?

Let us start fresh and put first things first. What is an argument? It is the root word of "argumentation" after all, so if we are going to learn about argumentation we better learn what an argument is. The last chapter talked all about argumentation—its history, its connections to theories of persuasion stretching back to the Greeks and the Romans, and even its connection to critical thinking. Not once, however—at least not very directly—did the last chapter come out and say, "*This* is an argument." With that said, *an argument is a statement or belief that is logically supported with reasons.* The key part of this definition is "logically supported with reasons," so we really need to focus on what that means. Let's begin by looking at a number of non-arguments:

"I like ponies."
"Vanilla is the best flavor of ice cream."
"Keeping whales in captivity is immoral."
"The U.S. government should ban the sale of assault rifles."
"You should avoid Wikipedia."

We need to point out that even though they may seem like arguments, each of the examples above are not arguments because they are not supported with reasons. Because they are lacking reasons, or grounds, they are only claims. You may have heard that a given statement "is just a claim without a warrant." What that means is that a given position is being advanced without any reasoning or supporting evidence behind it. Although we tried to provide some grounds for the three arguments briefly introduced in the last chapter (guns should be restricted, the U.N. should be focused on fighting global warming, and immigration reform is needed), it is also the case that these arguments were heavy on the claims and light on the supporting evidence. We will discuss this in more detail in Chapter Three, but an *argument,* according to Toulmin, consists of three parts:

1. *Claim—a statement or assertion.*
2. *Grounds—the reasons used to prove the claim.*
3. *Warrant—the logical inference between the claim and grounds.*[1]

Known as the Toulmin diagram based on the work of Stephen Toulmin and the 1950s and '60s, this three-part scheme lets us isolate the various components an argument must include in order to be "complete." There are other ways to think about arguments and argumentation, but the delineation based on the theme, the explanation, and the proof is very useful, whether talking about Iranian nuclear proliferation or the best flavor of ice cream. "Vanilla is the best flavor of ice cream" meets the criteria for a claim, but because it does not include *grounds,* or reasons supporting the claim (and subsequently a warrant), it does not meet the criteria for an argument. We could easily provide grounds for this claim, however. For instance, if we were to say, "Vanilla is the best flavor of ice cream because it tastes great and is the most popular," we now have an argument! The warrant in this case would be the reasoning that "ice cream which tastes great and is the most popular is the best flavor." You can probably see how helpful this three-art scheme is for distinguishing between a complete and a partial argument.

We could similarly construct an argument around the claim that keeping whales in captivity is immoral. For example, it would be an argument to say "keeping whales in captivity is immoral because captivity is physically and emotionally harmful to whales and whales do not deserve such treatment as sentient beings." Let us break this argument down into its constituent parts just to be clear.

---

[1] Toulmin, Stephen. (1958). *The Uses of Argument.* Cambridge: Cambridge UP, 2003. Also see, Toulmin, Stephen, Richard Rieke, and Allan Janik (1979). *An Introduction to Reasoning.* New York: Macmillan.

Claim—*keeping whales in captivity is immoral*
Grounds—*captivity is physically and emotionally harmful to whales and whales should not be subjected to such pain or experience such suffering*
Warrant—*causing physical and emotional harm to whales is immoral*

Visually, we can represent the relationships between claims, grounds, warrants, and arguments:

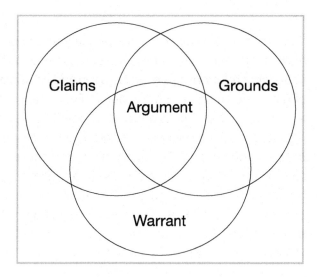

Figure 2.1 The Making of an Argument

You can see here what we have already described, but perhaps this makes things a bit more clear. Claims exist independently of grounds and warrants. The same is true for grounds, which can be asserted without a claim, though that would be rhetorically very awkward and ineffective. It is only when claims, grounds, and warrants intersect in the middle that you get arguments. Another way to think about it is that all arguments are claims, grounds, and warrants, but not all claims, grounds, and warrants are arguments. That is quite a tongue twister, but hopefully now you have a better idea of what constitutes an argument.

Knowing what constitutes an argument is the first skill needed for actual argumentation. And so it becomes even more important to learn the difference between an argument and a non-argument if you want to play the "game" of argumentation or participate in the world around you. After all, if a friend, coworker, or family member makes a claim without providing any reasons (i.e., grounds) to defend the claim, you will need to point out that they have not actually made an argument and, consequently, there is no game to play! But let us pretend that your friend, coworker, or family member actually does propose an argument, what then?

In a nutshell, the real trick of argumentation is determining the context of the argument and preparing a meaningful set of statements that includes a main thesis (claim), evidence in defense of the thesis (grounding), and a connection between the thesis and the evidence (warrant). If these statements also include a strong sense of *ethos*, *pathos*, and *logos*, then we are looking at a persuasive and compelling argument and a chance to create change and make a difference in the world.

Types of Arguments

Arguments come in all forms and varieties, but, generally speaking, there are three broad types of arguments.

Fact

The first type of argument you are likely to encounter is an argument of fact. Arguments of fact make supported claims about the past, present, or future. Arguments of fact assert that empirical or testable relationships exist between and amongst different people, places, or things. Arguments of fact are common in legal contexts. For instance, it is an argument of fact to accuse someone of a crime (e.g., "X person is guilty of Y crime"). To claim that someone is guilty, the prosecution must provide sufficient evidence (i.e., grounds) to convince the judge or jury, depending on the kind of trial. Arguments of fact also exist in the context of science. For instance, it is an argument of fact to assert that smoking causes cancer. Likewise, it would be an argument of fact to assert that the universe is expanding at an accelerating rate (an argument that won Saul Perlmutter, Brian Schmidt, and Adam Riess the Nobel Prize in Physics). But it is not just law and science where arguments of fact abound; keep your eyes peeled because arguments of fact are all around. They are in TV commercials (e.g., "X brand face cream will eliminate your acne!"), in politics (i.e., "Investing in clean energy will create stable and well-paying jobs"), and everyday conversations (i.e., "If we get to the movie early, we will have time to buy popcorn before the previews.") These arguments can usually be proven true or false, and they make claims based on a demonstrable assertion. "It is cold," is a different argument than "You look cold," which is a different argument than "We should all feel cold." Most arguments have an element of "fact-based logic" within them and can at least be supported, if not proven outright, by a set of facts regarding the proposition itself.

Value

Another type of argument you will inevitably come across is an argument of value. Arguments of value make evaluative claims. In other words, arguments of value make judgments based on

Argument	Description
Fact	Argues something is, was or will be. An empirical statement of relationship between two things. <u>Example</u>: Raising the minimum wage will harm job growth. <u>Example</u>: Lee Harvey Oswald did not act alone in the assassination of JFK.
Value	Makes an evaluative or comparative statement about something(s) based on criteria. <u>Example</u>: Corporeal punishment is unethical. <u>Example</u>: John Lennon was more talented that Paul McCartney.
Policy	Argues in favor of an action, movement or change. <u>Example</u>: The U.S. needs to overhaul its tax code <u>Example</u>: You should buy a hybrid car.

Figure 2.2 The Types of Argument

information or evidence that has to be interpreted and seen through a particular perspective. Unlike an argument of fact, which can be demonstrated by a computer or an encyclopedia, an argument of value is often determined by experts in the field, but can easily be decided in different ways depending on the judge and the process of judging. For instance, it is a claim of value, or judgment, to say that "A Snickers tastes better than a Kit-Kat." To prove this claim, and therefore to make an argument, the advocate will need to provide criteria for the value term "better." What constitutes "better," after all? And by which value premise should we judge the "better-ness" of a candy bar? Better for me might not be better for you. One person might love nuts more than any other food item and another might be so allergic that she or he does not know what nuts taste like at all and will hopefully keep it that way! That is why we need to agree on criteria for the word "better." We discuss how to do this in a subsequent chapter; the purpose here is to introduce you to value arguments. Know that, like fact arguments, value arguments are all around us, and they make for very fun, engaging, and often passionate discussions. For instance, claiming that, "abortion is immoral" or that "religion is corrupt" will likely stir strong reactions and spark some unique conversations. Patience, an open mind, and a system two orientation are crucial to keeping these kinds of discussions productive and educational for all involved.

Policy

A final type of argument you will come across is an argument of policy. Speaking generally, a "policy" is a definite course of action. It is not surprising to learn then that arguments of policy are often characterized by words like *should* or *need to*. Arguments of policy are common in politics, but policy arguments can be found virtually everywhere. It is likely the case that you have made arguments of policy on many occasions with your friends or family. For instance, if you have ever told your family members to vote for someone and subsequently offered up reasons why, you have made an argument of policy. Of course, arguments of policy are complex because they often involve groups changing their behavior or allocating resources in a certain way. In many instances, arguments of policy are built upon a collection of arguments of fact and arguments of value. When you encouraged your family members to vote for a particular candidate, you might have offered some supplementary arguments about how the candidate supports progressive change and protection of the environment (arguments of value), and you might have shared information about the candidate's voting record and experience on the job (arguments of fact). An argument of policy is a call for change—for the pursuit of a particular course of action that is not being taken in the present system, or *status quo*. Similarly, if you have ever told your friends not to take a class from a particular professor because she is a hard grader and she does not allow you to text during class, you have made an argument of policy (based on value arguments implied by "hard grader" and a fact argument about her texting policy). In fact, if you have ever asked anyone out on a date, you are familiar with arguments of policy on an interpersonal level (asking someone to marry you is one of the biggest *proposals of policy* you will ever make!).

Being able to detect different types of arguments is one of the most important skills involving argumentation. "What type of argument is it?" is an important first question to ask and to answer. Make sure you practice with your classmates on this one. Find a newspaper or listen to the radio and try to identify as many arguments of fact, value, and policy that you can. As we have been hinting, notice that the different types of arguments relate to one another in overlapping patterns. It is important to know the vocabulary of these types of arguments, but it is equally important to know that actual arguments combine these three types in complicated and contingent ways. Policy arguments are often based on value arguments. And value arguments are often based on fact arguments. For example, the U.S. and Iranian governments are highly distrustful of each other, and in recent years the United States government has accused the Iranian government of

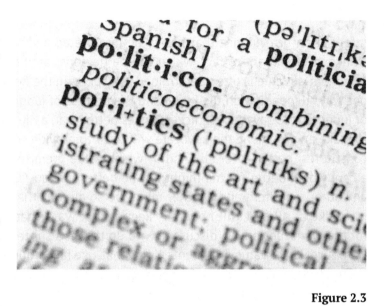

Figure 2.3

enriching uranium for the purpose of manufacturing a nuclear weapon. As a result, a number of lawmakers have argued that the U.S. military should intervene to prevent this from happening. But is it really true that Iran is seeking a nuclear weapon? And do they even have the capability? Furthermore, would it be bad or harmful if Iran acquired a nuclear weapon? And, finally, we have to ask whether U.S. intervention and war would be worth the risks. There are a number of countries in the world with nuclear weapons. Why should we prevent Iran from exercising the same right? What should we do? This is a major argument confronting the leaders of these countries and the world as a whole, and it depends on a cascading arrangement of facts, values, and policies. Without a sense of how argumentation works, these intense disagreements would have no means of resolving themselves absent serious military conflict.

Notice how each of the questions we just asked relates to one another. We first asked a question of fact (i.e., Is Iran pursuing a nuclear weapon?), followed by a question of value (i.e., Would it be harmful if Iran acquired a nuclear weapon?), and we concluded with a question of policy (i.e., What should be done?). Our ability to argue for a particular policy in many ways rests on our ability to argue fact and value. Therefore, being a strong policy advocate means being a successful fact and value advocate as well. It is good to know the three main types of argument, but we also want to reiterate that they overlap with one another and cannot be easily separated. A good argument generally rests on facts, values, and policy prescriptions. An argument with facts but not value structure or framework behind those facts is usually not very significant ("It is going to rain later because those clouds are approaching.") An argument with a cumbersome

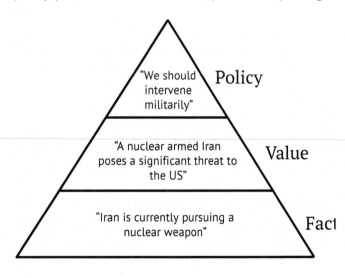

Figure 2.4 Fact, Value, and Policy

value structure but no facts is probably going to be one person's opinion and not very compelling ("The superior religion is the one I belong to because I have deep faith and conviction.") A strong policy argument is one that has both facts and values to support the premise ("The United States should not intervene in Iran unless we are acting with a group of nations including most of Europe, Russia, China, and Saudi Arabia because international consensus is a better way to help moderate a country with nuclear weapons than going in alone.") As we play with these examples, you should start to see how influential a good argument can be and how arguments perform a number of roles in our everyday lives.

Roles in Argumentation

As you now know, arguments (of fact, value, or policy) are made every single day—in Congress, in businesses and restaurants, and in dorm rooms and chat rooms around the world. On the other hand, we need to point out that not every argument is worth arguing about! For instance, if your boyfriend says, "I think murder should be illegal because it deprives one of life, liberty, and the pursuit of happiness," you are very likely (hopefully!) to agree. After all, murder *already is* illegal and as a result there is nothing to argue about. The same could be said for the following arguments:

> "The Earth is round. We know this from scientific experimentation and empirical observation."
> "All American citizens who are 18 years of age should be allowed to vote in local and national elections because it is their constitutional right!"
> "Plagiarizing your work is wrong because it is dishonest and fraudulent."

Each of these examples is an argument. The problem with them is that they do not seek a change in belief or behavior and, consequently, there is nothing substantial to argue about. Of course a crafty opponent seeking out an argument could take the position that those positions should be reversed and that the status quo is flawed. It would be hard to reverse tables like that with the first one (we will soon see how far you have to go to dispute the thesis that the Earth is not flat), but it should not be too hard to argue the position that the voting age should be raised to 21 and that plagiarism depends on the context and it can be OK to use someone else's work if you extend the appropriate credit (which mean it is no longer plagiarism, but that depends on the definition of plagiarism and at least initiates an argument). On the question of the geometry of the Earth, however, it should be no surprise that the overwhelming majority of rational people believe the Earth is round. Similarly, it is not hard to demonstrate that American citizens who are 18 years of age should be allowed to vote. They already can! And, of course, given a typical definition of plagiarism that includes the fact that the culprit does not cite the original source of the work, everyone *knows* that plagiarism is wrong—even the ones who do it, which is why they try not to get caught! In other words, we can all agree on these arguments unless there is an additional stipulation (i.e., a United States citizen who is over 18 should not be allowed to vote because she is a convicted murderer).

For an argument to be worth arguing, there must be at least two clear sides of the debate: the *advocate* and the *opponent*. When both sides agree on the argument, as in the case of the Earth being round, there is no *clash*, or disagreement surrounding the argument. Having at least two sides allows the game of argumentation, often called debate, to be played (as is the case with most other games). With that said, let us describe the two sides in detail.

The Advocate (The Affirmative Case)

The advocate is usually responsible for first proposing and defending the argument. There is one format of debate on the high school level (Public Forum Debate), where it is possible for the "con" side to begin the debate, but that is quite rare, and the standard model is that the side advocating change should begin the "round." In addition, the argument the advocate supports, or affirms, must challenge the *status quo*, or the way things currently are. As mentioned, the status quo is the present system or the current state of affairs, and it is assumed to be right or correct. This is important because many debates hinge on the idea that the status quo is flawed and needs to be changed. It is the advocate's job to convince the audience or the judge that it is time to make a change. In other words, the status quo is the best option unless demonstrated otherwise. Faith in the status quo is often referred to as *presumption,* and it is presumption that the advocate must overcome. In other words, presumption is the enemy of the advocate because it means that a "tie goes to the runner" and the advocate must prove that the runner (or status quo) is definitively "out." The advocate successfully challenges presumption, however,

Figure 2.5 Cultural Horizons

by meeting the *burden of proof*, which is the burden or expectation of a certain level of proof to disprove the status quo. Satisfaction of the burden of proof is necessary for a rational person, body, or judge to suspend faith in presumption and vote for the advocate. Let us illustrate this with an example.

Instead of arguing that the Earth is round, which as we discussed earlier is already almost universally accepted, let us take on the position of the Flat Earthers and argue that the Earth is actually flat. Now *here* is a position of advocacy! Think of all the scientists at NASA that we will be disappointing.

The status quo, being the way things currently are, includes the belief that the Earth is round (or an oblate spheroid, to be accurate). It is the most widely held position on the issue, and while scientists can be wrong, and often are, the claim that the Earth is round (or at least spherical) is widely seen as an empirical, observable, and uncontestable fact. Therefore, the position that we are arguing—the contention that the Earth is actually flat—puts us in a clear position of advocacy and virtually everyone else in a clear position of opposition to our radical argument (it is interesting to note that it was quite radical at one point in history to argue that the Earth was not flat). In this case, based on modern science, it is *presumed* that the Earth is round unless we can prove otherwise. So what will that require? In other words, what is our burden of proof?

Well, let us pretend that you and I stumbled upon a startling realization. Let us pretend that that the mathematical formulas that various scientists have used to prove the roundness of the Earth are wrong. Furthermore, we discover that, in actual fact, the moon landing was a hoax and that the hundreds of satellite images purporting to show Earth as a spheroid have all been manipulated to further this myth. Indeed, we contend, the Earth is actually flat and to argue otherwise is to play into the hands of NASA and the United Nations—the two conniving entities responsible for perpetuating this lie! In short, here is our argument:

> *Claim: The Earth is flat.*
> *Grounds: 1. Mathematical formulas used to prove the Earth is round are wrong.*
> *2. Satellite images showing the Earth as round have been edited and manipulated.*
> *3. The moon landing was a hoax created by the United Nations.*
> *Warrant: If Grounds 1–3 are true, the Earth must be flat.*

Would you be convinced by this argument? Even a little? Well, if yes, we would say that the advocate has met the burden of proof. And when an advocate meets the burden of proof we often say that the advocate has established a *prima facie* case. A case is *prima facie* (*prīmā faciē*) when, at first glance, the advocate has met the burden of proof and, therefore, has called into question the legitimacy of the status quo. Importantly, establishing a prima facie case does not mean the debate is over. Quite the opposite is true. A prima facie case simply means that the debate can begin. Otherwise, if the advocate fails to meet the burden of proof, the status quo prevails and the debate is over. So in our example, if you were not convinced by our case that the Earth is actually flat, then our case was not prima facie and the opponents (i.e., NASA) win (we are simplifying things quite a bit here).

The Opponent (The Negative Case)

Just like the advocate, the opponent has a number of responsibilities. Importantly, however, while the advocate has to overcome presumption, the opponent enjoys the benefit of defending the present system. In other words, the opponent is supported by the status quo. As the opponent or a member of the opposition, you simply have to negate the advocate; you do not have anything independent that you must justify. If you block the affirmation of change, you win. When you are the opponent this is a great thing for a number of reasons. First, the opponent is not responsible for developing a full argument or justification for change, even though some opponents may decide to do so. The key, though, is that the opponent is not expected to defend the need for any change. Why would she or he? After all, if it is not broken, do not fix it.

A second reason why it is nice to be the opponent is that change does not come easy. If there is one thing we have learned about humans it is that humans do not change readily. This

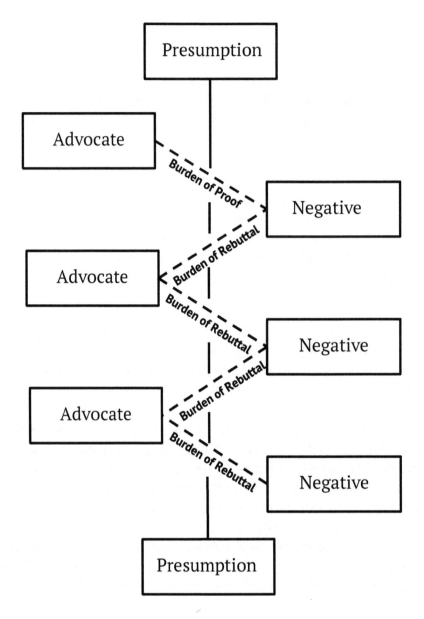

Figure 2.6 The Argumentation Process

is true for beliefs and behaviors alike. Even when presented with new information or facts that disapprove our beliefs, we go on believing them anyhow. Similarly, even when we learn that a particular behavior is bad or harmful we still go about doing it. The advocate's responsibility is convincing us otherwise—that we need to change our beliefs or our behavior. We have already learned that this is called the burden of proof and meeting the burden of proof is hard, hard work (as you will see). But this is good news for the status quo and the opponent.

Let's illustrate the opponent's position using our previous example. The opponents in the argument that the Earth is flat would be all those who believe the Earth is round. As mentioned before, this would include virtually all of the scientific community and, well, most everyone else. As the opponents, they would have to do nothing until we, the advocates, presented a prima facie case (as we tried to do earlier). If we failed to do so, then the opponents would not have any arguing to do because the case would be closed, so to speak. If, however, we succeeded in meeting the burden of proof (thus making a prima facie case in defense of the statement that the Earth is flat), the opponents (the scientists) would then, and only then, have to get out of their comfortable swivel chairs, don their lab coats, and get to arguing! Responding to a prima facie case in this way is often called the *burden of rebuttal,* and it is the responsibility of the opponent to rebut the initial argument only if the advocates, indeed, make a prima facie case.

To satisfy the burden of rebuttal, the opponent now has to think like the advocate. She has to build a case *against* the advocate's. Her job is to show that the status quo—the way things are—should still be upheld despite the advocate's prima facie case. Once she does this, then it is the responsibility of the advocate to *rebut* again. It goes back and forth, back and forth like this until a decision is made or a verdict is delivered or time runs out (see Figure 2.6).

The burden of rebuttal, also called the burden of rejoinder, propels the debate back and forth through a sequence of arguments, responses, and counter-responses. Importantly, it is extremely valuable to realize as a student of argumentation that not all arguments are resolved. In fact, in terms of a definitive proposition, very few are decided beyond a doubt. Even in the courtroom we talk about the "preponderance of evidence" or "beyond a reasonable doubt" or "satisfies strict scrutiny" because there is always a chance that an argument could go in the opposite direction of what we assume. So often we want final answers to our questions. Answers satisfy our need for explanation, for correct information and a conclusion. But some arguments persist throughout time, and we should be okay with that. The same will be true for some of your arguments. Answers *may never come.* What is important is that you engaged the topic, you learned about the issues involved, and you argued your point. All is never lost.

Hopefully now you are really starting to see how the game is played. To summarize, there are two positions: the advocate and the opponent. Both positions have responsibilities and duties to fulfill in order to win the argument. Both positions have advantages and drawbacks. Be sure to realize that you will inevitably be both an advocate and opponent at some time, which is why it is important to know each position. In addition, knowing how to be a skilled advocate will help you to become a skilled opponent and vice versa.

Argumentation vs. Debate: Overview and Format Descriptions

Argumentation is not the same as debate, strictly speaking. In fact, the two are quite different, with the former often referring to the general process of coming to a reasoned decision through written or oral deliberation and the latter often referring to a specific modality of, primarily, oral deliberation occurring within an artificial environment, governed by arbitrary rules and constraints, and adjudicated by a third party. The focus of this book is on argumentation, writ large. However, it's important for us to discuss debate in some detail.

There are a number of different types of debate in high school and college, not to mention all the less formal types of debate that occur every day with varying levels of competition and rules. The most common form of debate in the public sphere is political debate, and there is a vast literature on how political debates are established and conducted and moderated. Presidential and Vice-Presidential debates are fascinating events to study, including the connections to the two-party structure, the media, and voting behavior as a whole. Our intent here is not to weigh in on the precise details of political debates, but to gesture to the vast array of these contests and the number of events—often simply opposing speeches—that are classified as debate.

A more specific conception of competitive debate occurs throughout thousands of educational institutions in the United States and the world community, even spreading to places such as middle schools, home schools, community colleges, and summer debate "institutes" or "workshops" where students gather to improve their debate skills at a "debate camp." You will encounter debates throughout all walks of life, from a formal once-a-year debate held at a social club, church, or school over a traditional topic all the way to the nightly banter back-and-forth at the dinner table or even a bar. In some sense, every conversation with opposing viewpoints being presented against one another is a debate.

Competitive or "Formal" Debate

Competitive or "formal" debates involves two or more participants and at least one judge engaging in a back-and-forth "round" presenting arguments on either side of a specific proposition. Evidence is typically presented in different ways, and the competitors are usually allotted various amounts of time to speak, cross-examine one another, and prepare arguments.

The number of formats of competitive debate is immense and often very specific to a given region, league, or circuit. The most common forms of debate on the high school (and middle school) levels are: policy debate, Lincoln-Douglas debate, public forum debate, and Congressional debate. We will not list all of the details and practices of each type of debate here, but it is helpful to know about some of the differences and similarities and to think about how various arguments can be privileged and emphasized in distinct formats. It is also helpful to recognize how narrow competitive debate really is within the larger context of argumentation and all the environments where argumentation surfaces. If you do not participate in one of these formats, you will invariably run into someone who does, and it will be helpful to understand how arguments emerge and are framed in each of these contexts.

Figure 2.7 Debate Takes Many Formats

Congressional Debate

As implied by its title, this type of debate is designed to replicate the debates and deliberation that occur in the legislature over particular bills and propositions. The clash is not as much about evidence in this format because it is primarily about endorsing certain pieces of legislation, but there is debate over the proposed bills and propositions, and those floor speeches are used to determine the success of a given Congressperson in the competition.

Policy Debate

This type of debate is practiced widely among middle school, high school, and college students. In policy debate, two debaters make up one team, and a debate consists of an affirmative team and a negative team discussing a particular proposition. Usually the proposition is a major policy question and will be in effect for an entire season or a majority of the season. On the college level, CEDA (the Cross Examination Debate Association) practiced a form of policy debate that used to tackle two different propositions each season until it merged with the NDT (National Debate Tournament) and adopted one policy topic for the duration of the season. The National Forensics League (NFL) recently became the National Speech and Debate Association (NSDA), and that organization governs many high school debate activities and generates the topics for the various formats.

The basic format follows a series of four constructives that are about 10 minutes long (eight minutes in high school and nine minutes in college) and four rebuttals (five minutes for high school, six minutes for college). Each speaker gives a constructive and a rebuttal, and each constructive is followed by a three-minute cross examination period where the previous speaker is questioned by one of the opposing debaters. The purpose of the debate is for the affirmative to defend the proposition and the negative to negate the affirmative's defense of the topic. A lot of variety exists in the style and conventions governing policy debate as well as the other types of debate, but usually the time format mentioned above is used as well as an agreed-upon proposition or topic.

Lincoln-Douglas Debate

As opposed to the two-person teams in policy debate, Lincoln-Douglas or "LD" Debate is made up of single debaters, debating as individuals. Each debater is affirmative or negative, and the propositions are usually in effect for a few months. The topics are supposed to be more about values and debates or principles such as the individual and the community or justice and security. Recently, however, LD topics have started to include policy questions about specific instances of legislation and how to implement effective policy. The initial creation of LD was about discussing philosophical arguments more than direct policy, but that line has been hard to draw, and both policy debate and LD have experienced some slippage and taken on topics from each other's areas. The standard LD debate features five speeches,

Figure 2.8 Lincoln-Douglas Statue

with the affirmative speaker delivering arguments first and last (as well as in the middle) and the negative speaker talking second and fourth. There are cross examinations after the first two constructive speeches, and each debater is given a certain amount of "preparation time" to spend getting ready for the upcoming speech. LD is very popular among high school debaters, but it is also in operation on the college level with a smaller number of participating schools (NFA LD).

Public Forum Debate

Public Forum debate was designed to be more accessible and a type of debate that could be judged by anyone on any subject. Despite the original intent to make public forum debate focus on persuasion and not technique, a certain level of expertise has bled into the activity and turned the national circuit into a shorter version of policy debate. The constructives are only four minutes and the rebuttals just two, but there are long cross examination periods, even towards the end of the debate. The last cross examination, called the "grand crossfire" is particularly important for framing the debate, and each side can ask as well as answer questions. The topics in public forum are usually from the recent newspapers and involve a policy question.

Parliamentary Debate

Types of parliamentary debate are expanding on the high school level, and in some senses the title is a misnomer because it is not directly modeled on a parliamentary style, but this is the most common form of debate in colleges and universities in the United States. The affirmative is called the government or "the house," and the negative is the opposition. The two major organizations in the United States are the American Parliamentary Association (APA), governing

Figure 2.9 Opening of Canadian Parliament

events primarily on the East Coast, and the National Parliamentary Debate Association (NPDA), governing events in the West and mid-West. The APA is slightly more traditional, and the NPDA is slightly more aligned with policy debate in terms of the arguments being made and types of propositions being discussed. Evidence in "parli" is more off-the-cusp or generated in a short preparation period after the topic is discussed. Teams are made up of two participants, and the main distinction between this format and others is that the topics vary, even round by round. In some instances, the topic areas are announced a few weeks before hand, and in other instances the debaters come to the tournament not knowing the areas or the actual wordings until twenty minutes before the debate starts. There is little to no prep time in this format and the cross examinations occur in a modified way during the speeches.

Other

There are plenty of additional formats of debate and many that are not organized on a national or state level and may not be associated with educational institutions. British Parliamentary (BP), or "World Debate" is another common format that takes place around the world, usually in English. It is more about a team performing well than about proving and rejecting a particular proposition. BP features teams of four (or four teams of two) and is a type of propositional debate where the topic is announced prior to each round and the research focus is replaced with more of an emphasis on persuasion.

Argumentation and Debate: Genres of Argumentation

Many argumentation scholars would approach the term "genre" slightly differently than we are here. You have worked through a lot of the material on the nature and study of argumentation. Shortly you will be reading chapters on structuring and defending particular arguments. As the history and the structure come into the picture, you will not only have a sense of what an argument is, you will also be able to craft your own. The final step, one that begins right now, is to get a sense of the radical significance and operation of argumentation theory. We encourage you to learn the larger conceptions and contextualization surrounding argumentation by discussing argumentation and the self, argumentation and social movements, and more abstract notions of the public sphere and criticism within argumentation. To do it, though, we have to pivot from academic debate—where we are now—to the literal diagrams of specific arguments offered by Stephen Toulmin.

The pivot for this entire textbook, here at the end of Chapter Two, is to take some of the vocabulary from competitive debate and weave it back through the field of argumentation more generally, and begin to think about the links between human interaction, change, and argumentation. The two most common forms of debate at the collegiate level, including students who debated throughout high school and maybe middle school all the way through students who just picked up debate in the last year or two and are getting more involved, are CEDA-NDT policy debate and NPDA Parliamentary debate.

Both of these forms of debate involve a team of two students on either the affirmative or negative side of a proposition. To defend that proposition, the affirmative or government will begin the debate with a defense of a vision of the proposition, even if the vision includes discarding some or all of the proposition for a better approach to affirmation. Along the way, the negative will attempt to "win" the debate and compel the judge to vote for the opposition through a number of arguments. This is no different than our earlier discussion of building and negating a case, only the types of arguments have taken on certain dimensions and classifications to help us understand their basic objectives.

Framework

This genre asks how the arguments themselves should be adjudicated and what model is most appropriate for comparing and evaluating the debate. In some senses, the framework is the paradigm the judge uses to make a decision in the debate, but it is ultimately a question of how the debaters defend the background and justifications for their arguments. Paradigms are often discussed in terms of different models for judging, with the framework being a type of overarching or "meta-argument" that attempts to establish particular paradigmatic approaches that should be assumed by the judge or to prioritize certain aspects of a pre-given model of judging. The crucial questions to ask when thinking about these questions of framework are: "Who do we represent when we debate?" and "How do we make change?"

These are also significant questions for the larger study of argumentation because we often represent different constituencies when we advance arguments (ourselves, our families, our communities, our political parties, our state, our country, our religions, or even our fellow humans, to name a few). Moreover, depending on the agents or interests we represent, we also have to consider the changes that are possible from those different perspectives. Are we seeking to change someone's mind, influence a decision maker to pass or implement a given policy, spark a social movement, spark a new and unique way of thinking, or simply raise an issue that was previously not being considered?

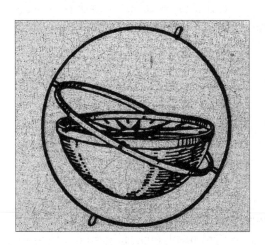

Figure 2.10 Framing Matters

The two common ways to conceptualize the framework issue are to think about an argument or a more formal debate as a particular deliberation over "micro-political" change or "macro-political" change. The micro-framing route asserts that the debate is about ideas, scholarship, and social criticism from the perspective of the immediate agency in the debate round itself. In other words, the framework is one of "local discourse," where the debaters represent themselves as critics or organic intellectuals and the arguments in question are about what those ideas and concepts mean to the immediate audience and the individuals in the room. The answer to the question, "How do we make change?" is either limited to the changes made possible by the speakers themselves in the local vicinity or the ways in which the arguments might "spill over" from the debate into other arenas such as local political platforms, small-scale social movements, petitions, protests, or social media campaigns. From that perspective, larger changes may occur, but they are hard to predict and they have a very specific starting point: the debate itself.

The other side of the coin involves a "macro-political" framing where the debate is primarily a deliberation about larger changes in society that are not directly influenced by the arguments at play, but the participants in the debate have agreed to suspend their immediate location and discuss a hypothetical decision-making body that is external to the debate itself. In other words, the macro-political frame lets the debaters imagine themselves to be actors in the world and decide how those actors should behave. Should the Supreme Court decide a certain way on an upcoming case? Should the local school board change its policies governing school lunches? Should the federal government adopt universal health care for all of it citizens? Should the United Nations expand its focus on environmental refugees? In many instances, these macro-political questions are addressed by allowing the debaters to pretend to act through the larger institution in question and to "fiat" that the desired policy is implemented.

This framework discussion is longer than the explanations of the other genres, but it is also the gateway to a broader understanding of how argumentation functions and what debate is all about. To govern the framework of a given debate is not to automatically prevail, but it is a massive step in defeating opposing positions in terms of their relevance and their degree of refutational responsiveness, or clash. This is exactly why the Presidential debates involve so much back-and-forth before the events can be held in the first place: determining who asks questions, what those questions will cover, and how each candidate will respond to the questions and engage with each other can make a huge difference in the outcomes. In some ways, the classic example of the power of framework and perspective can be seen in the example of Nixon vs. Kennedy where those audience members who heard the debate on the radio felt that Nixon had the upper hand and those who watched the debate on television thought that Kennedy was victorious. The relative importance of *ethos, pathos,* and *logos* can sway an audience in certain directions quite easily. We will return to the lessons implied by the framing of arguments, but at this point it is important to remember that arguments do not occur in a vacuum and the overall context of how certain positions are compared is extremely significant.

Figure 2.11 We are All Connected

Topicality

Topicality is the question of whether the case—the reason to change from the status quo—is actually within the parameters set up by the proposition. Does the case defend the topic? Is it within the limits of the wording of the proposition? If the proposition says, "Jane should go to the store," does the affirmative case demonstrate that it would be a good idea for Jane to go to the store, or, on the contrary, does the case prove that John should go to the store? If the answer is John, then the case is not topical. Likewise, if the case proves that Jane should go to the movies, then it is not topical. If the proposition says that Jane should go to the grocery store and the case simply proves that she should go to the store in general, then it may or may not be topical. If the proposition states that "Jane should go to the grocery store" and the case proves that Jane should go to the gym, then the case is not topical. Typically topicality is necessary to make sure that the debate takes place on the agreed upon issues and allows the opposition to prepare for the discussion. Education is usually enhanced when the affirmative case is within the agreed upon topic and the debate contains more clash on the direct question instead of procedural debate over whether or not the affirmative case is fair.

In many ways, topicality is a genre of argument that allows the negative team to keep the affirmative on target and to have an argument in instances where the affirmative is not on target. In some ways, this type of argument boils down to jurisdiction—does the judge have the jurisdiction to vote for the affirmative if the case does not defend the proposition at hand? If the question of the debate is one the centers on the proposition (is the proposition a good idea?), then an affirmative case that defends action outside that proposition is not a reason for the adjudicator to vote affirmative. Think about topicality as the boundaries set forth by the proposition. The burden of topicality is that the affirmative should defend some aspect of the proposition within those boundaries.

Disadvantages vs. Advantages

The advantages are the reasons why the case is a good idea or the positive results of advocating a change within the proposition. If the case is a restriction on gun ownership, then one advantage might be a reduction in gun violence and another advantage might be fewer accidents involving guns in the home. Disadvantages are arguments presented by the negative or the opposition and they are used to defend the status quo and argue against change. A disadvantage is a negative consequence of pursuing the affirmative case and ideally is something that is more significant than the advantages garnered by the case. A disadvantage to the case that defends more restrictions on gun ownership might be that such restrictions would violate the second amendment to the Constitution and the importance of protecting the Constitution outweighs the advantages of less gun violence and fewer gun accidents. Another disadvantage would be an economic argument that contends that gun sales and the gun industry are crucial to the financial stability of the economy and a downturn in the economy would be worse than the advantages.

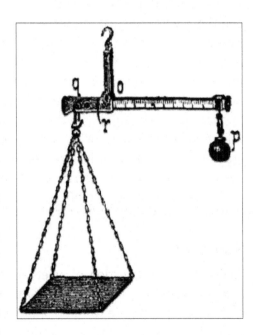

An important element of an effective disadvantage is that it outweighs the benefits of the affirmative case. That element of the disadvantage is called the impact—the consequence or problem brought about by

Figure 2.12

the enaction of the plan. A disadvantage also requires a link—how does the affirmative case cause the problem? It is also necessary to prove that the link is unique to the case, that it is not something that can be attached or attributed to the status quo as well. The "uniqueness" of a disadvantage is the portion of the argument that explains why the impact will not occur in the status quo—that the present system is on track to avoid the negative consequences of the disadvantage. So, for example, the economic disadvantage would argue that the gun industry is strong and growing in the status quo because guns are being sold regularly at a healthy profit. The link would state that future restrictions on gun ownership would reverse that trend and result in a weaker gun industry and less economic growth overall. The impact, ultimately, would be that a collapse of the gun industry (or at least a slowing of its profitability) would damage the economy, risk a prolonged economic recession, and create financial hardship for the country that would translate into fewer jobs, a lower standard of living, and greater hardships, including poverty and mental depression.

Counterplan

The counterplan is a type of argument that agrees that change is necessary—there is a problem that needs to be confronted—but the way in which the case goes about trying to resolve that question is not the best path. A counterplan is another way to solve the problem that avoids some disadvantageous consequence of the affirmative case. Typically the negative defends that the status quo is the best option and change is not needed, but a counterplan allows the negative to also manipulate the present system in some way and reject the affirmative case in favor of the counterplan.

Depending on the topic, the counterplan could do anything from acting through a different agent to using a distinct mechanism to solve the problem, or it could go further in the opposite direction of the affirmative to draw out the link to a disadvantage. If the proposition is that "Jane should go to the store," than a counterplan might be "Jane should shop on the Internet at home." Of course the counterplan cannot simply be a rival policy that does not compete with the affirmative case—it has to clash. Without competition, the affirmative debater or debaters can simply say, "Let us do both." Doing both the affirmative case and the counterplan is called a permutation, and it is a way to demonstrate that the counterplan does not compete with the case. Ultimately, the negative must prove that the adoption of the counterplan alone is better than the adoptions of the plan and all or some of the counterplan. These norms involving counterplan theory are not solidified principles, and all of this argumentation is open to debate.

Kritiks

Kritiking is the debate genre of radical criticism or the praxis of critique. Primarily rooted in critical theory coming out of the disciplines of Rhetoric and of Philosophy, Kritiks are arguments that undercut the deeper assumptions being made by the affirmative case. The affirmative's language, value structure, and ideology could all be seen as flawed from different perspectives that argue about the methodology being used rather than the implementation of a particular policy.

Kritiks can originate from thousands of directions, including more popular criticism based the work of Foucault or Marx and obscure arguments about the nature of time or the consequences of adhering to something like international realism or a calculative mindset that relies too heavily on the state. How do these kritiks address the problems they reference, let alone tackle the specifics of the affirmative case? The specifics are fleshed out in the link to the kritik, whereas as the kritik's solution is posited in an "alternative" way of approaching the world and the case.

Figure 2.13 You Are

Kritiks are tightly interwoven with framework because it makes a big difference whether the debate is about legislative role-playing or endorsing a certain form of scholarship. It is also possible to go beyond this type of kritik into a realm that is more about personal perspective and the individual standpoints in the debate. How does a student perform a given identity and what relations of oppression are tied up in those constructions and lived experiences? Much of these performance arguments are about aesthetics, but there is an emerging vocabulary about these kinds of identity politics, also called performance affs or projects.

There may be a number of other genres of argument, and there are certainly positions that combine some of the types of debate arguments discussed here. Every format has a different take on these types of arguments and which ones are more acceptable than the others. What really makes sense to each format varies and this is a very broad overview. Nonetheless, many types of debate are using issues like these, and it is almost always the case that the affirmative has to defend the proposition for change, but also gets to speak first and last.

Learning Activities: Chapter Two

1. Identify if the following is a claim of fact, value, or policy:
   a. Lower taxes increases consumption.
   b. It is irresponsible to raise taxes during a recession.
   c. We should lower the marginal tax rate.
2. Locate an argument of fact, value or policy in the media. Analyze the argument carefully. Does the advocate meet the burden of proof? In other words, are you convinced? Why or why not?

3. Identify the advocate and opponent on the following issues and summarize their positions.
   a. The Federal Government should legalize prostitution.
   b. Global climate change is a hoax.
   c. The United States military needs to withdraw its troops from Iraq and Afghanistan.
4. Find a partner in class and together, select an article or story from the news that contains a controversial issue or debatable topic. Choose a position on the topic and assign the other position to your partner. Articulate several claims in support of your position. Have your partner articulate their position after.

Figure Credits

CHAPTER 3

The Structure of Arguments

I n Chapter Two we briefly discussed the basic components of an argument. You will recall that an argument has three essential parts: claim, grounds, and warrant. Together, the claim, grounds and warrant create a *unit of argument*. But you most likely did not know that you can make an argument even more complex and more convincing by adding *backing, rebuttals,* and *qualifiers*.

In this chapter we are going to examine arguments and their make up more thoroughly. In many ways, we are about to *dissect* arguments and diagram their constituent parts. Because arguments are the central building block of argumentation, it is absolutely necessary that you understand how they are constructed and how they can be critically assessed. To do this, we think it is best to help you learn more about the Toulmin Model of Argumentation.

Once we have worked through the details of the Toulmin diagram and come up with a set of elements that must be present to constitute an argument, we will then expand the notion of "warrant" or "reasoning" in the primary triad into the larger field of logic. Exploring the foundations of logic helps add to our understanding of the structure of argument as we

recognize that errors in the claim, the grounds, and certainly the warrant can generate a "fallacy" in our thinking. What is logic, and how does it contribute to argumentation? How can we connect logic to rationality and reason? These questions bridge the gap between psychology, sociology, and communication as we discuss different ways of reasoning, distinct modes of thought, and even considerations of the irrational and non-rational.

Finally, we will cap off our expanded discussion of logic and reason with a brief journey into "logical fallacies." What makes up a fallacy in logic, and when is it useful to think about different types of errors in the application of logic?

The Toulmin Model of Argumentation

It seems that every area of intellectual study has its legends. Physics celebrates the genius of Albert Einstein; chemistry celebrates Marie Curie; mathematics has Leonhard Euler. And, likewise, we owe much of our understanding of argumentation today to the work of the great British philosopher Stephen Toulmin (1922–2009).

A student of the philosopher and logician Ludwig Wittgenstein, Stephen Toulmin was educated at Cambridge University. Toulmin spent most of his professional career as an educator and scholar in Europe and the United States. While he published quite prolifically during his career, he is most well known among scholars of rhetoric and argumentation for his book *The Uses of Argument* (1958), in which he provided six components for constructing and analyzing arguments. These six components are formally known as the Toulmin Model of Argumentation.

The Toulmin Model contains two triads, or groups of three. The first triad, which we briefly introduced earlier, consists of the three most basic argument elements: claim, grounds, and warrant. The second triad, a new set of characteristics for arguments, consists of the qualifier, rebuttal, and backing. We will address the secondary triad shortly, but it is important to spend additional time clarifying each element of the primary triad first. If you learn the first triad, you will have come a long way toward understanding the requirements of a complete argument.

The Toulmin Model of Argumentation

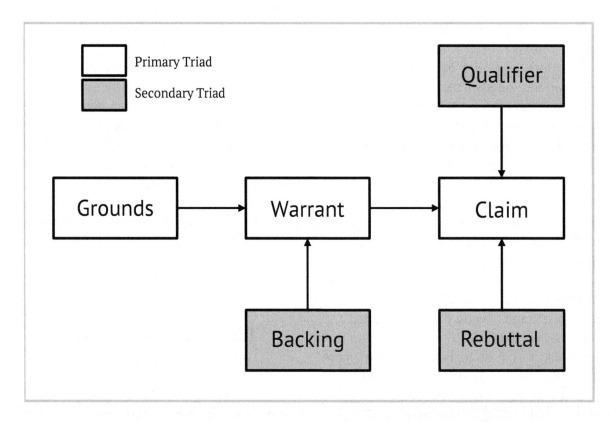

Figure 3.1 The Toulmin Model of Argumentation

The Primary Triad

The primary triad of the Toulmin Model is composed of the claim, grounds, and warrant. Importantly, in Toulmin's original model the grounds are represented as leading to the warrant with the warrant leading to the claim. Toulmin placed the grounds before the claim as a way of illustrating a specific relationship between the elements, namely that grounds provide the basis for the claim. In other words, the grounds lead to the claim. However, it is important to know that when we argue with our friends or coworkers, for example, we often start with claims and follow with grounds. Think about it: rarely when arguing do you begin with evidence; instead, you most likely make an assertion or statement (e.g., "The Yankees are better than the Angels this year") and then provide the reasons that support it (e.g., "because they have a more productive offense, an experienced team leader, and a deeper bullpen"). To emphasize the practical uses of argumentation in our daily lives, our discussion will try to emphasize both the original (and more theoretical) and the more common (and practical) representation of the Toulmin Model.

The Claim

The claim states the position of the advocate and, as such, contains the specific challenge to the status quo. The claim is the thing being argued. It is the thesis or conclusion the advocate purports to prove. The following are examples of claims:

> *Claim 1*: You should boycott all companies that use child labor.
> *Claim 2*: Edward Snowden is a patriot.
> *Claim 3*: Violent video games lead to violent behavior.
> *Claim 4*: I am a British citizen.

Each of these examples is a claim. The first one is a claim of policy and the second example is a claim of value. The third and fourth are both claims of fact. Each claim clearly states the position or thesis of the advocate; each claim could go against the status quo, and therefore, each claim is potentially worth arguing about. In short, there is the potential for *clash* (see Chapter Two for a review of clash).

The Grounds

Stephen Toulmin referred originally to the grounds as the "data," which makes intuitive sense when you realize that the grounds represent the evidence or proof of claim. Whenever you assert something, you need to prove it. You need to "ground" it in evidence, in other words. How else are people supposed to believe your claim? Grounds are the instances of evidence (e.g., statistics, testimony, empirical fact, reference to an expert or authority, etc.) that demonstrate why a claim is true. Let us illustrate this by using Claim 4 listed above. This was the claim Stephen Toulmin used originally in *The Uses of Argument.* We can prove the claim "I am a British citizen" with the following grounds:

> *Ground 1*: I was born in Bermuda.

If you did not know, all persons born in Bermuda are legally considered British citizens. Therefore, we can "ground" or prove the claim "I am a British citizen" by showing that "I was born in Bermuda." In short, being born in Bermuda is the proof that one is, indeed, a British citizen. Importantly, by providing grounds, we have now created an argument. Nevertheless, whether or not we have met our burden of proof depends on a number of other things, including the strength of the warrant.

The Warrant

The warrant is the most conceptually difficult element of Toulmin's primary triad to understand, but it is also arguably the most important. Think of it this way: the warrant is the logical bridge between the grounds and the claim. The warrant is the *logic* that connects the grounds to the claim. For example, the warrant for the argument "I am a British citizen because I was born in Bermuda" is:

Warrant 1: A person born in Bermuda will legally be a British citizen.

Notice how the warrant in this case connects the grounds to the claim through a particular form of reasoning. Because one who is born in Bermuda is legally a British citizen, one can claim she is a British citizen if, in fact, she was born in Bermuda. Importantly, the warrant is often unstated in arguments when it (the warrant) is obvious or undisputed. For British citizens, especially those familiar with their own country's laws and immigration system, the warrant "a person born in Bermuda will legally be a British citizen" would likely be obvious and, therefore, would not need to be explicitly stated. Instead, one could simply argue, "I am a British citizen because I was born in Bermuda." Presumably, most British citizens would know the warrant implicit in this argument. It would be like saying "I am an American citizen because I was born in Alabama." To Americans, the warrant "a person born in Alabama is an American citizen" would be obvious. In other words, a warrant can be left unstated if it is a form of reasoning so well known by the parties to the argument or so commonplace that it does not need to be restated.

Let us illustrate the concept of the warrant further with another example. Pretend we came across the following campaign advertisement: "Put California back to work: Vote Jim Duprie." Catchy political slogans like this one are quite common, but we rarely analyze the logic within them.

The claim in this example is that one should vote for Jim Duprie. The reason why, or the grounds, is that California will be put back to work. The logic, or warrant, here is obvious: Jim Duprie can and will put "California back to work." Notice how the campaign advertisement did not need to explicitly state the

Figure 3.2 A Typical Campaign Advertisement

warrant in this case. We were able to deduce it on our own. And such is the case with warrants in many instances. On the other hand, as we will see, there are many scenarios in which the warrant is *not* so obvious. Furthermore, there are many instances in which the warrant is disputed, debatable or fallacious (i.e., illogical.). For instance, will electing Jim Duprie actually put California back to work? The campaign advertisement does not provide any proof that Mr. Duprie can or will. We are left to just assume it is true. But should we? In cases like this one the warrant needs to be supported with *backing*, which is an element of Toulmin's secondary triad.

Before moving to the secondary triad, however, let us summarize the primary triad of the Toulmin model. The building blocks of argumentation are arguments. At their most basic, arguments are composed of claims, grounds, and warrants. A complete argument requires all three elements. The claim is the position or thesis on the issue. The grounds support the claim by providing evidence for why the claim is true. The warrant is the logic used to connect the grounds with the claim. Using Toulmin's original example again, all three elements can be represented like this:

The Primary Triad of the Toulmin Model

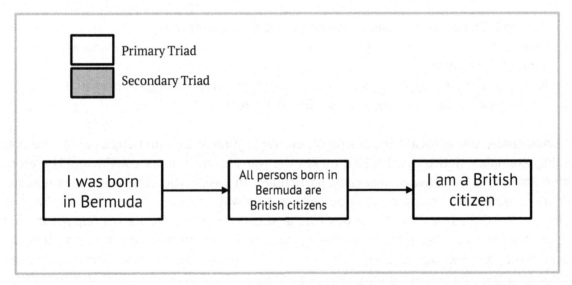

Figure 3.3 The Primary Triad of the Toulmin Model

In everyday use, this same argument might be communicated like this:

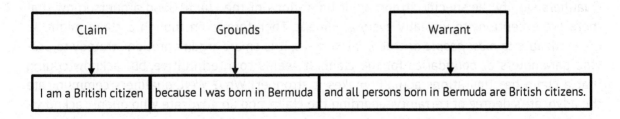

The Secondary Triad

The secondary triad of the Toulmin model builds off the primary triad and consists of backing, qualifiers, and rebuttals. These three elements are not absolute requirements of a complete argument, but they are certainly the difference between a mediocre and somewhat flat argument and one that really matters and can actually change the world.

The Backing

As we discussed previously, in cases where the logic, or warrant, of an argument is disputed, unclear or debatable, an advocate must provide additional "backing" in support of the warrant. You can think of the backing as the grounds for the warrant. Just as the grounds prove the claim, the backing proves the logic. The backing, therefore, is crucial in many situations. Returning to Toulmin's example, if, for instance, the opponent did not know that a person born in Bermuda is legally a British citizen, or the opponent disputed this fact, the advocate would need to prove the truthfulness or validity of the warrant. In short, she would need to provide backing. The following examples would serve as backing for the warrant "all persons born in Bermuda are British citizens:"

> *Backing 1:* The advocate could showcase the legal statute or provision.
> *Backing 2:* The advocate could provide examples of people born in Bermuda who are, in fact, British citizens.
> *Backing 3:* The advocate could acquire expert testimony from a judge or magistrate that verifies that persons born Bermuda are British citizens.

Importantly, the advocate could strengthen her argument by using any or all of the preceding examples. Notice that backing makes the warrant much more convincing. Therefore, while backing is not always necessary, particularly in cases when the warrant is obvious, widely accepted or undisputed, it is our advice to always be prepared to provide backing when you are the advocate and to always demand backing when you are the opponent. After all, the backing provides support for the warrant, which is another way of saying that the backing supports the logic undergirding the entire argument. Some arguments may be more compelling than others, but a minimum requirement of any argument is that it be logical. Backing is truly important.

Qualifiers

Qualifiers signify the specific strengths or limitations of the claim. Good arguers know that there are exceptions to virtually every argument. Therefore, even though a claim might be generalizable *to most people* or true *in most cases,* it is smart argumentation strategy to provide parameters or boundaries for the claim. It seems counterintuitive, but acknowledging that a claim has limitations actually makes it stronger! Why? Well, qualifiers communicate the advocate's degree of certainty regarding the claim, and an advocate who openly acknowledges that there are potential exceptions or a degree of mild uncertainty is better placed to defend the claim against an opponent looking to exploit one or two exceptions as a way of discrediting the entire argument. Some examples of qualifiers include: *all things being equal, in most cases,* or *generally speaking.* Toulmin qualified his claim "I am British citizen" in the following way:

> *Qualifier 1*: "I am a British citizen, presumably."

The word "presumably" serves to qualify the claim "I am a British citizen." What might be the purpose of using a qualifier in this instance? Well, there's a big difference between the claim "I am a British citizen" and the claim "I am a British citizen, presumably." The first claim is much more certain than the second one. Using the qualifier "presumably" may make sense if, for instance, you wanted to claim British citizenship because you were born in Bermuda but were not certain if, because laws may have changed, or because you left Bermuda shortly after birth, being born in Bermuda indeed warranted British citizenship. In short, qualifiers are a way of saying, "this is what I believe, but I am aware that there could be an exception or limitations."

Rebuttals

Rebuttals help to strengthen the advocate's claim by pre-empting any potential counter arguments from the opponent. To *preempt* is to take actions to protect or defend something before it is harmed. For example, if you wanted to build a sand castle near the beach but you knew the tide was going to rise and ultimately destroy your sand castle, you might think to build the sand castle farther from the ocean, beyond the reach of the rising tide. Or you might decide to build a wall around the sand castle that could withstand the tide. Both strategies would provide protection for your castle *before* it was threatened.

In argumentation, preemption involves addressing the counter arguments of your opponent before they can even advance them. If you can frame their arguments for them, you will have an advantage in refutation and you will control the terms of the discussion. Toulmin referred to such efforts as the rebuttal. Addressing a counter argument before it is given is helpful because it allows one to mitigate the harm a counter argument may have on the advocates' position. Returning to Toulmin's original argument, a rebuttal for the claim "I am a British citizen" would be the following:

> *Rebuttal 1*: "A person born in Bermuda will legally be a British citizen, unless she has betrayed Britain and has become a spy for another country."

Rebuttals are not required in argumentation. However, they are useful in situations when the advocate wants to preempt any counterargument from the opponent. In the case of being a British citizen, including the rebuttal "unless she has betrayed Britain and has become a spy for another country" strengthens the argument because it gives the advocate the opportunity to address it and disprove it before the opponent uses it against the affirmative case.

Figure 3.4 Flag Map of Bermuda

Let us now summarize the secondary triad of the Toulmin model. Backing, qualifiers, and rebuttals are used to support and strengthen the elements of the primary triad. Backing helps to support and justify the warrant; rebuttals and qualifiers strengthen the claim by (1) preempting counter arguments and (2) providing boundaries around the certainty and generalizability of the claim, respectively. In many cases, elements from the secondary triad are not needed, but you will want to know them well nonetheless as they can help strengthen any case.

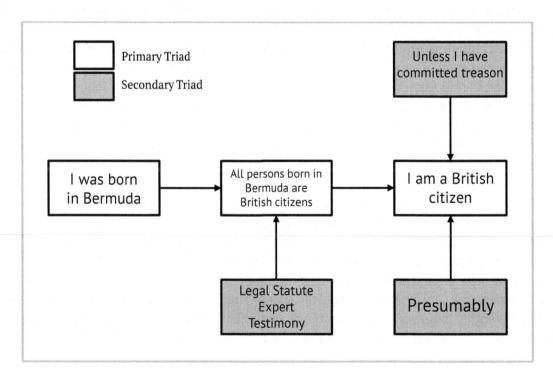

Figure 3.5 The Primary and Secondary Triad of the Toulmin Model

Written more practically, the entire argument could also look like this:

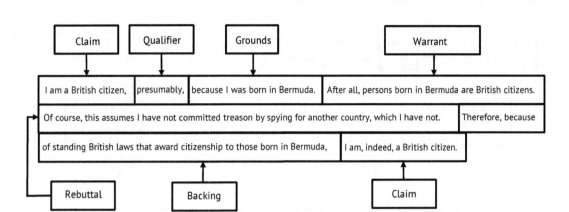

Examples

Let's demonstrate the usefulness of the Toulmin Model for analyzing arguments a bit further by looking at an example.

Argument for Breastfeeding

The American Medical Association strongly recommends breastfeeding for infant children. Still, for a number of reasons, some women choose not to. Other mothers are simply not able to breastfeed their children. In any case, there are strong opinions on the issue. Advocates point to the health benefits associated with breastfeeding; opponents argue that the health benefits have been overstated and that no significant difference exists between breastfed and non-breastfed children. Considering this, let's pretend that someone made the following argument:

> *Unless they are physically unable, I think all mothers should breastfeed their babies for the first year. I understand that breastfeeding poses challenges for some women and infants, but it is often the case that many of those challenges can be eliminated with just several visits with a lactation specialist. Breastfeeding for the first year decreases a child's risk of obesity. Breastfeeding for the baby's first year may lower a baby's risk of sudden infant death syndrome (SIDS). Furthermore, extended breastfeeding is associated with increased bonding between mother and child! This research was conducted by impartial experts and is clear proof that breastfeeding benefits both the mother and child. All mothers want their children to be healthy. Therefore, I believe a mother should breastfeed her baby for the first year.*

Are you convinced by this argument? It certainly sounds convincing at first sight, but as you probably know, we need to take a closer look. What happens if we dissect this argument and analyze the justification for the claim? The good news is that all of the elements of the Toulmin Model are there, and we can diagram them like this:

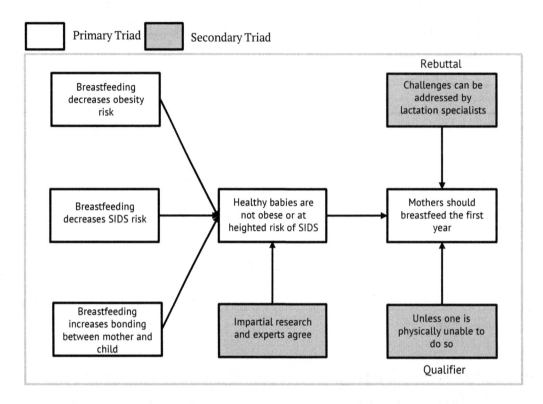

Figure 3.6 Primary and Secondary: Breastfeeding Example

Now that the argument resembles the familiar structure of the Toulmin Model we are better positioned to critique it. You can see clearly that the advocate has provided three reasons, or grounds, to support her claim "*all mothers should breastfeed their babies for the first year.*" The first reason she lists is that breastfeeding reduces a child's risk of obesity. Her second reason is that breastfeeding may reduce the risk of SIDS. And, finally, her third reason is that breastfeeding is associated with increased bonding between mother and child. Also notice that the claim is bounded with the qualifier "unless they are physically unable." This specifies the parameters or generalizability of the advocate's claim in an important way. The advocate wants the opponent to know that her claim does not apply to all mothers, only those who are physically able. This is an important and wise distinction to make because, as we mentioned, some mothers are simply not able to physically breastfeed their children.

Diagramming an argument this way also allows us to see how the grounds relate to the claim through the warrant, which is "*healthy babies are not obese, are not at heightened risk of SIDS, and are closely bonded with their mothers.*" The assertion that mothers want their children to be healthy is a relatively uncontroversial one. But what exactly constitutes "healthy"? And is the advocate asserting that children who are not breastfed can't be healthy? Obviously, this warrant needs backing, which the advocate provides. The assertion "*this research was conducted by impartial experts and is clear proof that breastfeeding benefits both the mother and child*" is clearly intended to allay any concerns that the warrant is justified. Still, to our eyes, the advocate could strengthen her argument by demonstrating that breastfed babies enjoy *unique* health benefits relative to non-breastfed babies.

Logic and Reasoning

Hurrah! You have moved through the most important structural elements in your study of argumentation: the Toulmin model. Understanding that an argument needs to have a claim, grounds to support the claim, and a warrant that explains how the grounds work to demonstrate the claim is essential. Now we are going to add some additional depth to the fluid that makes the Toulmin model work, the *thought process* of creating a warrant. What thoughts do we use to come up with various justifications for an argument? How can we show that the evidence connects back to the claim being made? To assess that process, we need to discuss three concepts that relate back to thinking. What does it mean to think? And, more specifically, what does it mean to think logically, reasonably, and rationally? At the end of Chapter One, we introduced the concept of critical thinking; now we are concerned with the actual nuts and bolts of deploying such modes of thought—the structure behind the mechanics of argumentation. To aid in our pursuit, it is helpful to focus on these three definitions as we discuss the various thought processes that go into argumentation:

Logic

> *Logic is the set of formal principles that directs thought toward a linear, step-by-step assessment of, and response to, a situation or problem.*

Reasoning

> *Reasoning is a method of thought that gathers specifics to form a conclusion or applies a known premise to particulars.*

Rationality

> *A condition of thinking that emphasizes current knowledge and reliable experiences to maximize expectations of accuracy.*

Despite some consistency in the definitions of these three related terms, it is actually difficult to pin down exactly what they mean and how they play out in practice. If someone asks you to "be more logical" or "let's just be reasonable in this situation," you might have a vague sense of what is being requested, but it would be hard to specify in writing the particulars of the expected behavior. What does it really mean to "not act erratically"? You might say you were being asked to "act responsibly" or "think before acting," but it would be hard to get more specific than that until a given situation presented itself.

Take the given situation of global climate change and what to do about it. Once we determine who might be doing the action and what the proposal looks like, we can try to calculate whether it would be worth taking the potential action. To do so, we essentially have a debate in our heads (or with another interested person) about the necessity of, for example, a major carbon tax imposed on all individuals and corporations in the United States. To sum up this kind of problem, we might ask: Should the United States impose a major carbon tax on individuals and corporations in the U.S.? The main reason would be to address the crisis of climate change. Once the situation is posed as an advocacy statement where change is being prescribed to address a certain problem, we can work through the debate as a way to bring logic to bear on the particulars.

Staging a small debate is a good way to work through logic, reasoning, and rationality. Logic would tell us that if the extent of the problem is massive, then action must be contemplated. Secondly, if the primary cause of the crisis is the production and consumption of fossil fuels, the kind of action we need is something that promises a dramatic reduction in such behavior. The United States is a big consumer, perhaps justifying a carbon tax in the U.S. as a way to spur global change. In addition, another justification for the tax comes from the premise that the U.S. is the kind of actor that can influence others to follow, including India and China. All of these steps require dividing the larger statement into a series of smaller problems and determining the plusses and minuses of each given dilemma. Sound reasoning also requires looking at a problem from multiple perspectives, meaning that we would want to take into account, for example, the economic effects of a major carbon tax and the risk that jobs would be lost or productivity would slow.

By using these stages of "hypothetical actions attached to various risks and rewards," we place the situation inside a debate to try to determine the best course of action. The example is complicated, but so are the notions of logic, reasonability, and rationality. Despite our attempts to capture the meaning of these concepts without relying on one term to define another, in terms of providing clear definitions that do not rely on equally slippery terms referring to "correct forms of thought" (sanity, competence, understanding, etc.), there is not a universal definition or structure for any of these terms. Nevertheless, that should not deter us from a more detailed exploration.

Logic

Logic, in its etymology, stretches back to formal speech and the application of reason to specific problems. That makes sense from our perspective because the strength of an argument is often based on its degree of logic and how the logical progression of the argument moves from step to step. One important limitation on logic—and a way to narrow its meaning—is that logic relies on outside pieces of information to be accurate in order to proceed. Logic assumes that the inferences in question are fully valid unless otherwise qualified. In other words, logic does not ask if the reasoning behind the inference is sound or not—it simply wants the abstract form or variable.

In the American Legion's Oratorical Contest that takes place every year for high school students, judges are given instructions for evaluating contestants and ranking the quality of speeches. In the "suggestions to judges," among a number of categories, judges are asked to assess "Logic (Correctness of inference)." The way a score is determined for a participant's use of logic is by asking:

- Are illustrations supported by logic or facts?
- Are conclusions properly drawn?
- Are there inconsistencies in the use of an application of logic?
- Are inferences made without proper support or logic?[1]

These are excellent questions to ask any advocate and go a long way toward determining the validity of a particular statement. That said, we need to go further into what constitutes logic beyond some hard-to-quantify instinct that may hint at logic's presence or that logic is in play. The key word here that should draw our attention is *inference*. Inference is not used regularly in the area of argumentation *except* to talk about logic. Then, when we do hear about an inference in the context of logic, we come across a very interesting tug-of-war between two meanings: an inference as a guess and an inference as a conclusion based on evidence. Those meanings are almost opposites—a guess is typically a shot in the dark or a very rough estimate, whereas a conclusion based on evidence has been tested and has a relatively high degree of accuracy. We need to heed this binary in the meaning of inference and borrow the idea of "probability." What makes a statement more or less probable? Can we seek out the variables that are hard to isolate and assign a degree of probability to the statement? Using probability, we can conclude that logic is a means of testing an inference so that it moves from the realm of guess to the realm of premise.

> *We need to heed this binary in the meaning of inference and borrow the idea of "probability."*

Formal Logic

Formal logic evaluates inferences by creating equations out of arguments. Philosophers will claim it is about determining truth in and through language. Mathematicians will emphasize the form of the argument and the variables for uncertainty. Communication scholars will simply cringe at the simplifications made in a given sentence to fit it into a formal equation. As the name implies, this type of logic is highly structured, agreed upon by a larger community, usually from the sciences, and often associated with the bridge between mathematics and philosophy—going further into numbers would lead to statistics, and going further into ethical theory would lead to morality and maxims for living. To go even further, taking arguments from a formal setting and putting them into symbolic logic (symbols as forms) is only a question of representation—are pieces of an argument effectively represented by symbols within the given equation?

Reasoning

As noted above, reasoning relates to the use of the mind to work through something that is unknown, whether the unknown is a solution, a sense of truth, or a greater understanding. When we are unsure, we have been taught to apply reason that we have learned in the abstract or through experience to resolve our uncertainty. Why do blue and yellow make green when mixed

---

[1] "Suggestions to Judges," 77th Annual H.W. Dare Maness High School Oratorical Contest, Department of South Carolina, *American Legion*, March 12, 2016. On file with authors.

together? To get to the bottom of that question, lots of things have to happen, the least of which is an actual "experiment" where blue paint and yellow paint are mixed together in roughly equal parts and brushed onto a white canvas. From the experiment, we can reason that the color green is positioned on a light spectrum equidistant from blue and yellow. We can also reason that our eyes will detect differences in shade and will recognize green as its own color—something other than a shade of blue or a shade of yellow. Our reasoning is based on past experience, what we have learned about the properties of color within a light spectrum, and empirical observation. In other words, when we apply facts and values that we believe to be valid to something uncertain, we can clarify that uncertainty through the use of reason.

The best way to categorize reasoning is to think about inductive and deductive reasoning because they both imply a particular starting point and an end point to their respective thought processes.

	Direction	**Orientation**	**Form**	**Practice**
Inductive reasoning	Bottom Up	Future	Specifics to general premise	Seek out examples to generate a rule
Deductive reasoning	Top Down	Past/Present	General premise to specifics	Apply a series of rules to particulars

The more examples you can think of to demonstrate the differences between inductive and deductive reasoning, the better. If you observe a number of children with chicken pox who all attend the same school, you might contend that the school is the starting point where kids are making contact with chicken pox and contracting it themselves. That would be inductive because you start with individual cases and move to the general conclusion. If you have a general premise about chicken pox being more likely at a certain school during a certain time of the year, you might surmise that some of the students at the school have chicken pox. There, you are using deductive reasoning because you are starting with a general conclusion and moving to the specific examples.

What is important for our purposes is that you understand how we can move up a chain of logic or down a chain of logic to try to be as reasonable as possible. We move up a chain of logic by carefully assessing the specifics of a situation and then linking those specifics to each other in order to generate a larger premise. We move down a chain of logic by taking a generalized conclusion and applying that to a very specific situation. This is where we find the standard syllogism. Dora is a cartoon character. All cartoon characters are immortal. Dora is immortal. Regardless of the potential error in the premise (some cartoon characters are not immortal), our syllogism follows the statements in a deductive way—we start with two observations that we assume to be true and then derive a third statement about a particular case. Interestingly, a syllogism is also defined simply as an inference or a conclusion, leading us to our discussion of rationality.

Rationality

Western humanists want to define rationality as the extension of Descartes' "I think, therefore I am," an appeal to social convention and sound judgment that leads to predictable and sensible decision-making. If you are rational, then, you rely on logic and you are "clear-headed." We have started to outline some of the standard procedures for thinking in a correct (and usually predictable) way. There is an intricate balance between creativity and effectiveness. When we think about logic and reason, we are implying a certain sequence of thoughts and a measured "rationality." So we arrive at our third term, often defined using the first two and posing the same problems of ambiguity when attempting to reveal what exactly is rational. If we are not defining rationality as the "demonstration of logic" or the "possession or reason," we are still talking about expected human behavior and conduct that stems from sound arguments. Argumentation, including a structure involving data, claim, and warrant, may be the missing link that can unite the floating signifiers of logic, reason, and rationality. Logic, reason, and rationality mean understanding and enacting sound arguments. So let's try to lay out some mechanisms for implementing this thought process. What steps can we take to assist in the application of logic, sound reasoning, and rationality to a given example? As the beginning of a list, we suggest that you "Must Have..."

C. "C" is for Collective understanding and Consensus building. To know that we have acted reasonably, we should not be especially surprised at the outcome or the conclusion. Being shocked or surprised at a decision usually indicates that it is not as logical or rational as the alternatives. Thus, if you were able to obtain collective support for a decision, even consensus from a group of stakeholders, you would be headed in the right direction.

E. "E" is for Experimentation. Do you really know what the question is in the first place? Experimentation can help clarify what is being asked. Experiment with the question at hand before you lock in on a response. Logic is measured and utilized step by step; it can take time to apply. Experiment with different answers and different variables to put your reasoning to the test. Share different conclusions with others and gauge the reactions.

R. "R" is for Risk and Reward. Should we drive across the country? Should the international community ban arms sales? Should we send our children to private school? Should we take out larger loans to enhance our educational opportunities? Should we let non-violent offenders out of prison? Should we see a documentary or science fiction? Should we study another language or take another science class? Or, as we asked earlier, should the United States tax the consumption of carbon? All of these decisions matter in some way or another—that is why they are in dispute, they are contentious. Supporting or not supporting each decision requires deliberation and a conclusion. Often (but not always), we want to make the most reasonable decision possible. Laying out the risks and rewards and comparing them to one another can help make a decision that is more in line with the consequences and thus more rational.

T. "T" is for Test. You have to test the variables that are not certain. Any uncertainty needs to be isolated and given a number or a range—applying percentages and quantifying uncertainty can go a long way toward clarifying the decision itself. Test the possible outcomes by altering the different variables and creating an equation for the dilemma. In some instances, creating a fairly rigid equation out of a complicated and uncertain scenario can bring some necessary clarity to the process.

A. "A" is for Application. The principles that are agreed upon—use past experience, use empirical data, use research from credible sources, be cautious, take risks that are proportional to the reward, etc.—should be applied uniformly and consistently. Once the ground rules are set in place (ideally before the particular situation arises), you should follow them closely, in sequence, without bias or altering the rules to conform to the particulars. Any alterations in the application should be reflected in the procedures going forward.

I. "I" is for Identify. Identify the main assumptions and then make a chain from each assumption back to the proposed solution. Each assumption should have a reasoned connection—a linear relationship—to the next piece in the chain. The beginning of the first link and the end of the last one should return to the same variable. Once the primary assumptions can be identified, those can be split up into sub-assumptions. Each smaller question that can be identified and treated as a separate problem should be examined on its own and then added into the larger equation. Ultimately, moving through the logical chain step by step can provide a check on tangents or conclusions gone awry.

N. "N" is for Note and Notice. You should take notes on everything you notice along the way—what each step is, how you addressed it, using what parameters, where you are taking leaps, where you are certain of the results, what similarities you detect with other scenarios, what differences, etc. When you find comparisons, also ask about exceptions. Do the exceptions prove the rule, as we like to say, or do they point to a flaw in the reasoning? The more exceptions that can be applied to the situation to either reinforce or complicate the decision, the better.

T. "T" is for Try again. Try going through the logical steps again and see if they feel the same, if the conclusion is the same, and if there are places where you have second thoughts. You might also shift some of the variables in the formula just slightly to see what differences are produced in the outcome. It does not hurt to run through the thought process multiple times to check for errors. It can be extremely informative to change the variables until the decision changes and isolate the threshold for that change.

Y. "Y" is for You. You guessed it: certainty! The nine-step process is a quest for certainty. You are striving for certainty in the variables you are putting into the equation, and then you are creating an equation that is as simple as possible and reduces uncertainty where possible. All of these concepts—logic, reasoning, and rationality—have an inherent subjectivity in their implementation, an interaction we will take on directly in Chapter Six on the self.

Fallacies

Not a reference to grammatical fallacies popularized by websites promising to improve one's writing, these fallacies are flaws in an argument. Some scholars consider the study of fallacies to be a branch of informal logic, whereas others view the fallacies as a set of rules determining correct and legitimate arguments. For our purposes, the "fallacies" are pitfalls in reasoning that have various consequences from diluting a certain position to nullifying it altogether. There are literally dozens of potential fallacies, and they take many forms. We have isolated a few that directly relate to our inquiries and have extreme manifestations to be avoided in most instances.

Many of the fallacies appear in Latin, taking the form of "*argumentum ad* _____." The *argumentum* reference is to "argument" or "appeal," and the *ad* means "toward" or "to." Thus, knowing that *misericordium* refers to fear or emotion, we can deduce that *argumentum ad misericordium* is an unnecessary appeal to fear or an unwarranted argument based on emotion. The Latin phrasing does not imply that these moves are automatically fallacies or flaws in logic; they are simply arguments that rely on a certain thought process or formation (authority, fear, character, tradition, etc.). The phrasing over time, however, has been linked to these fallacies such that an "appeal based on attacking a person" is seen as an invalid or erroneous appeal in terms of an *argumentum ad hominem*. Keep that distinction in mind as we move through this section—the distinction between highlighting what the argument is based on and assuming that relying on that formation is wrong—because in some instances, a so-called fallacy is not a fallacy at all, but actually an argument that supports the overall position in a helpful way.

There are probably as many fallacies in logic as there are positions to be advocated, and it may not be constructive to bog down in creating an exhaustive list. Many fallacies overlap, and some are issues simply of execution in the argument. For example, one popular fallacy is the "appeal to authority," although we also encourage advocates to defend their positions with evidence and the use of experts in the field. Thus, "*ad verecundium*" might not indicate a flaw at all. We have listed a few of the more useful fallacies to think about and a way to summarize the very issues that the Toulmin model and the three-part discussion of logic, reasoning, and rationality are all trying to avoid. Most of the fallacies to avoid are quite obvious and do not appear in serious discourse very often (with the exception of recent political debates). This would include not answering the question at all, omitting major pieces of information from the calculation, assuming that if something is true once it will always be true, linking two events together solely because they occurred in sequence, relying on disqualified or heavily biased sources, intimidation as an argument strategy, or blatantly changing the subject. Here are four that you should consider among the others:

1. *Ad Hominem*
This is an attack on someone's character and is used to challenge the source of the argument, not the argument itself. As you get deeper into this appeal, it can become more nuanced in terms of the importance of ethos and how to challenge the values held by a particular author. If Heidegger, for example, was a member of the Nazi party, should that influence how we treat his writings? What if he joined the Nazis under pressure? What if his writings challenge the nationalism of the Nazis in some ways? How important is the author or the speaker to the argument itself? You can see here, in one of the more accepted fallacies, that it is not so cut and dry and that differences in the context can change the degree to which a certain appeal is fallacious.

2. *Ad Nauseam*

This is the use of repetition, often excessive repetition, to emphasize an argument. Repeating something does not make it true, and continuing to repeat something will actually reduce the force of the original statement by desensitizing the audience to the claim. In some cases, repetition can strengthen one's position, but there is a point at which that backfires, creating a flawed appeal. The best way to view this fallacy is that it becomes more of an error in logic the more it is relied upon as the primary evidence or grounds. Repetition is not evidence—it can offer emphasis and express prioritization, but it does not stand in for data itself.

3. *Ad Populum*

Also called "band-wagoning" or "following the crowd," this is an argument based on what others believe or do. Peer pressure is often based on this appeal to the crowd, because certainly if "all the cool kids are doing it," you should, too. It does not necessarily hurt an argument to show who else agrees with it (the idea of an endorsement, for example), but concurrence from the crowd does not constitute solid evidence by itself and should not be used as the main validation for a position.

4. *Ad Baculum*

This is an appeal to fear and is common in attempts to justify certain policies that ostensibly prevent the threat in question. If the threat is exaggerated or, even worse, fabricated completely, then an argument using fear of the threat as its justification is severely flawed. In most instances, there is some need to take into account the risks or consequences of the action, but such fears need to be tempered in terms of any unnecessary escalation or intensification of the fear. The appeal to fear may make a situation worse if the actions serve to create a bigger threat than the one present in the first place. There may not be a "monster in the closet," but if we act as if there is and use the light in the room as a way to ward off the monster, we can generate more anxiety and functionally create the monster itself.

Chapter Summary

The point of this chapter was to introduce the beginning argumentation student to the building blocks of argument using the classic Toulmin Model of Argumentation. Arguments are composed of claims, grounds, and warrants. Arguments are strengthened and made more persuasive through qualifiers, rebuttals, and backing. We hope the utility of the Toulmin Model is clear at this point. Arguments can, at times, be exceedingly convoluted. Skilled debaters are able to often obscure fuzzy logic in fancy or intimidating language. Often anger or shouting is used to obscure arguments as well. Too often in our society we confuse "might" with "right." The Toulmin Model allows debate participants to critically assess arguments in a clear and easy way. For advocates, the Toulmin Model reveals the strength and cogency of the case one is making. For opponents, the Toulmin Models helps to uncover weaknesses in logic or support. In either case, breaking down arguments into their constituent parts is a very useful and practical skill. We recommend you practice it regularly.

The second portion of the chapter worked through the concepts of logic, reasoning, and rationality. You should have a sense of how these three terms rely on each other and are slightly different. The connection between using sound logic, being reasonable, and acting rationally is often argumentation in that a "good" argument will show traits of all three of these thought processes. We provided some helpful details and examples for logic, reasoning, and rationality before we introduced the idea of "fallacies" and how they operate. In general terms, fallacies take many forms, which we have explained and offered four in more detail. If you can link the primary and secondary triads of the Toulmin model to the forms of thought discussed in the second half of the chapter, you will have greatly expanded your toolbox for critical thinking and analysis.

Learning Activities: Chapter Three

1. Explain the relationship between the claim, grounds, and warrant of an argument. Then, explain how that argument can be strengthened by the elements of the secondary triad of the Toulmin Model.
2. Read the opinion section of a major newspaper like *The New York Times* or *The Washington Post*. Find an article that presents a case of fact, value, or policy. Once you have located an article, analyze each argument using the Toulmin Model. Diagram the author's arguments using the two Toulmin triads. Does the author make a reasoned argument? Is the author's position logically warranted?
3. In recent years a number of high-profile celebrities have amplified the argument that vaccinating children against common but potentially deadly viruses can lead to a number of harmful side effects, including autism. The basis for this argument was a damaging report published in the eminent medical journal *The Lancet* that purported to show a link between early childhood vaccination and autism. While the report in *The Lancet* has since been retracted for using misleading data and falsifying its conclusions, the so-called "anti-vaccination movement" has persisted. Read the following argument opposing childhood vaccinations and place the elements of the primary and secondary triad into a visual Toulmin Model.

   According to the Centers for Disease Control and Prevention, one in 68 children are now diagnosed with autism spectrum disorder (ASD). Furthermore, autism rates have increased concurrently with vaccination rates in the U.S. This is an alarming trend that might appear coincidental. However, we now know from a landmark study published in The Lancet *that vaccinations in early childhood increase a child's risk of developing some form of autism. Autism can severely impair a child's verbal and nonverbal communication, making it hard for them to interact socially. Not only do vaccinations increase a child's risk of developing autism spectrum disorder, they expose them to a range of other harmful health effects. Hopefully, with a number of influential celebrities now supporting our cause, mothers around the world will learn the harmful effects of vaccinations.*

4. Other than "rationality" or "logic" give some examples of warrants. How do warrants vary culture by culture? Do you think superstition or premonition could be considered a warrant? In what ways would they and give examples.

5. Does religious faith constitute a warrant and how is it demonstrated? What types of claims and grounds might you find in an argument based on religion? What direction should someone take in an attempt to refute such arguments?

6. Discuss three weaknesses with the Toulmin model. Give examples of arguments where those weaknesses are most evident. Can you use the Toulmin model to diagram an argument critiquing the model? What would the warrant and ground be to go along with the claim: We should not use Toulmin to understand the structure of argument?

7. Of the three parts of the secondary triad, what would be the most important part and the least important part? Why? For all forms of argument? Give an example of an argument that makes no sense without some type of qualifier. Give an example of a weak argument with lots of grounds and backing. Discuss the phrase "quality over quantity" in terms of the Toulmin model.

8. What goes into a good claim? Give examples of good and bad claims? Are the good claims stronger because of implied ground and warrants? What makes a good claim that would be distinct from evidence or reasoning? Come up with two opposite claims and discuss why one might be better than the other. Would it make sense to talk about an argument with grounds and a warrant but no claim? Can you provide an example?

9. Given the argument that "dogs are better pets than cats because they relate more to their owners," what would be the claim, the grounds, and the warrant/s. Make an argument in the other direction. Which one prevails and why?

10. Assess the following scenario. You are in a survival situation in a remote forest with only about a day's worth of food remaining. Prospects for hunting or foraging are slim, and you need to use your dwindling supply of energy to build a shelter for the night. What are your thoughts on how to proceed? How will you ration your remaining food? What questions do you have about the scenario that would clarify your answers? Write down your questions and any responses you have to these questions.

11. Given your answers to the questions posed in the survival setting above, pick a few variables to change about your own survival skills and then answer the questions again. For example, imagine that you have expert skills at hunting and foraging in order to feed yourself for some period of time, making variables on "getting out" and "being rescued" the prominent consideration. At that point, assume you had hiked into the region about twenty-five miles and were at least that far from any road or occupied building in any direction. Assume that the chance for being located if you stay in one place is relatively small and that no one will be actively searching for you (at least for the next two to three days). Then, once you have thought through the scenario and developed a plan, outline what the main variables will be. How do they change if you are injured and need medical attention? Where are you drawing your information from as you make decisions and ask questions?

12. Lay out the logic, the reasoning, and the rationality surrounding the survival scenario with as much attention to distinguishing the three from each other as possible. What system of logic governs a survival situation? When is reasoning necessary to estimate or gauge an uncertainty? Is there a limit to "acting rationally," and what does that actually require?

13. Go through the same scenario but include two other people with you—a stranger and a loved one. You decide to stay in one place, but food is very limited. How will rations be distributed? On what basis?

Figure Credits

CHAPTER 4

Proving Your Claims: Conducting Research in the Digital Age

Recall that arguments consist of claims, grounds, and warrants. Claims are supported by grounds, or evidence, and the logical inference that connects the claim with the grounds is the warrant. The warrant is an essential element of any argument. Think about it: If a warrant is not logically sound or valid, which is to say reasonable or acceptable, then the argument will be easily defeated. It's important, then, that your arguments always be logical. The focus of this brief chapter, however, will be the grounds. How do we build, develop, and maintain arguments? What materials do we use and what process do we use for construction?

Think of the Eiffel Tower, that iconic monument in Paris that we all know so well. In addition to its beauty, the Eiffel Tower is a marvel of civil and mechanical engineering built in the 1880s. At its base, the Eiffel Tower is 100 meters or 382 feet wide (its base is a 4 × 100 meter square), but at its highest point it is only as big as a thin pipe. How does something so small stand so resolutely 985 feet and 11 inches high in the air?[1] Well, there is a lot of mathematics involved, but in short, it has a strong base that was designed specifically to support the tallest part of the tower. This is not just true of the Eiffel Tower, though. In fact, you will find that many tall structures are widest at their bases. If the opposite were true, then many of the structures around the planet would be more unstable and vulnerable to things like earthquakes or strong winds. The bottom of a well-crafted pyramid can withstand the weight of the top.

Just like the foundation of the Eiffel Tower is integral to its strength, the evidence used to support a claim is similarly important to the strength of an argument. If the evidence we provide is not able to ground or *prove* a claim, then the integrity of the entire argument is placed at risk. Indeed, it is much easier for an opponent to topple an argument that is poorly supported than one which is firmly grounded. It is not an exaggeration to say that *the strength of your argument is determined by the quality of the grounds you choose.* However, choosing between good, bad, and mediocre grounds is not so easy, particularly in the age of Internet research. Countless advocates have lost arguments because of poorly chosen grounds and a lack of evidence. Therefore, if you want your arguments to stand tall and firm like the Eiffel

---

[1] Of course, once the 66-foot television antenna was added, it took the Tower to over 1,000 feet!

Tower, you will need to know how to ground your claims and demonstrate your overall argument successfully.

Researching in the Information Age

Information is all around us and bombards us with messages every day. Perhaps this is why we live today in what experts refer to as the "Information Age." Indeed, among the many characteristics that typify the Information Age is the overwhelming availability of data, messages, advertising, "chat," newsfeeds, and text of all kinds. Books, documents, data, archives, and even entire libraries are now available to all those with a connection to the Internet. This is why there has never been a better time to want to know something. Questions do not have to go unanswered for long periods of time like they used to in the past. Popular search engines like Google make every day searches easy and fast. What is the population of Moscow? How many countries are recognized by the United Nations? What is the average expenditure on health care per capita in the United States? Especially for factual questions, like how many miles from the Earth to the Sun, you can very quickly find fairly reliable answers. The answers are not always fully accurate, but most sources provide helpful information and shed light on subjects of all kinds. Furthermore, the Internet makes it possible for us to find information virtually everywhere: while we ride in subways, dine with family members, or hang out with friends. And what a revolution this is! In previous generations, information was often hard and/or costly to find. Books were expensive and people had to travel to read them. As a result, elite classes of people were given access over those without privilege. In the Information Age this is no longer as universal (even though estimates are that today roughly 4.2 billion people—60% of the world's population—are not connected to the Internet![2]). For many of us, information is just a click away. This subject—access to information—gestures to a big debate over the digital divide and the ways the gap between the wealthy and the poor is reinforced or broken down through the Internet. It would be an outstanding exercise to chart the various characteristics and vectors of those living in poverty across those individuals who have an inability to access information over the Internet. Certainly there would be a great deal of overlap, but what direction is the trend?

With all of this said, it is important that we acknowledge that the Information Age presents an equal number of curses as it does blessings. For instance, more information is not necessarily a good thing. And *more information* is not the same as *more knowledge*. There is a big difference. With the increased number of documents, websites, and pieces of data available it becomes much more difficult to parse and sift through them. Information overload and source qualification issues provide just one paradox of the Information Age: There has never been more information, but there has also never been more *misinformation*. The point of this chapter is to assist you with the research process in the Information Age. If the goal is to be successful advocates, then an essential skill to develop along the way is the ability to ground the claims we make so that we prove our arguments. Whether you are a consultant, a politician, a debater, or even just a concerned citizen, you will find yourself making arguments that are tested—tested

---

[2] From "ITU releases 2014 ICT figures: Mobile-broadband penetration approaching 32 per cent Three billion Internet users by end of this year", by S. Acharya, 2014. © ITU. http://www.itu.int/net/pressoffice/press_releases/2014/23.aspx#.U-ja_6OTG1i

Figure 4.1 The Library is Changing

with questions, disbelief, even evidence to the contrary. You will need to defend the claims you are making with effective evidence of your own—data, logic, experience, empirical studies, examples, explanation, or simple intuition. The most important component of argumentation is clash—how arguments compete with one another—and the core element of good clash is based on the grounding. Where are you obtaining your evidence and how does it ground your argument?

The Problems with Google

Whether we care to admit it, Google has had an impact on each of our lives, often for the better. It is such a simple tool but such a profound idea. The founders of Google realized that with the abundance of information comes the increasingly difficult challenge to search for the relevant details. So Google was created. And how great is Google? You and I are now able to search something easily and quickly. It is often the first place we go to learn something quickly, and it has now become a verb: "Go Google it!" The larger problem, however, is that many people, including advocates for particular arguments, *stop* at Google rather than *begin* at Google. This would not be a terrible thing if all the information on the Internet completely accurate. But it is not. There is no such thing as a "tree octopus," (go Google it) for example. The same "source qualification" issue is true for Wikipedia, another Internet resource that has probably improved the quality of our lives by making more information more accessible to more people. Many people turn to Wikipedia first to learn details about a subject, and there is nothing inherently wrong with this approach to gathering information. Again, the problem comes when we stop searching after we have found a little something on our topic on Wikipedia or the first results page on Google or Bing or Yahoo or some other popular, profit-driven search engine or website. Such preliminary search results can include fraud, missing source citations, and even political agendas and have the potential to weaken our arguments rather than support them.

Thus, there are incredible benefits to being able to search quickly and broadly using Google. It is odd that we would even talk about a private information company in a chapter about conducting academic research. Yet Google drives some of this conversation precisely because it gives you a chance to get an "overview" on a particular issue and often helps to fill in the pieces of an argument. Learn a few of the tricks and be persistent (very few things replace the time involved in learning about a subject, reading the material, and digesting the main nodes on the map. At some level, that time needs to be invested, regardless of the particular search engine).

A common refrain is to avoid Google and Wikipedia altogether. This is not our position, but we definitely advise caution. Diversify your research by gathering as much information from as many different sources as possible. In our opinion, it is much better to embrace the wonderful aspects of the information age, including research tools like Google or the many personal blogs that generate equivalent web traffic to the venerable *New York Times*. You just have to be aware of the location of the information and treat the process with an open mind and some healthy skepticism. Information from a personal blog on Iran's nuclear ambitions may not be as accurate or reliable as data being reported by both the U.S. State Department and the United Nations. Keep in mind, as much as you can, that "experts" and peer-reviewed scholarly journals are not without flaws themselves. In fact, one aspect of the information age is that it is easier to catch plagiarists and fraudsters today than it has ever been because more text is being uploaded into various databases and is easily searchable. In addition, it has been revealed that even our most respected publications, including our scholarly journals and scientific literature, have occasionally been infiltrated by plagiarists. Clearly, personal blogs are not all bad and everything written in a so-called "scholarly" journal is not all good. We simply advise caution and the following few important research tips that will help you find the best grounds to support your arguments.

Tips for Finding Evidence

The ability to conduct thorough, credible research to ground a particular claim (or series of complementary claims) is a lifelong skill that takes years of diligent practice. Research is a specialized skill. Indeed, there are many people who do research for a living. Law firms, political campaigns, think tanks, and scientific corporations have individuals working for them whose main responsibility is to conduct research (incidentally, if research is something you enjoy doing, consider looking into it as a career). Importantly, you can begin to perfect your research skills now, and argumentation is at the heart of any good research program or objective. Gathering research without a larger argument is like collecting something without a sense of the larger context or how common those items might be. In an attempt to avoid the tendency to simply "collect" without purpose, we have provided you with seven tips to help you find the grounds you will need to support your claims and prove your arguments.

Remember, before you work through these seven tips, there are some planning suggestions you should follow to make the most out of your time and effort. Make sure you stay organized and take notes all along the way. This means having a document open where you are saving full citations, search terms, and any other useful information. Don't be stuck recreating your bibliography at the last minute because you failed to keep all of your citations in one place from the very beginning. Also, make sure you know exactly what your assignment is. How long is the paper you are writing? About how many sources are expected? If you are putting together a controversy brief for a debate, have you divided your research assignments up with your group, and what are you responsible for locating? As you find your material, take notes on each article or source and keep track of what quotations look particularly helpful. And the final step before you dive into the more specific tips is to keep a running list of all your search terms and add synonyms along the way. As you read more material, you will find more search terms that will help the process—keep track of those terms in a secure place.

Research Tip #1: Use Reference Librarians

Reference librarians are the unsung heroes of the research process. These are individuals whose job it is to provide a person with direction and guidance at various stages of the research process. Perhaps the greatest time to utilize the skills of reference librarians—and make no mistake, they are very skilled—is at the beginning stages of advocacy. Reference librarians know the sources that exist, and more importantly, they know how to find them. Your library likely has several reference librarians on hand just waiting to help. Even better, many libraries today can provide researchers with digital reference librarians. In many cases, this entails logging on to the library's website and simply contacting a reference librarian through instant messaging, Skype, or Google chat to get the help one could otherwise get face-to-face. So why should you seek out a reference librarian?

The main reason you should seek out your nearest reference librarian is that they are specialists in research and they will usually be able to provide some very useful help. Of course your teacher can help you along the way as well, and she or he also likely knows quite a lot about the research process. But reference librarians generally know more about the sources themselves: if they exist, where to find them, how to read them, and how to evaluate them. Think of research librarians as expert chefs of evidence and think of everyone else as casual, at-home cooks. The at-home cook could probably prepare a wonderful and tasty chicken parmesan. An expert chef, however, could not only prepare a wonderful and tasty chicken parmesan, he or she could also tell you about the history of the dish, the variances on chicken parmesan around the world, details about ingredients and, most importantly, how to make one yourself. And *that's* the difference between reference librarians and, say, your typical teacher (although you might be surprised at how skilled most teachers are at conducting research—it never hurts to ask for assistance). In sum, when beginning to develop and create grounds for a particular argument or position, take advantage of the expertise that is available and keep in mind that reference librarians are educated on how to educate others to conduct research.

Figure 4.2 Chicken Parmesan

Reference librarians will also help you to focus your research. As mentioned, the sheer amount of information available is overwhelming. It is truly difficult to tell the difference between credible grounds, evidence, or support on one hand, and that which is specious, unsupported, or fringe on the other. Once again, Google may have great potential as a research tool, but not everything *on* Google is great. It is often the case that in the process of conducting a Google search one ends up with many useless, misleading or questionable sources. In such cases it is up to the researcher to make the decision between good and bad sources. And this takes practice. It is particularly challenging when you are new to a subject or argument. Reference librarians can help narrow the search by helping to divide the topic into smaller pieces or make suggestions on what aspect of your research area is the most pertinent.[3]

Think of it this way: If we were to go fishing off the Pacific Ocean and we decided to lower a wide net into the water, we would very likely trap a number of fish in the net. In addition, we would likely trap some plastic (sadly), some foliage, some seaweed, and maybe some inedible ocean creatures. We would then have to sift through it all to find the fish we wanted to eat. And we could do this, but it would take some time. On the other hand, we could use a fishing pole or even several fishing poles to catch exactly the fish we wanted. It might take a bit longer because we would only have at most a few lines in the water, but we would be more likely to catch just the specific fish we were looking for to eat. For sure, we would be less likely to catch the debris or inedible creatures we did not want. Think of Google as the big net approach and think of an assisted search using reference librarians as the fishing pole strategy. With more years of experience and skill, it is likely you will be able to successfully search a large database or search engine like Google for sources you have in mind. This may be because you have learned the subject so well that you are intimately familiar with the organizations and authors that produce the data you need to prove your claims. Until then, it is our strong recommendation you seek out expert assistance and guidance in the form of reference librarians and other experts. Why sift through all the debris and distraction on the Internet to find a few gems when you could receive help? Learn from the experts and find ways to improve your research skills along the way.

Research Tip #2: Investigate the Source of Information

If you truly follow Tip #1, you should also learn a few tips of your own along the way—learn to fish instead of just eating the meal. Reference librarians can help you find the sources you need to ground your claims, and for this reason, along with others, we strongly advise using these types of research experts throughout the research process. If you cannot find a librarian, seek out a teacher or scholar in the field, perhaps even an argumentation instructor or a debate coach, all of whom are well-trained in the practices of researching grounds for a claim. Ultimately, however, you will need to do some investigatory work on your own. In short, it is essential that you trust and verify the sources of information you choose to use in your argument. This is important for many reasons, primarily because unverified and illegitimate sources can produce inaccurate, exaggerated, and even false information.

First, much like the axiom "you can tell a lot about a person by the friends they keep," we believe the reputation of an advocate becomes inextricably bound to the sources he or she chooses to cite. This works to the advocate's advantage when the sources selected are good, which is to say trustworthy, credible, and/or verifiable. Strong sources can be a sign of a strong argument (though not always). If, on the other hand, an advocate chooses to use or include sources that are untrustworthy, biased, or misleading, the reputation of the advocate and the argument can

---

[3] Here are Google "hacks" or tips to improve/focus one's Google searches. Examples include: http://www.thedailybeast.com/articles/2013/09/15/13-hacks-to-improve-your-google-search.html or http://www.techlila.com/google-search-tips/.

be diminished. It is important then to "put yourself with good company." Seek legitimate and qualified sources for your evidence and think about where your grounds are being derived. Keep in mind, it is always important to investigate your sources of information thoroughly. Tracking down a source is as much for argumentation scholars as it is for news journalists. You can begin by asking the following questions: *Who* is the source of the information? *What* is the information? *Why* is the information being produced? In some ways it mirrors *ethos*, *pathos*, and *logos* in that the source itself is the credibility, the content of the evidence is the substance or material, and the background behind its production is the connection to the audience from the source itself.

You need to know *who* the author of a source of information is. It may be an individual author, a series of authors, or an organization like The White House or The American Enterprise Institute. In any case it is important to investigate the history of the author. What are their past publications? Have they written several books or articles or is this their first? Also, what is their reputation? Is the author or organization affiliated with the particular cause or commercial interest? For instance, the American Enterprise Institute is a well known think-tank that produces research and information, often in favor of conservative causes. The Brookings Institution is a centrist think-tank. And yet The Center for American Progress is a well known think-tank that produces research more aligned with progressive causes. Knowing the affiliation of an author's organization therefore becomes very important for you because while you may be striving to remain politically neutral, your sources may be politically biased in one direction or another. All sources probably have some level of bias built in, and most sources are attempting to "sell themselves" as an important location for information, but some biases are extremely pronounced and tilt the message being promoted toward a less legitimate category of evidence. Examples of medical articles like those downplaying the risks of smoking on lung cancer that are funded by the tobacco industry can occur in lots of industries and on lots of topics. It is important to find sources that are knowledgeable and experienced in the area, but the line can easily be crossed from "expert" to "politically motivated." It can be hard to uncover particularly egregious forms of bias, but one way is to look for other qualified sources talking about the author or organization in question. An illegitimate source will often be criticized from within the field. You can also "follow the money" and research how the author gets paid or where the organization receives its larger donations. If there is a clear link between financing and publishing, then a bias may exist.

You will also want to investigate the content of a particular source. *What* is being argued or presented? Are the conclusions logical? Do the conclusions align with previous research or other sources? Has the source you are citing been researched itself? In other words, did the author you are potentially citing cite his or her sources? And if he or she did, are those sources legitimate? Your sources of information do not need to agree with each other in exact detail. Just because one source comes to a different conclusion than the others does not mean it is wrong or it is fake or untrustworthy. You need to stay skeptical and seek out independent support for you main claims. In the process of doing rigorous research you will come across many articles, books, or other documents on the same subject matter. After spending some time reading this information and cataloging where it is coming from, you will detect certain arguments and consistencies. As a result, you should develop the ability to be skeptical of any source that deviates significantly. Again, this does not mean the source should be thrown out. But it should warrant your attention. In summary, know *what* is being said. You should also pay close attention to *what is not* being said, too! If an argument does not mention how much a major policy being advocated will cost, you have to think it could be exorbitant and question the omission. Arguments occur in between the lines as well.

Another important question to ask is *why* a particular source exists. Doctors, lawyers, advocates, and experts of all kinds produce and publish research to support their goals and positions. But without knowing an author's goal or position it becomes difficult to place complete trust in their research. We previously mentioned think tanks like the American Enterprise Institute and the Brookings Institution. These are just two of the better-known think-tanks that exist. There are many more, some that are devoted to a single issue and others that are evaluating and assessing a major area of a field. The most well known are in the area of politics and domestic and international policy, such as the Center for Strategic and International Studies (CSIS), the RAND Corporation, or the CATO Institute. Think-tanks are all in the business of predicting, analyzing, and imagining various arguments. They are, if nothing else, argumentation centers! There are hundreds if not thousands if we include state and local think-tanks, and many of them are producing literature and documents that speak to a particular field or issue. Yes, think-tanks exist in theory to produce quality research, but it is also important to remember that think-tanks are created to produce a particular type of re-search. This could be research that supports a political cause, promotes a certain ideology or organization, or directly supports a commercial interest. The hard part in all of this is that rarely does a think-tank, author, or organization declare their political affili-ation or interests openly. In many cases they remain hidden. Therefore, we as advocates, who need grounds to support our claims, must ask why a particular source exists in order to start to uncover the various interests that are supporting a certain type of infor-

Figure 4.3 Validate Your Sources

mation. Who benefits from a positive economic report? Who might benefit from a negative one? Is it possible that a commercial enterprise, such as the pharmaceutical industry, could have funded a report or website? If so, is the research always one-sided? These questions will greatly strengthen the overall argument because you will pick and choose what to support and advocate based on more reliable evidence.

Research Tip #3: Follow the Breadcrumb Trail

There is a difference between primary, secondary, and tertiary sources of information. The primary source of information is recognized as the original source. The primary source is the document or report that first detailed or outlined a conclusion, thesis, or position. The Declaration of Independence, for example, is a primary source. Martin Luther King Jr.'s *Letter from Birmingham Jail* is another example of a primary source. A secondary source of information, on the other hand, is one that references, describes, or summarizes an original source. For example, in the context of law and litigation, previous court rulings, known as precedents, are often invoked to justify current decisions or outcomes in a case. Because the second ruling was based on the first, or original decision, any subsequent publications of the second court ruling would be an example of secondary sources of information. A secondary source is usually more scholarly and is about a collection of primary sources and other secondary sources. The line is a bit fuzzy here—a newspaper article might be primary source (the original instance of the information) or the secondary source (summarizing events). Classifying sources helps to ensure you have a diversity of support and you are thinking about the various layers of opinion that are informing (often clouding) the details. A summary of the Declaration of Independence would be another example of a secondary source. Tertiary sources are even further removed from the original source. Think of a tertiary source as a summary of a summary or an explanation of a review.

There is nothing inherently wrong with citing secondary or tertiary sources, although it is best practice to cite the primary source of information. This is for several reasons. First, just like the game "telephone" where a message is passed from person to person to person and, inevitably, evolves with each passage, sources of information "evolve" each time they are summarized by other people. The result can be a misinterpretation of an original source. Of course we always want to ground our claims using the most accurate interpretation of the source as possible. This is why we recommend to "follow the breadcrumb trail" back to the original source. We can use Wikipedia as a good example of how to do this.

If you want to know something quickly and with a degree of depth, Wikipedia is a good place to go. It is not the final place to research a topic, but it is like decent fast food—you know what it will be and it is served relatively quickly. Many teachers tell their students to avoid Wikipedia, and for good reason. There are certainly examples of fraudulent or inaccurate information reported as fact on Wikipedia. In addition, there are examples of individuals editing Wikipedia pages when they are not fully informed enough to do so. Still, we believe Wikipedia is a good place to start if a reference librarian is not available or when the consequences of having shaky grounds are not severe (a friendly debate with a colleague, for instance). One thing that many people forget, however, is that Wikipedia provides footnotes for many of the claims on a particular page, and instead of following the footnote to the primary source of information, people (much to our mutual frustration) cite Wikipedia *as the* source. This is a problem because (a) citing the primary source is always best practice and (b) Wikipedia itself is not a source, it is an aggregator of other sources, often anonymous or made up of a crowd of people. There is simply no reason to stop at an online encyclopedia, particularly when the original sources are made available at the bottom of the page. One simply has to follow the trail to the original source. We recommend you do this at all times when researching and even for fun. Sometimes you will find that the Wikipedia page's interpretation of an original source is not at all accurate! The good thing about Wikipedia is that it can be fixed at a moment's notice, unlike books, which need to be edited, republished, and then re-circulated. Our point here is to encourage you to go deeper into each and every source you find. Follow the footnotes or endnotes, look up the other relevant sources in the bibliography, search for other work by that author or published by that organization, and pursue more research about your initial topic. Once you find one or two good sources (even by luck or through some skilled browsing), you should be able to use those to find more. Once you find where the best fruit on the tree is hanging, you should be able to find more in the same vicinity or at least at the same height.

Not only can you track down positive reviews and assessments of a particular author's work (a pro-dict), you also determine who to avoid and who is especially biased. That can be useful if your opponent is relying on one or two authors whom you can expose based on comments by colleagues, reviews of their work, other erroneous statements they have made, etc. The bottom line here is that you cannot be content to find a quotation by an author or organization—you have to find out how credible that source is before you hang your hat on his or her conclusion. Especially with secondary or tertiary sources, find out exactly who you are dealing with and why they wrote the things they published. Keep in mind, one good way to follow this advice is to look at the footnotes and bibliographies of the people you are citing. If their sources are qualified, numerous, and in agreement, it is more likely they are reliable sources. The best way to make a source reliable, however, is to find someone else who is credible saying the same thing.

Research Tip #4: Identify the Experts

You'll save yourself a lot of time and energy if you learn who the experts in the field you are arguing about are. Once again, reference librarians are great for this, but so are your teachers. If a reference librarian is not available and your teacher is not familiar with the particular field of argument, then you need to reach out to other experts on your campus or school. You will want to interview them, and hopefully they can tell you which books to read or which authors to follow. In this way, you are kind of like a detective. To figure out who committed the crime you need to interview so-called "persons of interest." These are the people who likely have the information you need. A person five miles from the crime scene would probably be of little use. A person 500 yards from the crime scene would be better, but a person 500 feet away would be better still. A person five feet from the crime scene would be ideal. As a researcher you want to be gathering information from the people five feet from the crime scene, so to speak. Unless you are arguing about a new or burgeoning topic, there are likely experts—people who are considered respected authorities—on virtually any subject. These people often have shaped the knowledge of the subject in profound ways. Similarly, they might be prolific authors or critical voices.

Finding the experts not only improves the quality of the information you read or investigate, but it also increases the chance that you'll find the relevant documents you need. And as an additional benefit, you are likely to come across primary rather than secondary sources of information, though this is not always the case. There are simply so many voices out there that you have to be patient unearthing the more legitimate sources. And there are so many conflicting opinions.

Figure 4.4 Investigate Carefully

It is easy to get bogged down by the cacophony of voices you might find on the Internet. For this reason and others, we strongly recommend you seek out the experts. Again, talk to your reference librarians, your teachers, or potentially resident authorities you know or other experts you are able to contact. These people can point you in the right direction.

Research Tip #5: Redundancy

If you want to win an argument, you need to ground each of your claims. We are hoping that you know this already. As you also may know, one source—one piece of evidence—is rarely enough to do the job. If the Eiffel Tower had only one point of contact with the ground as opposed to four, it would collapse. It is basic physics, really. Likewise, the need to have multiple sources of evidence and a variety of grounds is true for claims and ultimately arguments. Just like the Eiffel Tower, your arguments will benefit from the concept of redundancy (or at least mutual support, coverage, and some overlap).

With regard to structuring arguments, redundancy, much like in engineering, refers to the duplication or reapplication of essential elements. Duplicating essential elements (such as contact points with the ground in the case of the Eiffel Tower, or grounds to prove a claim in the context of argumentation) increases the structural integrity of the object, or argument, through reinforcement. If one element breaks, another is there for support. If two break, hopefully there is a third. Providing multiple forms of evidence increases the strength of an argument because the grounds reinforce each other. Furthermore, if one channel of evidence is weak or disproven, others are there to make sure the entire structure does not collapse, so to speak.

It is important to point out that in some instances one ground may be sufficient. For instance, if a prosecutor were to claim a defendant committed a crime and proceed to show video surveillance footage of the defendant actually committing the crime, the defendant's guilt would be hard to disprove, unless the defense attorney were able to argue some form of extenuation. A *prima facie* case here could be met with just one claim and just one ground. However, this is rarely the case. You are far more likely to need many grounds to prove each of your claims. Be redundant with your grounds. Once you have discovered one form of evidence, keep going. Your argument will be stronger because of it and you will be better able to withstand any potential attacks from your opponent.

It may be the case that you have limited space or can only introduce a few pieces of evidence. In that instance, it does not hurt to have backup. And, if you collect multiple pieces of evidence in the first place, you will be able to select the most compelling pieces for the final draft of the argument.

Research Tip #6: Know the Opposition

In addition to knowing the evidence that supports your arguments, it is imperative that you know as many of the arguments and the evidence behind them that disprove your arguments. In other words, you need to know the arguments of your opposition. This is known often as opposition research, where one investigates the sources and data that contradict one's own position.

There are a number of really important benefits to conducting opposition research. The first is that you have an idea of your own weaknesses. As a result, you can conduct additional research to buttress or strengthen your position. This will make your argument more appealing and increase your chances of victory. In addition, another benefit of conducting opposition research is that you will learn, to some degree, how your opponent will argue their position. This enables you to focus your criticism toward your opponent's weaknesses. The spy camera may be a little much, but you need to carefully research your opponent's position and know what the other side is going to say before you finish setting up your position—that's the best way to pre-empt any competing arguments before they are introduced.

An equally important, though less empha-sized, benefit to opposition research is that by studying the arguments of your opponent you will become a more well-rounded and edu-

Figure 4.5 Know the Opponent

cated individual. Too often we form opinions and positions and then proceed to reinforce those positions by only reading those documents that agree with us. As a result, we may find ourselves in an "echo chamber," as some have called it, where we are surrounded by the reverberations of our own beliefs. Nothing contradictory or challenging penetrates the echo chamber. You can imagine the harm in this: If we are constantly told we are correct in everything we believe and do, we move swiftly in the direction of zealotry and dogma. On the other hand, democracy relies on the plurality of voices and ideas, so it is not productive for society to be caught in a series of echo chambers—we need deliberation and dissent to move forward in positive ways. Opposition research, or exposing oneself to alternative perspectives generally, has the great benefit of protecting one from the perils of being stuck and only hearing the claims of like-minded voices.

Research Tip #7: Know the Nuts and Bolts

We have one final research tip to send you on your way. Remember that there is no real sub-stitute for time and effort—concentrate on your searches, stay organized, and follow any leads that arise. For many search engines, there are ways to narrow your searches to better locate the specific articles you are seeking. Find out the "tricks" of each search engine and make sure you utilize them when appropriate. For example, just putting quotations around a particular phrase you are looking for can prevent extraneous articles from littering the results of your search. Using "privacy violations" in quotation marks will find articles that use the phrase instead of articles that might talk about privacy in one section and violations in another (not the exact piece you are looking for). In LexisNexis, an excellent search engine that most libraries have access to, you should learn your way around the various libraries inside Lexis and practice using some of the search tricks that are available. Within Lexis, you will find a library for legal searches that will bring up court cases and law reviews, a separate library for newspapers and other recent sources, and a library that allows you to combine all the various options (ALLNWS). Once you have selected the library you want to use, you can also restrict the dates you are searching in order to look for material published in the last two months, the last year, the last five years, on a specific date, etc.

When searching for articles on Lexis, it may also benefit you to apply some of the more sophisticated search techniques to further your process of narrowing. No one wants to sift through thousands of articles to find that ten that really matter. Make your searches do the work. Two additional ways to improve your searches on Lexis (and a few other search engines that use similar terms) involve the "within" function and the "atleast" function. "Within" allows you to search for a word that is within a certain number of characters from another word. In other words, if you are searching for articles about gun control and you want the word "restriction" to appear in the article near the word "gun" or "guns," you can search for "restriction w/10 guns." The "w/#" stands for "within a specified number of characters," in this case ten. An article that talks about restrictions toward the beginning and then later mentions guns would not come up in the search. Only articles where "restrictions" and "guns" are within ten characters of each other will be retrieved by the search. You can change the number that appears after the "w/" to alter how big the range is between the two words. If you simply want an article that mentions "China" and "currency" fairly close to each other, use "China w/50 currency." If you want "China" very close to "currency" in terms of "China is manipulating its currency," you could shrink down the number after the "w/" to five or ten. Another quick trick to keep in mind here is that the "*" or the "!" may act as a wild card so that you can search for different manifestations of the same root word. If you are looking for "restriction," "restrict," "restricting," or "restrictions," you can simply search for "restrict*" in Google or "restrict!" in Lexis and all of those words will be retrieved.

"Atleast" is also a useful trick when using Lexis and can greatly help to narrow down your searches. "Atleast# (term)" is a search configuration that will look for the term in parentheses to appear at least the number of times specified by the number appearing after the "atleast." So, if you are looking for articles that talk about Paraguay more than in passing, you might search for something like "Latin America and atleast5 (Paraguay)." If an article only mentions Paraguay twice, it will not be retrieved. This function allows you to find articles that are more in-depth and more focused on your particular search phrases. Combining date restrictions, wild-card characters, "within," and "atleast" can go a long way toward improving the effectiveness of your searches.

Chapter Summary

The point of this chapter has been to stress the importance of finding high quality and credible evidence to ground one's claims. Research in the Information Age is beset with difficulties. Therefore, we advised the beginning student of argumentation to proceed with caution: not all that exists on the Internet is to be believed. To help navigate the research process we provided six research tips. First, use reference librarians to help locate sources of information. Second, investigate those sources critically and thoroughly. Third, always strive to locate the primary sources of information. Fourth, save yourself some time and effort by locating the experts. Fifth, be redundant and sixth know the evidence against your position.

Learning Activities: Chapter Four

1. Research one of the following topics using the six research tips discussed in the chapter:

   > Abortion rights
   > Drug legalization
   > Containment of Iran
   > Militarization of civilian police forces
   > U.S. military intervention in Iraq
   > Gun control

2. How can a solid research agenda prevent some of the more outlandish positions within each of the topic areas above?

3. Search the following terms using:

   > Gay Rights
   > Arab Spring
   > The History of Hip Hop
   > Particle Accelerator

   What do you make of the results? Are they different for each search engine? What are the first results in each? Why do you think these results are the first to appear?

4. Locate an argument in the media (print, Internet, or TV). What sources of information do they provide? Are they strong sources of information? What makes them strong or weak sources of information? How do the sources used affect the argument?

5. Find an article on one side of the gun control issue, the abortion issue, the welfare issue, or the states' rights issue. How did you find that article? How qualified is the source? How would you go about finding an article on the opposite side of the proposition? Can you locate the footnotes in one of your articles and track down an article from the footnotes that appears promising. Which is better, the original article or the one from the footnotes? Why?

6. Find an article with very little credibility. What argument is the article making? Is the argument hard to believe or is the course simply lacking legitimacy? Which is worse? Find another article that has more credibility but makes what you would consider to be a bad argument. Why is it a bad argument?

7. Go back through the seven research tips and explain what can happen to distort your research if you do not deploy each one three different search engines.

8. Do an extremely broad search on Lexis-Nexis so that you retrieve over 1,000 hits—try something like "keystone pipeline" or "Paris terrorism attacks." Now, use some of our suggestions to try to narrow the results to about a dozen articles. restrict the dates, use a secondary term and look for it "within" a certain number of characters/words from the primary term, and then use "atleast" to find articles focused on your search term. Do this again with three or four topics until you feel comfortable with these tricks.

Figure Credits

CHAPTER 5

Case Construction and Flowing

So far we have discussed some essential aspects of argumentation, critical theory, and debate. We have learned about the history of argumentation and the way we process arguments both emotionally and cognitively. We have learned about the various roles and responsibilities in argumentation. In addition, we have learned the difference between an argument and a non-argument. We even used the Toulmin Model of argumentation to illustrate the relationship between the primary and secondary elements of an argument. At this point it becomes important to combine all of these aspects about argumentation into a practical cluster to discuss how an advocate or an opponent builds a case. Think of cases as individual arguments combined together in support of an overall position or "grand argument."

Writing the Controversy Brief

Case construction begins with what is known as a controversy brief. A controversy brief is a document that summarizes both positions on a give issue—the affirmative and negative. This allows one to develop his or her position on a given issue. The first step in creating a controversy brief is to state a proposition that specifies the controversy in question and divides ground evenly between the affirmative and negative sides. Controversial issues are not hard to come by—society is built on controversy in many ways—but it is difficult to craft a well-written proposition that contains balanced arguments on either side. In other words, it is not hard to list a set of controversial areas, but it can be quite challenging to come up with the exact wording of a proposition within those areas that generates reasonable space for a debate. To give you a sense of the kinds of controversies we are talking about, we will provide a short list here of some possibilities. These controversies are contemporary even though some of them have been with us for a long period of time. Generally they implicate particular policies but also connect to a number of values and deep-seated beliefs. As you work through the list, imagine how you might convert each area into a proposition or topic statement:

Sample Controversies:

abortion rights
gun control
counter-terrorism
religion in schools
universal health care
alternative energy

taxing the wealthy
the use of drones for targeted
killing
employment discrimination
affirmative action
arms sales

Once you have selected a controversy, you will need to complete the following steps on your way towards case construction:

1. Write a proposition.
2. Write an overview.
3. Interpret key terms.
4. Structure arguments.

1. Write a Proposition

You can think of a case as a series of individual arguments that, working together, prove one's position on a given issue. One's position on an issue is often referred to as a *proposition*. Like arguments, propositions can take the form of a fact, a value, or a policy (see Chapter Two for a review of fact, value, and policy). Propositions summarize the overall position of the advocate or opponent in a concise statement. In other words, a proposition states the issue, position, or idea being argued. So, without a proposition (often referred to as a "resolution" in debate contexts), there is no argument. Therefore, case construction begins with the creation of a proposition.

The sure-fire way to create a good proposition is to start with a mechanism that has the ability to confront one of the major problems that emanate from the controversy area. If the controversy area involves, for example, the issue of employment discrimination, you might start with a mechanism that "increases protections from discrimination for employees," or one that "expands restrictions and strengthens penalties on discrimination in the workplace," or even "implements a policy that substantially reduces employment discrimination." From there, you can decide if you want an agent to join the wording (the United States, the United States Federal Government, Congress, the Supreme Court, businesses, States, etc.).

Once you have an agent of action or you decide to use the passive voice and not specify an agent, you add that portion of the wording to the mechanism (also called the stem, particularly if it includes some other adjectives or phrases). From there, you either fill in the remainder of the topic with a particular objective or you leave that choice up to the individual students involved. In other words, you could write a proposition that increases statutory restrictions on employment discrimination in the military through Congress or you could write one that simply asks the affirmative to defend further restrictions on employment discrimination. Now take a look at your larger proposition to get a sense of what it means and where it takes both sides. If you feel good about it and can imagine having some good debates on it, move forward to the next step.

2. Write an Overview

The general overview does not need to be much longer than a page or two. The main points on either side of the proposition should be highlighted and previewed. Each side (the pro and the con or the affirmative and the negative) should have a distinct cover letter of that side of the controversy brief that serves as an overview of the arguments. This is the "executive summary," where the authors briefly explain the most important arguments on either side of the proposition. Start by re-stating the proposition and then make the overall argument as succinctly and clearly as possible. The goal is to provide a few main claims with a short warrant or two and a gesture to the best evidence the either supports or negates the proposition.

3. Provide an Interpretation of Key Terms

Every proposition will have some key terms that can be defined in slightly different ways. Depending on the definition, the topic will mean different things and the burdens and expectations of the affirmative and the negative will shift. It is important to isolate those phrases and define each one in a reasonable, yet strategic way. These "interpretations" should be argued in a way that makes sense and can be defended as a relatively central definition for the term or phrase in question, but also in a way that helps that side prove the particular point. In other words, if the proposition is "the United States should pass a national policy to address racism," the word "address" means a lot to how the proposition is interpreted. The affirmative may want to define "address" as "acknowledge racism" or "provide education on the problem of racism." Those are relatively easy arguments to defend. If the negative wins a counter-interpretation that states that "address" means to "resolve racism" or even "substantially reduce the prevalence of racism" it becomes a much harder burden for the affirmative to meet. Set up the definitions of key terms in a way that helps prove or disprove the statement.

In this section of the controversy brief, it would not hurt to have a clearly articulated interpretation of a term or phrase and then an explanation as to how that interpretation influences the larger meaning of the proposition as a whole. The last step should then explain how that broad interpretation of the proposition that rests on the particular definition in question makes it more likely that the topic will be affirmed (or denied, depending on whether this is the "interpretation" section for the pro or the con side). In addition to the interpretation, it might help to have an explicit connection back to the larger topic and a definition from a published source, even an online dictionary. Whether the interpretation is supported by dictionary definitions, definitions from experts in the field, or even a definition created by the authors of the controversy brief, it is valuable to have some stable definition and an argument as to why that definition is the most accurate and what it means for the topic as a whole. In other words, do what is necessary in this section to defend the definition and interpretation as fair and then explain how it helps one side or the other in terms of the topic.

This section is typically not part of the numbered arguments in the brief because it is about the parameters of the proposition itself and will play a role in all of the more substantive arguments. It will help, however, to allude to the various meanings and their importance in the specific arguments in the brief.

4. Provide Arguments in Sequence

The actual arguments have arrived! This section is the protein of the controversy brief and should make up the bulk of the document. Essentially the numbered arguments on each side of the controversy brief are well-developed argument choices that each independently offers a defense of the proposition or a challenge to it. There are many ways to organize and format this section, but the important element is to set up the claim, grounds, and warrant for a series of thoroughly explained arguments for or against the proposition. Here are some useful steps to follow in this section of the briefs.

a) Numbering in order

It helps to number each distinct argument. You can use sub-structure within each argument if you want, but that depends on how much material there is under the same claim. If you have separate claims and distinct evidentiary support, you probably have two different arguments. The goal is to put the strongest argument as the first one, then the second strongest, and so forth. This is an arbitrary standard in some ways, but it does help to give the controversy brief a sense of prioritization among the arguments. In other words, try to put the best arguments at the top, effectively ordering your arguments based on importance and priority.

b) Argument Range

A thorough controversy brief should shoot for ten or more distinct arguments, and each argument should include at least a paragraph or two. Within that explanation, the argument should provide evidence and a connection back to the proposition. Why does that argument matter? It does not hurt to use the Toulmin model as a test of each argument to assess its completion. At a minimum, a complete argument should have a claim, grounding, and warrant (i.e., logic) connecting the point of the argument to the various forms of evidence being deployed.

c) Structure

The structure of how the arguments are set up is very flexible as long as there is a distinct argument that relates back to the statement, includes evidence, and explains why it matters. That argument could be put together in paragraph form or some other way of organizing the information. It may help to use bullets underneath each number—just remember to include analysis under each argument, however, so the brief is not just a collection of pieces of evidence without additional warrants and no connection back to the statement. It can also help to summarize the claim of each argument at the top of each number (providing a tag line for each argument).

d) Citations

Don't forget to cite your sources along the way! As you will discover, it is important to note that every outside source must be accompanied by full reference information so that the citation can be easily located in the references section of your essay. Moreover, it helps to include qualifications for the sources being used and justify them (as well as other forms of evidence) where possible. See Chapter Four for tips on finding quality research.

Why Do We Use Controversy Briefs?

There are a number of reasons why controversy briefs are so instrumental to the argumentation process. The first reason we use controversy briefs is they allow us to ask the right questions. By laying out all of the issues and each of the perspectives on a given issue, we learn what is at stake. We notice the stakeholders and the concerns of all the parties involved. This, in turn, helps us to ask the pertinent and relevant questions necessary to understanding the issues and, ultimately, arguing in favor of or in opposition to a proposition.

Controversy briefs also help us understand why each argument matters. This means two things: First, why does each argument make a difference? What is the impact? Assume you win your argument—then explain why it is important. Give each argument some weight. Second, why does each argument prove the proposition true or false? Go back to the wording of your statement and connect the statement to each argument. In many cases, I am left saying, "Sure, this argument makes sense in a void, but I do not know how it speaks to the specifics of the proposition."

Controversy briefs also help us to weigh and compare positions, which helps us better understand our own positions. This in turn allows us to discover means of pre-emption, or refuting an opposing argument before it is made. And lastly, controversy briefs help us determine the precise location of clash, which, as you will recall, is required for any debate. It sounds silly, but the controversy brief lays out the controversy and as with anything, it becomes easier to compare and contrast two things once they are seated next to each other. For this reason, and the others we just discussed, we strongly recommend that you begin the case construction process with a controversy brief.

Case Construction

Recall from Chapter One the story of Zack Kopplin. Zack wanted to challenge the Louisiana Science Education Act (LSEA) because he felt, for a number of reasons, that the LSEA threatened science education in Louisiana schools. As a result, Zack spoke out against the LSEA and, in short time and with the help of many others, he became the face of opposition to the legislation. To succeed, Zack needed to define his position. Zack needed to find arguments that supported his position. He needed to organize and articulate these arguments in such a way that made his proposition persuasive. In short, Zack needed to build a *case* against the LSEA.

In his TED talk, titled The Cost of Teaching Creationism, Zack laid out his case against legislation like the LSEA. He argued that such legislation would allow for creationism education in public schools. In just under 10 minutes, Zack made the following case for eliminating the LSEA and increasing the funding for science education.

Proposition: The LSEA should be eliminated.
    Claim 1: Teaching creationism will confuse students about the fundamental nature of science.
        Ground 1: Science is testable.
        Ground 2: Science is falsifiable.

Ground 3: Science is expandable.

Warrant: Creationism confuses scientific understanding because it is not testable, falsifiable, or expandable.

Claim 2: Teaching creationism will not equip Louisiana students to make the breaking scientific discoveries needed to solve our most pressing challenges.

Ground 1: Drought can only be solved through scientific study.

Ground 2: Disease can only be solved through scientific study.

Ground 3: Climate change can only be solved through scientific study.

Warrant: Creationism does not provide students with the knowledge and skills to solve drought, disease, and climate change.

Claim 3: Strong science education will increase our ability to address future threats.

Ground 1: Science education funding has a high return on investment.

Ground 2: Scientific discoveries stay with us forever.

Ground 3: Strong science education funding will help unlock new/hidden technologies.

Warrant: A high return on investment, permanent discoveries, and the development of new technologies will help us address future threats.

Zack's case emerges to contain three central arguments in support of his proposition. The proposition in this case is one of policy. In such a short speech Zack was likely unable to fully explicate his case. For instance, the details regarding the evidence he provided and the claims he made could be fleshed out in a more detailed essay or manuscript. Furthermore, in a more detailed essay, Zack could utilize some of the secondary elements of the Toulmin Model you are already familiar with. Qualifiers, for example, may help him circumscribe his claims in such a way that increases their effectiveness. Backing could help support the strength of his warrants, and rebuttals could help make the counterarguments of his opponents seem less persuasive.

With this said, we are able to discern the essence of Zack's case by rewriting them in the shortened, more condensed format above. This format is often referred to as a *case brief*. Case briefs distill complex cases to their essential elements. This makes reviewing, studying, and critiquing individual arguments and propositions much easier. For this reason, we recommend you practice converting the cases you come across in the news media or arguments with your friends into case briefs. Case briefs are different from controversy briefs in that case briefs lay out just the affirmative or negative case, whereas controversy briefs lay out both sides. You will recall that controversy briefs are must-do first steps for any advocate. Controversy briefs summarize the entire argument, from all sides. In this way, they help provide the "lay of the land," so to speak. Because of this, controversy briefs always precede case briefs. We provide opportunities for you to practice this essential skill at the end of this chapter. In what follows we are going to walk you through the process of case construction for propositions of fact, value, and policy. We will include several sample case briefs along the way.

To make the successful case in favor of a proposition of fact, value, or policy the advocate or opponent must meet certain requirements. In argumentation, and particularly in debate, these requirements are often referred to as *stock issues*. Stock issues represent the blueprints for successful fact, value, and policy case construction. Importantly, the stock issues are different for each type of proposition. This means that case construction for fact, value, and policy represents three distinct challenges. We like to think of case construction for fact, value, and policy as three different variations of the same game. For example, cricket and baseball are similar in many respects even though the terminology, strategy, and governing rules of the two sports vary considerably. One is not necessarily better than the other; both games are rewarding and fun to play. Nevertheless, fully appreciating the two games requires an understanding of how each game is played. To be a successful advocate, you will need to know the stock issues of fact, value, and policy case construction. Fortunately, they are simple, intuitive, and easy to remember.

Both the advocate and opponent need to complete some "prep work," or *case development,* before addressing the stock issues. The good news is that the process of case development is the same for fact, value, and policy propositions. In short, the advocate develops her case by (1) summarizing the significance of the issue at hand, (2) discussing the historical context related to the proposition, and (3) defining key terms within the proposition that are central to understanding the advocate's or opponent's position. After case development, one can then begin to address the stock issues. Importantly, addressing the stock issues is where the argumentation occurs. But, before one can begin to argue her case, one needs to establish a clear understanding of the debate at hand.

Case Development

Case development is important because it helps to provide clarity, which is essential in argumentation. For example, stating the significance of the issue summarizes the debate as it has existed until the intervention of the current debate. Significance asks, "Why are we talking about this issue?" or "What is the larger importance to society?" or "What do we know and what do we not know?" Think of summarizing significance as catching someone up to speed on the issue. Before a person can participate in an argument, she needs to know the issue! This is why we recommend you begin your arguments, particularly your written arguments (where you presumably have more time and space) by addressing the significant elements of the debate so that everyone participating is on the same page, so to speak.

Taking some time to address the historical context of the debate also helps in this regard. Providing historical context helps to showcase the advocate's understanding of the issue not only as it exists today but as it has existed throughout time. Our understanding of history certainly influences our understanding of the present. And rarely do issues exist in isolation. Therefore, in making clear our understanding of how things developed or how things are related to others, our opponents in argumentation can better understand how we view our own positions as well as theirs. Deciding what to include in a historical account of a particular issue is challenging to beginning debaters. Ultimately, however, one needs to provide history that is both (1) relevant and (2) prudent. In other words, strive to craft a historical account that includes information that is necessary as well as that which is advantageous to your case.

Defining the central or ambiguous terms within our proposition provides additional clarity in argumentation. Words are powerful and have the ability to shape our thoughts and perspectives. Words are laden with meaning, power, and relationships. Words seemingly as simple as "truth" and "real" are actually quite complex, as they conjure different emotions and feelings in people. The ambiguous nature of language imbues poetry and creative writing with its magic. In argumentation, however, where often our purpose is not to be enthralled through evocative stories or impressed with bombastic prose (at least not often), ambiguity in language can be a distraction. We need to be unequivocal with our words and meanings so that our positions, and of course our propositions, are similarly unequivocal.

By way of example, let us examine the following proposition of fact:

Acme Car Corporation purposely hid information from their investors and consumers about the questionable safety of their vehicles.

Which terms within this proposition are not immediately clear to you? Perhaps after reading the proposition more critically, one begins to wonder what the advocate means when she says "hid," for example? And who *exactly* did the hiding for that matter? Acme Car Corporation? But who is that, *exactly*? Is it the entire corporation, or is it just the assembly line workers? These are questions that need to be answered before we can argue this proposition. For this reason, we believe it is perfectly reasonable to ask an advocate to define any term within a proposition. Returning to the example of *The Acme Car Corporation,* the advocate would most likely need to define the following terms: "Acme Car Corporation," "purposefully hid," and "information." He or she may then proceed in the following manner:

Acme Car Corporation: By "Acme Car Corporation," I am referring specifically to the leadership of the corporation, and the CEO in particular.

Purposefully hid: I define "purposefully hid" as intentionally and strategically covering up, destroying, or manipulating something in such a way that other people are no longer able to find it.

Information: In this context, the word "information" refers to the data and internal communications that prove Acme Car Corporation's cars were unsafe to customers.

Defining terms in this way clarifies any potential misunderstanding regarding the advocate's proposition. Now the opponent can better understand what the advocate is really arguing. Indeed, based on the definitions she provided, it seems the advocate is arguing that "The leadership of the Acme Car Corporation, including the CEO, intentionally and strategically covered up the data and internal communications that proved Acme Car Corporation's cars were unsafe to customers."

Arguing the Stock Issues

After the advocate has developed her case by summarizing the significance of the debate, providing historical context and, finally, by defining her terms, the advocate now needs to address the stock issues that establish the legitimacy of the proposition. As we mentioned earlier, each type of proposition (fact, value, and policy) requires different forms of proof. In other words, each type of proposition has unique stock issues that establish a successful case. To prove the stock issues of a case proposition, one needs to provide arguments. It is at this stage of case construction that we employ the elements of the Toulmin Model we learned in Chapter Three.

Building a Case for a Proposition of Fact

Recall that arguments of fact are those that make declarative statements about that which is, was, or will be. Propositions of fact are the same. Propositions of fact can make the case that something happened or will happen, that something is true or false, or that a relationship between two or many things exists. The following are examples of propositions of fact:

A vegetarian diet is healthier than an animal-based diet.
Processed food is made to be addictive.
A meteorite killed the dinosaurs.
Social media use decreases social intelligence.

To make the case in favor of a proposition of fact an advocate must complete the process of case development we described in the previous section. After this, he or she must address the stock issues of fact argumentation. There are two stock issues needed to construct a case in support a proposition of fact:

Stock Issues for Fact Argumentation
1. Does the evidence reasonably support the purported fact?
2. Can the purported fact be explained by extenuating circumstances?

The first stock issue of fact argumentation requires the advocate to locate and provide sufficient evidence to prove his or her purported fact beyond reasonable doubt. In other words, the first stock issue deals with the evidence that is needed to satisfy one's burden of proof. This often requires an advocate to provide satisfactory data, statistics, testimony, or other forms of evidence that compels the opponent to suspend faith in presumption. In short, the first stock issue of fact argumentation requires the advocate to confirm the existence of the stated fact through evidence.

The second stock issue of fact argumentation requires the advocate to demonstrate the absence of any legitimate *extenuating circumstances*. Extenuating circumstances are additional considerations or alternative accounts that mitigate or reduce the impact or legitimacy of an argument. It is not sufficient to simply provide compelling evidence. The advocate must also demonstrate that the evidence is clear and incontrovertible proof of the purported fact in the manner the advocate described.

Let us use a simple case to illustrate. Pretend we wanted to argue the following proposition: John Smith committed the bank robbery. To prove this proposition, we need to satisfy the aforementioned stock issues of fact argumentation. First, what evidence supports the purported fact that John Smith committed to bank robbery? Let us pretend that after a thorough investigation, we found John Smith's fingerprints on the gun used to rob the bank. We also found searches for "bank robberies" on his home computer. Last, we discovered text messages on his confiscated phone wherein Mr. Smith discussed planning to leave the country the day after the bank robbery occurred. Considering this, we conclude that John Smith committed the bank robbery for the following three reasons:

1. Fingerprints on the weapon.
2. Researched bank robberies on home computer.
3. Planned to leave the country the day after the bank robbery.

We decide that these three arguments are sufficient to satisfy our burden of proof (stock issue one). However, we must now prove the absence of any potential extenuating circumstances, which may mitigate the impact of our arguments. For example, for what other reasons might John Smith's fingerprints be on the weapon? Also, what other reasons might he have researched bank robberies from home or planned to leave the country?

Well, it is possible that John Smith's hands were on the weapon because the gun belonged to him. John likes to shoot targets at his local firing range as a hobby. But this doesn't prove that John Smith used the gun during the robbery. In addition, John may not have researched bank robberies at all. It could have been anyone with access to his home computer, including his brother who is visiting from out of town. And maybe he was planning to leave the country because he wanted to visit his family in Guatemala. Perhaps that could explain the text messages on his phone. Considering these extenuating circumstances, then, it appears that John Smith may not have been the bank robber. Perhaps our attention should turn to his brother.

As we just demonstrated, if the advocate is able to provide evidence in support of a fact, but cannot demonstrate the absence of compelling alternative considerations or extenuating circumstances, the advocate cannot establish a prima facie case. The wise advocate, therefore, considers alternative perspectives of every argument. Conducting opposition research helps in this regard (see Chapter Four).

Let us now examine a more complicated proposition of fact to further demonstrate the stock issues of fact argumentation. In particular, let us use an essay written by a student of ours to show what a complete proposition of fact case looks like.

Outline: Prosecuting Prostitutes Does Not Deter Prostitution

by Jennifer L. Cruz

<u>Key Terms</u>

Prosecution: any negative legal action against someone who has been accused or convicted of committing a crime.

Prostitution: the performance of a sexual act in exchange for profit—which may or may not be monetary compensation.

Prostitute(s): any person who performs a sexual act in exchange for profit, whether or not they directly receive that profit.

Deter: an overall prevention or discouragement of the continuation of the prostitution market as a whole.

Arguments

Claim 1: Prosecuting a prostitute can fail to deter the prostitutes' continued involvement in the prostitution market.

> Grounds 1: Anyone with a prostitution conviction on their record will be denied employment with the U.S. federal government (U.S. Office of Personnel Management, n.d.).

> Grounds 2: Jobs requiring background checks require disclosure of convictions within the last seven years minimum, and some background checks have no time constraint (Federal Trade Commission, 2002).

> Grounds 3: If a prostitute wants to enter a different job market, in some cases they must first pay fines associated with their prostitution acts. Their inability to pay these fines through any means other than prostitution can result in their continued involvement in the prostitution market (Sanders, 2004).

> Warrant: Prosecuting prostitutes creates a stigma around prostitutes and, once labeled, prostitutes are less likely to acquire gainful employment.

> Backing: Prosecutorial action aimed at prostitutes can cement the idea that prostitution is a prostitute's only option, rather than deter it (Sanders, 2004).

Claim 2: Prosecution efforts aimed at prostitutes can actually aid the continuation of the prostitution market.

> Grounds 1: Prosecuting prostitutes creates vacancies in the supply of prostitutes (Shively, Kliorys, Wheeler, & Hunt 2012).

> Grounds 2: Sex traffickers fill those vacancies in the prostitution market with sex trafficked people (Shively et al., 2012).

> Grounds 3: Once a sex trafficker has successfully profited from the prostitution of a person they trafficked, they will continue to seek profit by prostituting that person and by trafficking even more people off whom they can profit in the prostitution market (Dempsey, 2010).

> Warrant: Prosecuting prostitutes creates a temporary vacuum into which a sex trafficked victim is likely to inhabit.

> Backing: The brief loss in supply caused by prosecuting prostitutes does nothing to deter the prostitution market as a whole, and in fact can initiate the sex trafficking of people beyond the number of prostitutes prosecuted.

Claim 3: When prostitutes are prosecuted the overall demand for the prostitution market is not deterred.

> Grounds 1: The prostitution market is driven by demand (Shively et al., 2012).

> Grounds 2: When consumers realize purchasing sexual acts will not be prosecuted, the risk of soliciting a prostitute goes down and the demand for prostitution goes up (Jakobsson & Kostadam, 2011).

> Grounds 3: In response to consumer demands going up, the prostitution market will increase supply (Shively et al., 2012).

Warrant: If prostitutes are prosecuted, but not consumers, there is no prevention or discouragement for consumers to solicit the services of prostitutes therefore the prostitution market proliferates.

Backing: When consumers have been prosecuted and not prostitutes, street prostitution has been reduced between 50–75% (Shively et al., 2012).

Opposition Arguments

Summary: People will avoid becoming a prostitute for fear of being arrested (Hayes-Smith & Shekarhar, 2010).

Challenge: This argument both denies the existence of people forced, coerced, or defrauded into entering the prostitution market, and then it assumes all people will decide that the cons of prostitution will outweigh the pros regardless of their socioeconomic status, education, alternative opportunity, etc.

Summary: The decrease of supply by prosecuting prostitutes will decrease the prostitution market because prostitutes are less likely to return to the prostitution market.

Challenge: Because the demand for prostitution has not decreased, the removal of one person leads to more people entering the prostitution market, including sex trafficked persons. Additionally, prosecuting prostitutes has been shown to lead to some prostitutes' continued prostitution by leaving them with little to no viable alternatives.

Summary: Prosecuting a prostitute disrupts a micro prostitution market, and if enough micro prostitution markets are shuttered eventually the global prostitution market will be deterred.

Challenge: Disrupting one micro prostitution market has been shown to only last temporarily, and usually just leads to the market moving to another area. Even if one micro prostitution market is completely shuttered, because the market is driven by demand more micro markets will emerge to take its place.

Works Cited

Dempsey, M. (2010). Sex trafficking and criminalization: In defense of feminist abolitionism. *University of Pennsylvania Law Review, 158,* 1729–1778.

Federal Trade Commission. (2002). Fair Credit Reporting Act. Retrieved from http://www.ftc.gov/sites/default/files/fcra.pdf

Hayes-Smith, R., & Shekarhar, Z. (2010). Why is prostitution criminalized? An alternative viewpoint on the construction of sex work. *Contemporary Justice Review, 13*(1), 43–55. doi:10.1080/10282580903549201

Jakobsson, N., & Kostadam, A. (2011). Gender equity and prostitution: An investigation of attitudes in Norway and Sweden. *Feminist Economics, 17*(1), 31–58. doi:10.1080/13545701.2010.541863

Sanders, T. (2004). The risks of street prostitution: Punters, police, and protestors. *Urban Studies, 41*(9), 1703–1717. doi:10.1080/0042098042000243110

Shively, M., Kliorys, K., Wheeler, K., & Hunt, D. (2012). *A National Overview of Prostitution and Sex Trafficking Demand Reduction Efforts, Final Report.* Retrieved from https://www.ncjrs.gov/pdffiles1/nij/grants/238796.pdf

U.S. Office of Personnel Management. (n.d.). *Background investigations suitability adjudications.* Retrieved from http://www.opm.gov/investigations/background-investigations/suitability-adjudications/#url=Referral-Chart

Case: Prosecuting Prostitutes Does Not Deter Prostitution

by Jennifer L. Cruz

Although prostitution is referred to as the world's oldest profession, there is little regard given to prostitutes. While they are punished for not abiding by the laws, they are rarely afforded the laws' protections. This applies to people who were forced, coerced, or otherwise entered or stay in the prostitution market against their will. Regardless of how a prostitute entered the market, 89% want to leave but can't (Farley et al., 2003). Therefore, to speak of prostitution is to speak of sex trafficking.

Between January 2008 and June 2010, the U.S. Department of Justice reported that 82% of investigated incidents of human trafficking were for sex trafficking, and almost half of the sex trafficking victims were minors (Banks & Kyckelhahn, 2011). According to the Swedish government, "trafficking in human beings could not flourish but for the existence of local prostitution markets" (U.S. Department of State, 2004, p. 2). Human trafficking, so consequently sex trafficking, is the fastest growing criminal enterprise and behind only drug trafficking as the most profitable (Harris, 2012). Even though almost half of sex trafficking victims are minors, when they reach the age of majority in most countries they are no longer deemed victims but willing participants. The shift of responsibility onto the person whose body is being exploited works in the favor of traffickers. If a prostitute is taken off the street, traffickers simply put another in their place. Put simply, prosecuting prostitutes does not deter prostitution.

In ancient Athens male prostitutes were forbidden from holding public office, taking legal action in court, or addressing the assembly—some of the capstones of citizenship in Athens at the time—or they would be dealt punishments up to and including execution (Nowak, 2010). Legally, female prostitutes could not be raped, so their attackers faced no penalty. Athens still profited by requiring prostitutes to pay a special tax for their income. Though prostitution seemed legal prostitutes were stripped of their rights. Historically, prostitutes have been punished with little to no retribution against those who exploited them (Nowak, 2010). There are several recent examples of societies' and governments' differing reactions to the prostitution market.

Despite the fact that the Condition of Women in the Russian Federation was approved in 1996, which classified prostitution as a form of violence against women, the Russian public's opinion of prostitutes is much lower than the opinion of their customers (Alikhadzhieva, 2009). Results of a public opinion survey found that 95% of respondents felt hatred, hostility and disdain, or disgust toward prostitutes, and that violence against prostitutes was an absolute right of consumers and pimps (Alikhadzhieva, 2009). Despite wanting prostitution stopped, some said it was completely normal for a man to use a prostitute (Alikhadzhieva, 2009). In Sweden, on the other hand, the purchase of sex is illegal while the sale of sex is not. While the majority of Swedish citizens want prostitution eradicated, they feel it is more warranted to prosecute consumers rather than prostitutes, and this has led to a decrease in street prostitution (Jakobsson & Kostadam, 2011). In the U.S., treatment of prostitutes varies from county to county.

Even before prostitution was criminalized in the U.S., the legal system prosecuted female prostitutes on charges like nightwalking at a greater rate than men engaging in the same acts (Johnson, 2014). The Mann Act of 1910 criminalized who today we consider sex traffickers (Public Broadcasting Service, 2005). Within fifteen years of the passing of the Mann Act prostitution was criminalized in every state, but prosecution was overwhelmingly reserved for prostitutes with little action against consumers or sex traffickers (Johnson, 2014). Even now some states do not consider purchasing the services of a prostitute to be a crime (Johnson, 2014). Nationally, prostitutes are still prosecuted far more frequently than consumers or traffickers.

Before the claims of the proposition that prosecuting prostitutes does not deter prostitution are discussed, the terms must be operationally defined. "Prosecution" refers to any legal action against someone who has been accused or convicted of committing a crime. This can include but is not limited to incarceration, arrest, citation, fines, deportation, community service, violent punishments like lashing, etc.

"Prostitute(s)" refer(s) to any person who performs a sexual act in exchange for profit, whether or not they directly receive that profit. The profit does not have to be a monetary sum; it can also include but is not limited to favors, food, shelter, protection, drugs, etc. If the profit goes to a pimp, madam, boyfriend, or other person, the person performing the sexual act is still a prostitute. Because of a wide variety of sexual preferences and fetishes, a sexual act in this context is defined as any act performed for the gratification of the consumer.

"Prostitution" is the performance of a sexual act in exchange for profit as described above. If the consumer pays for a sexual act not consented to by the prostitute, the act is both rape and prostitution. Therefore, minors who cannot legally consent to sexual acts can still be considered prostitutes.

Lastly, "deter" refers to an overall prevention or discouragement of the continuation of the global prostitution market as a whole. If an individual prostitution operation moves from one area to another, or if one prostitute leaves the prostitution market, the prostitution market as a whole has not been deterred.

The proposition that prosecuting prostitutes does not deter prosecution is expanded into a primary inference thusly: Taking negative legal action against any person who is accused or convicted of performing a sexual act in exchange for profit does not prevent or discourage the continuation of the global market as a whole wherein the performances of sexual acts are exchanged for profit.

There are three main claims that will be established: prosecuting a prostitute can fail to deter the prostitutes' continued involvement in the prostitution market, prosecution efforts aimed at prostitutes can actually aid the continuation of the prostitution market, and when prostitutes are prosecuted the overall demand for the prostitution market is not deterred.

Prosecuting prostitutes creates a stigma around prostitutes and, once labeled, prostitutes are less likely to acquire gainful employment. There are many jobs and industries in which a prostitute is not allowed to work after prosecution. Anyone with a prostitution conviction on their record will be denied employment with the U.S. federal government (U.S. Office of Personnel Management, n.d.). Jobs requiring background checks demand disclosure of convictions within the last seven years minimum, and some background checks have no time constraint (Federal Trade Commission, 2002). Before some prostitutes can even be considered for other employment, they have to pay off fines associated with their prosecution for prostitution (Sanders, 2004). Their inability to pay these fines through any means other than prostitution can result in their continued prostitution.

There are some who argue that prosecuting prostitutes is a deterrent because people will avoid becoming prostitutes for fear of being arrested (Hayes-Smith & Shekarhar, 2010). This idea denies the existence of people forced, coerced, or defrauded into entering the prostitution market, and assumes all people will decide that the cons of prostitution will outweigh the pros regardless of their socioeconomic status, education, alternative opportunity, etc. In fact, as previously shown, prosecuting prostitutes can have the opposite effect of a deterrent by leaving prostitutes with little to no viable alternatives.

Not only is prosecuting prostitutes an ineffective deterrent of the prostitution market as a whole, it can also support the continuation of that market. According to a report released by the National Criminal Justice Reference Service, "market forces of prostitution [drive] demand for human trafficking of women and girls" (Shively, Kliorys, Wheeler, & Hunt, 2012, p. 11). One market force of prostitution that drives the demand for sex trafficking is the loss of supply, which in many cases is a result of the prosecution of prostitutes. Sex traffickers promptly fill these voids because sex trafficked victims are forced to comply. Once a sex trafficker has successfully profited from the prostitution of a person, they will continue to prostitute that person and traffic more people into prostitution (Dempsey, 2010). Prosecuting a prostitute can create a temporary vacuum into which a sex trafficked victim will likely inhabit, thereby continuing the market.

It can be argued that the removal of one prostitute from the prostitution market via social programs aiding that person does immense good for that person (Barrows, 2009). This supposedly supports the idea that the decrease of supply will decrease the prostitution market because prostitutes are less likely to return to the prostitution market. However, because the demand for prostitution has not decreased, the removal of one person leads to a new person entering the prostitution market. On a macro level a loss in supply does nothing to deter the prostitution market as a whole, and in fact can initiate the sex trafficking of other people.

When prostitutes are prosecuted consumers have no reason to stop soliciting prostitutes, therefore the overall demand for the prostitution market is not deterred. If consumers realize their actions will not be prosecuted, the risk of soliciting a prostitute goes down and the demand for prostitution goes up (Jakobsson & Kostadam, 2011). Rising demand leads to increasing supply, via sex trafficked victims or prostitutes who feel they cannot leave. The economics of the prostitution market dictate that "wherever demand occurs, supply and distribution emerge" and even though demand is not the only influence on the market, "removing or reducing demand reduces or eliminates markets" (Shively et al., 2012, p. iv). Without reducing the demand, the prostitution market as a whole will continue.

One could try to argue that prosecuting a prostitute disrupts a micro prostitution market. However, this is temporary and usually only moves the prostitution market to another area (Shively et al., 2012). Even if one micro prostitution market was eradicated, the global market would continue and soon another person would emerge as a replacement. Conversely, prosecuting the consumers has reduced street prostitution in Sweden by 50–75% (Shively et al., 2012). Considering Sweden began prosecuting consumers at the same time it stopped prosecuting prostitutes, this decrease cannot be attributed to the prosecution of prostitutes.

By demonstrating that prosecuting prostitutes can fail to deter a prostitute's continued involvement in the prostitution market, can aid the continuation of the prostitution market, and does not deter the overall demand for the prostitution market, a prima facie case has been made for the argument that prosecuting prostitutes does not deter prostitution.

References

Alikhadzhieva, I. (2009). Public opinion about prostitution and measures to prevent it. *Sociological Research, 48*(4), 82–90. doi:10.2753/SOR1061-0154480404

Banks, D., & Kyckelhahn, T. (2011). *Characteristics of suspected human trafficking incidents, 2008–2010.* U.S. Department of Justice, Office of Justice Programs, Bureau of Justice Statistics. Retrieved from http://www.bjs.gov/content/pub/pdf/cshti0810.pdf

Barrows, J. (2008). An ethical analysis of the harm reduction approach to prostitution. *Ethics & Medicine, 24*(3), 151–158.

Dempsey, M. (2010). Sex trafficking and criminalization: In defense of feminist abolitionism. *University of Pennsylvania Law Review, 158,* 1729–1778.

Farley, M., Cotton, A., Lynne, J., Zumbeck, S., Spiwak, F., Reyes, M., & Sezgin, U. (2003). Prostitution and trafficking in nine countries: An update on violence and posttraumatic stress disorder. *Journal of Trauma Practice, 2*(3–4), 33–74.

Federal Trade Commission. (2002). Fair Credit Reporting Act. Retrieved from http://www.ftc.gov/sites/default/files/fcra.pdf

Harris, K. (2012). *The State of Human Trafficking in California.* California Department of Justice, Office of the Attorney General. Retrieved from https://oag.ca.gov/sites/all/files/agweb/pdfs/ht/human-trafficking-2012.pdf?

Hayes-Smith, R., & Shekarhar, Z. (2010). Why is prostitution criminalized? An alternative viewpoint on the construction of sex work. *Comtemporary Justice Review, 13*(1), 43–55. doi:10.1080/10282580903549201

Jakobsson, N., & Kostadam, A. (2011). Gender equity and prostitution: An investigation of attitudes in Norway and Sweden. *Feminist Economics, 17*(1), 31–58. doi:10.1080/13545701.2010.541863

Johnson, E. (2014). Buyers without remorse: Ending the discriminatory enforcement of prostitution laws [Notes]. *Texas Law Review, 92,* 717–748.

Nowak, M. (2010). Defining prostitution in Athenian legal rhetorics. *The Legal History Review, 78,* 183–197.

Public Broadcasting Service. (2005). *The Mann Act: Full text.* Retrieved from http://www.pbs.org/unforgivableblackness/knocko ut/mannact_text.html

Sanders, T. (2004). The risks of street prostitution: Punters, police, and protestors. *Urban Studies, 41*(9), 1703-1717. doi:10.1080/0042098042000243110

Shively, M., Kliorys, K., Wheeler, K., & Hunt, D. (2012). *A National Overview of Prostitution and Sex Trafficking Demand Reduction Efforts, Final Report.* Retrieved from https://www.ncjrs.gov/pdffiles1/nij/grants/238796.pdf

U.S. Department of State, Bureau of Public Affairs. (2004). *The link between prostitution and sex trafficking.* Retrieved from http://www.defense.gov/home/features/2008/0608_ctip/do cs/Prost itution%20Fact%20Sheet.pdf

U.S. Office of Personnel Management. (n.d.). *Background investigations suitability adjudications.* Retrieved from http://www.opm.gov/investigations/background-investigations/suitability-adjudications/#url=Referral-Chart

Stock Issues for Value Argumentation

Instead of making an assertion about something that is, was, or will be, let us assume an advocate wants to make some form of an evaluative assessment or comparison. We make assertions like these frequently. It is quite common for people to project their tastes, moral standards, and critiques about aspects of society onto others. We do this when we say a film was "poorly directed," or when we say a meal was "deliciously prepared." We make value statements in political or social contexts as well.

The process of case construction for a value proposition is similar to fact argumentation. In more detail, the advocate must first complete the process of case development. After that, the advocate must then address the stock issues. There are three stock issues needed to construct a case in support of a proposition of value:

Stock Issues for Value Argumentation
1. Value premise.
2. Value criteria.
3. Value maximization.

The first stock issue of value argumentation considers "by what value premise should the present debate be evaluated?" To establish a value premise is to advance one value as superior or more important in relation to competing values—as *the* lens through which one should analyze the proposition. For example, if one were to assert that "Theme Park X is more enjoyable than Theme Park Y," a likely value premise supporting this assertion might be "enjoyment." This illustrates an important realization regarding the value premise: The value premise is often based on the value term (i.e., "enjoyable") within a given value proposition, but this is not always the case. An advocate or opponent may choose, for strategic purposes or otherwise, a value premise not within the proposition. For instance, instead of "enjoyable," the advocate could choose "economical" as a value premise. In either case—"enjoyment" or "economical"—the value premise is the basis of the argument: It is the value being proposed.

After the value premise has been clearly established, the advocate must next move to satisfy the second stock issue of value argumentation: value criteria. If we continue using the theme park example, we can illustrate the concept of value criteria in detail. Let us say that the value premise for the proposition "Theme Park X is more enjoyable than Theme Park Y" is "enjoyment." Once we establish the value premise, it is imperative that we provide sufficient criteria that certify the presence or absence of "enjoyment." In other words, once we have decided that "enjoyment" is the focus of our argument, we need to quickly decide what constitutes "enjoyment." How *do* we know if a theme park is enjoyable, after all? Value criteria provide us with the ability to define, measure, or evaluate a given value premise. Considering this, value criteria in support of the value premise "enjoyment," might include the following:

1.   A theme park is enjoyable when it creates a friendly and safe atmosphere.
2.   A theme park is enjoyable when there are rides and attractions that appeal to all ages.
3.   A theme park is enjoyable when it is not cost prohibitive.

We should point out that there is not a "right" or "wrong" set of criteria for a given value premise. The three criteria we listed above could be easily substituted with another set. For instance, we could have used the following criteria for "enjoyment":

1.   A theme park is enjoyable when it makes one laugh.
2.   A theme park is enjoyable when it brings family together.

Deciding on the most appropriate criteria for a value premise becomes a matter of strategy. The advocate will want to advance a specific set of criteria for the stated value premise. These criteria should reinforce one's position in the debate. For instance, on the proposition "Theme Park X is more enjoyable than Theme Park Y," where the value premise is "enjoyment," the advocate will want to choose criteria for "enjoyment" that *apply* to Theme Park X and *do not* apply to Theme Park Y. Unsurprisingly, it is common for the criteria proposed by the advocate to be at odds with what the opponent wishes to propose. With that said, ultimately the advocate and opponent must agree upon a common set of criteria. If two sets of criteria are used to evaluate the same value premise—one for the advocate and one for the opponent—then the two positions will be unable to agree upon the outcome of the argument. They will, in effect, be arguing two different things.

Once the advocate has established the value premise and the value criteria, he then needs to show how the value criteria are satisfied or met by the subject of the proposition. This is the essence of the third stock issue for value argumentation: value maximization. For example, if an advocate were to propose that "Theme Park X is more enjoyable than Theme Park Y" and that the value premise "enjoyment" is defined by the following criteria:

1.   A theme park is enjoyable when it creates a friendly and safe atmosphere.
2.   A theme park is enjoyable when there are rides and attractions that appeal to all ages.

3. A theme park is enjoyable when it is not cost prohibitive.

The advocate must demonstrate the following:

1. Theme Park X is enjoyable because it creates a friendly and safe atmosphere.
2. Theme Park X is enjoyable because there are rides and attractions that appeal to all ages.
3. Theme Park X is enjoyable because it is not cost prohibitive.

If the advocate is able to demonstrate that the criteria are satisfied by Theme Park X *to a greater* degree than Theme Park Y, it follows logically that the advocate will have shown that Theme Park X *maximizes* the value premise of "enjoyment" more than Theme Park Y. Therefore, based on the stated value premise of "enjoyment," the proposed criteria, and the demonstration that the criteria are present to a greater degree at Theme Park X relative to Theme Park Y, we can conclude that, indeed, Theme Park X is more enjoyable that Theme Park Y.

As we did for fact argumentation, let us now examine a more complicated proposition of value to further demonstrate the stock issues of value argumentation. In particular, let us use an essay written by a student of ours to show what a complete proposition of value case looks like.

Brief: It is Unethical to Knowingly Produce Addictive Foods

by Carly Donohue

<u>Key Terms</u>

Knowingly: Full and conscious awareness
Food: processed foods that have been processed on a mass scale—this includes changing the composition of food, such as canning, cooking, freezing, and dehydrating
Addictive: the psychological response in the brain that leads to overeating, cravings and subsequent withdrawal symptoms

<u>Value Premise</u>: Unethical
<u>Value Criteria</u>: Deceit, manipulation, harm

<u>Value Maximization</u>:
Claim 1: Producing addictive food is deceitful.
    Ground 1: Marketing and advertising healthy options in attempt to direct consumer choices.
        Warrant: Health and nutrition claims have been shown to increase consumers' perception of healthfulness and willingness to purchase the products (Harris, 2011).
    Ground 2: Products marketed to be healthy still lack nutritional value, usually being full of sugar (Seabrook, 2011).

Warrant: The FDA is working on revising nutritional requirement so companies will no longer be able to have health claims on packaging if they do meet the requirements (Harris, 2011). Backing: FDA was authorized to improve food labels because companies were making unregulated health claims to advertise and market products.

Claim 2: Addictive food increases consumption though manipulation.
> Grounds 1: Research shows that foods are being designed to surpass the rewarding properties of traditional foods by increasing fat, sugar, salt flavors and additives to high levels (Gearhardt, Grilo, DiLeone, Brownell & Potenza, 2010).
> Warrant: Food scientists have constructed a way to trick the brain into wanting more called "vanishing caloric density" (Moss, 2012).
> Grounds 2: Food is being designed to keep consumers to keep buying their products by leaving them craving more and eating more.
> Warrant: Food manufacturers are combining sugar, fat and salt to create 'highly palatable' that prompts a positive cognitive response and consequently that fat and sugar consumption of trans fatty acids directly contributes to the occurrence of heart diseases (World Health Organization, 2012).
> Backing: Additives in processed foods are carefully formulated in an effort to prompt a pleasurable response in the brain (Kessler, 2010).

Claim 3: Addiction to processed foods is harmful to one's health.
> Ground 1: Causal relationship between salt intake and Hypertension (Meneton, 2005).
> Warrant: Americans consume up to 75 percent of their daily recommended sodium intake from processed foods like "tomato sauce, soups, condiments, canned foods and prepared mixes" ("Shaking the salt," 2014).
> Ground 2: Rising obesity rates correspond to the increase in the availability of highly processed foods (DeBres, 2005).
> Warrant: Foods dense in fat, sugar and salt prompt release of dopamine, which acts to motivate people to overeat overeating high-calorie foods.
> Backing: The patterns of consumption associated with convenience food has been known to harm the mechanisms that regulate energy balance, which leads to excess eating (Monteiro, Levy, Claro, Ribeiro de Castro & Cannon, 2010).

References

American Heart Association. (2014, March 05). Shaking the salt habit. Retrieved from http://www.heart .org/HEARTORG/Conditions/HighBloodPressure/PreventionTreatment of HighBloodPressure/ Shaking-the-Salt- Habit_UCM_303241_Article.jsp

DeBres, K. (2005). Burgers for Britain: A cultural geography of McDonald's UK. Journal of Cultural Geography; *22*(2), 115–139.

Gearhardt, A., Grilo, C. DiLeone, R., Brownell, K., & Potenza, M. (2010). Can food be addictive? Public health and policy implications.

Harris, J., Thompson, J., Schwartz, M., & Brownell, K. (2011). Nutrition-related claims on children's cereal: What do they mean to parents and do they influence willingness to buy? *Public Health Nutrition, 14*(12), 2207–2212.

Kessler, D. (2010). *The end of overeating: Taking control of the insatiable American appetite.* (p. 21). Random House LLC.

Meneton P., Jeunemaitre X., de Wardener HE., & Macgregor GA. (2005). Links between dietary salt intake, renal salt handling, blood pressure, and cardiovascular diseases. Physiological Reviews; *85*(2), 679–715.

Monteiro, C., Levy, R., Claro, R., Ribeiro de Castro, I., & Cannon, G. (2010). Increasing consumption of ultra-processed foods and likely impact on human health: Evidence from brazil. *Public Health Nutrition, 14*(1), 5–13.

Moss, M. (2012, February 20). The extraordinary science of addictive junk food. *The New York Times*, Retrieved from http://www.nytimes.com/2013/02/24/magazine/the-extraordinary-science-of-junk-food.html?pagewanted=2&pagewanted=all

Seabrook, J. (2011). Snacks for a fat planet. New Yorker, *87*(13), 54–71.

Case: It is Unethical to Knowingly Produce Addictive Foods

by Carly Donohue

Contemporary Americans are fixated on instant gratification, especially when it comes to food. They are inclined to choose foods that are quick and easy to consume in between long hours at work, school, and extracurricular activities. Prepackaged foods are inexpensive and widely accessible, but the drawback to the ease and low cost of these foods is that they are heavily processed, contain little nutritional value, and have a greater addictive potential than whole foods such as fruits, vegetables, and lean proteins (Avena & Gold, 2011). These processed foods trigger a cognitive response in the brain that has been shown to satisfy the same cravings that drive tobacco, alcohol, and drug consumption (Beil, 2012). While processed foods may be packaged for the consumers' convenience, they have also been conveniently designed to stimulate food cravings. Thusly, consumers are unaware that these foods are being produced at the expense of their trust and health for profit. In this paper, I will argue that **it is unethical to knowingly produce addictive foods.**

The introduction of processed foods came about as a way to extend shelf-life, diversify diet through different flavors/colors/texture in food, and generate income for food manufacturing companies (Fellows, 2009). This innovation preceded the existence of food quality and safety standards. The first regulations were set in 1906 by The Food and Drug Administration to protect consumers and establish food standards (FDA History, 2013). Food labeling wasn't required by the FDA until 1990 and is just now working toward a more comprehensible labeling system to eliminate misleading claims and confusion by providing consumers with clear, factual information (Pomeranz, 2011). The processed food industry was destined to change as new technology developed. Along with the growth of the industry, the buying power of major retail companies and superstores has exploded, which has resulted in strategies to increase their competitiveness to stay on top (Fellows, 2009). Now, the food industry is going as far as designing food to trigger a cognitive response in the brain that has been shown to likely satisfy the same cravings that drive tobacco, alcohol, and drug consumption (Beil, 2012). The purpose of this is to induce addiction by making it so that consumers have to keep buying to satisfy the craving (Kessler, 2010).

In order to provide clarification in terms of my contentions, I will define key terms. "Knowingly" refers to the full and conscious awareness of food producers that their products are addictive for consumers (Moss, 2012). In other words, the food industry, food and beverage producers and retailers, purposefully choose ingredients with a motive. The term "food" refers to processed foods. Processed foods are foods that have been processed on a mass scale—this includes changing the composition of food, such as canning, cooking, freezing, dehydrating. For these procedures to be effective, preservatives are used to maintain consistency, color, or flavor. Preservatives can be as defined as any chemical added to food to extend shelf life (FDA, 2013). In the process, flavor and color are compromised so added color and flavor is used to maintain taste and aesthetic. Given that definition, examples of packaged foods and ready-to-eat foods include soup, frozen meals and pizza, bread, chips, granola bars, dressing and sauce, cereal, etc. "Addicting," refers to the psychological response in the brain that leads to overeating and cravings. In this case, addiction is constituted by "inability to control consumption, increased motivation to consume and persistent consumption despite negative consequences" (Ziaddeen, H. & Fletcher, 2012). "Unethical," to be defined more specifically in criteria, broadly refers to undesired outcomes and/or behaviors such as deceit, manipulation and harm.

The value premise for the present argument is "unethical." In order to be able to identify the presence or absence of the value premise "unethical," the following value criteria will be used. In more detail, something is "unethical" when it meets the following three conditions: (1) it is deceitful, (2) manipulative and (3) harmful.

"Harmful effects" here on refers to any adverse effects on health. For example, weight gain, obesity, hypertension, overeating, or addiction are harmful effects. Utilizing deceptive practice is in reference to using advertising and marketing that is misleading or confusing to sell a product. For example, putting a health claim on a food label that is unproven or confusing with the intention to influence consumption. The manipulative tactics begin with advertisements and continue as food companies add ingredients to induce cravings. In short, something is "unethical" when it is deceptive, manipulative and has a harmful effect on one's health.

The food industry knowingly produces addictive foods that have harmful effect on health. Is it ethical for the food industry to knowingly sell food products that carry health implications? The food industry has become so competitive that they may have lost sight of the consumers' interest in pursuit of their own interest. It is questionable whether the food industry should have a moral obligation to provide food that is healthy or at least provide the information to make healthy choices (Early, 2002).

Americans are consuming processed foods and putting their health at risk. There are well-documented studies proving a causal relationship between salt intake and

Hypertension (Meneton, 2005). According to the American Heart Association, Americans consume up to 75 percent of their daily recommended sodium intake from processed foods like "tomato sauce, soups, condiments, canned foods and prepared mixes" ("Shaking the salt," 2014). There is also a connection between processed foods and obesity; rising obesity rates correspond to the increase in the availability of highly processed foods (DeBres, 2005). This is in part due to the subsequent series in the brain that follows the release of dopamine prompted by food that is dense in fat and sugar. Ultimately, this process weakens the dopamine response so as result more food must be consumed to satisfy those receptors (Kenny, 2013). The patterns of consumption associated with convenience food has been known to harm the mechanisms that regulate energy balance, which leads to excess eating (Monteiro, Levy, Claro, Ribeiro de Castro & Cannon, 2010).

The food industry knowingly produces addictive foods using deception. So, are consumers really in control of choosing foods best for their health when marketing and advertising attempts to direct their choices for other reasons? The aforementioned puts companies' trustworthiness at stake and with that comes the possibility of losing money. Further, these products marketed to be healthy still lack nutritional value, usually being full of sugar (Seabrook, 2011). The problem with the food companies trying to get into the "nutrition business" by making "healthy" versions of junk food is whether these foods are going to be able to make the claim that their food is healthy. It is misleading when, in fact, health and nutrition claims have been shown to increase consumers' perception of healthfulness and willingness to purchase the products (Harris, 2011). The FDA is working on revising nutritional requirement so companies will no longer be able to have health claims on packaging if they do meet the requirements (Harris, 2011). As of 2009, the FDA was authorized to improve food labels because companies were making unregulated health claims to advertise and market products.

The food industry knowingly produces addictive foods by manipulating ingredients to influence consumers to eat more. Is it ethical to add ingredients to food for the purpose of increased consumption? Food companies depend upon food scientists to create product that allure consumers and entice by stimulating, then satisfying cravings. In fact, food scientists have constructed a way to trick the brain into wanting more called "vanishing caloric density" (Moss, 2012). Vanishing caloric density works by tricking your brain into thinking the food you're eating has no calories by making it melt down quickly (Moss, 2012). The processed food industry quite literally has the creation of cravings down to a science, designed to keep consumers to keep buying their products by leaving them craving more and eating more.

The food industry knowingly sells products that are harmful to public health, deceiving people with false claims, and manipulating food choices by using added ingredients for increased consumption to ensure the highest profit margin. This is unethical. Consumers are being put in situations in which processed foods that should be most limited happen to be highest in profit margin, meaning that the food industry would lose money if consumer demand went down (Brownell, 2009). The food industry makes it appear that the consumer's best interest is in mind with use of clever marketing and advertising, but their only concern is making money, a similar tactic used by the tobacco industry (Brownell, 2009). But the difference is that consumers rely on the food industry. According to U.S. Judge H. Lee Sarokin, "the choice between the physical health of consumers and the financial well-being of business, concealment is chosen over disclosure, sales over safety, and money over morality"(as cited in Brownell, 2009, p.). Once food companies have corrupted a consumer's diet with addictive products that cause poor health it is only a matter of time before what they're doing will no longer be seen as acceptable to ethically support.

References

American Heart Association. (2014, March 05). Shaking the salt habit. Retrieved from http://www.heart.org/HEARTORG/Conditions/HighBloodPressure/PreventionTreatmentofHighBloodPressure/Shaking-the-Salt-Habit_UCM_303241_Article.jsp

Avena, N., & Gold, M. (2011). Food and addiction–Sugars, fats and hedonic overeating. *Addiction*, *106*(7), 1214–1215. doi: 10.1111/j.1360-0443.2011.03373.x

Beil, L. (2012). The snack-food trap. *Newsweek*, *160*(19), 44–47

Brownell, K. D., & Warner, K. E. (2009). The perils of ignoring history: Big tobacco played dirty and millions died. How similar Is big food? *Milbank Quarterly*, *87*(1), 259–294.

DeBres, K. (2005). Burgers for Britain: A cultural geography of McDonald's UK. *Journal of Cultural Geography*, *22*(2), 115–139.

Early, R. (2002). Food ethics: A decision making tool for the food industry? *International Journal Of Food Science & Technology*, *37*(4), 339–349.

Fellows, P. J. (2009). *Food processing technology: Principles and practice*. (3 ed.).

Gearhardt, A., Grilo, C., DiLeone, R., Brownell, K., & Potenza, M. (2010). Can food be addictive? Public health and policy implications.

Harris, J., Thompson, J., Schwartz, M., & Brownell, K. (2011). Nutrition-related claims on children's cereal: What do they mean to parents and do they influence willingness to buy? *Public Health Nutrition*, *14*(12), 2207–2212.

Kenny, P. J. (2013). The food addiction. *Scientific American*, *309*(3), 44–49.

Kessler, D. (2010). *The end of overeating: Taking control of the insatiable American appetite*. (p. 21). Random House LLC.

Meneton P., Jeunemaitre X., de Wardener HE., & Macgregor GA. (2005). Links between dietary salt intake, renal salt handling, blood pressure, and cardiovascular diseases. *Physiological Reviews*, *85*(2): 679–715.

Monteiro, C., Levy, R., Claro, R., Ribeiro de Castro, I., & Cannon, G. (2010). Increasing consumption of ultra-processed foods and likely impact on human health: Evidence from Brazil. *Public Health Nutrition*, *14*(1), 5–13.

Moss, M. (2012, February 20). The extraordinary science of addictive junk food. *The New York Times*, Retrieved from http://www.nytimes.com/2013/02/24/magazine/the-extraordinary-science-of-junk-food.html?pagewanted=2&pagewanted=all

Pomeranz, J. (2011). Front-of-Package food and beverage labeling new directions for research and regulation. *American Journal of Preventive Medicine*, *40*(3), 382–385.

Seabrook, J. (2011). Snacks for a fat planet. New Yorker, *87*(13), 54–71.

U.S. Food and Drug administration. (2013). *History*. Retrieved from http://www.fda.gov/AboutFDA/WhatWeDo/History/default.html

Stock Issues for Policy Argumentation

Propositions of policy, like policy claims, assert that something should be done. Policy propositions advocate an action or change. This is why policy propositions often contain the words "should" or "needs to." Sample propositions of policy include the following:

> *The United States federal government should legalize prostitution.*
> *Animal testing should be prohibited in all cases.*
> *The United States Congress needs to repeal the Affordable Care Act.*
> *The Louisiana Science Education Act (LSEA) should be eliminated.*

Propositions of policy are quite common in our everyday discourse and happenings (e.g., "We should invest in a retirement account"). Policy proposals are also common in legislative contexts. Indeed, one of the chief responsibilities of lawmakers is to create and oppose policies that ultimately govern a state or nation.

The process of case construction for a policy proposition is similar to fact and value argumentation in that appropriate case development is required before addressing the stock issues. Afterward, the advocate must then address the stock issues. There are three stock issues needed to construct a case in support a proposition of policy:

1. Harm.
2. Inherency.
3. Solvency.

The first stock issue of policy argumentation requires the advocate to demonstrate a harm or problem with the status quo. We must stress that it is absolutely essential for the advocate to succeed in establishing harm. Policies are warranted or palatable only when a problem exists. The familiar cliché "if it's not broke, don't fix it" applies here. Without a present and significant problem, there simply is no need for a new policy.

The advocate succeeds in establishing harm by demonstrating that a harm is both:

1. Imminent in nature.
2. Significant in nature.

First, the advocate must show that the harm imminent or is either happening presently or will happen in the near future. This is crucial because if a harm occurred in the past, there is little we can and should do about it now. Alternatively, if a harm is said to not occur for many years or decades in the future, policy action today will seem hasty and unwarranted. For these reasons, the advocate needs to demonstrate that a harm is currently happening or is likely to happen in the immediate future.

Second, the advocate needs to also demonstrate that the harm is or will be significant in nature. If an advocate succeeds in showing that a harm is presently occurring or will occur in the near future and yet that harm is not significant or substantial, policy action may seem unnecessary. Therefore, it is not sufficient to show that a harm is happening or will happen; the advocate needs to show that the harm is having or will have significant and/or lasting effects. In other words, the harm needs to appear great.

The second stock issue of policy argumentation requires the advocate to demonstrate that a present and significant harm is *inherent*. To argue something is inherent is to argue that something exists in a fixed or permanent state. Something is *not* inherent when it is a passing trend or statistical anomaly. To say something is inherent, therefore, is to say that something is *innate* or *ingrained* and is therefore unlikely to dissipate on its own. Successful policy argumentation requires the advocate to demonstrate that a harm is inherent. This is important for two reasons. First, if a harm is shown to be inherent, then the it becomes clear the harm will remain unchanged or mitigated. If the advocate succeeds in showing that a harm is significant—having great effect—then the inherent existence of the harm appears unacceptable. Second, if a harm appears unacceptable, then action will appear warranted and desired. So, in summary, the advocate needs to show a harm, which has already been shown to imminent and significant, is inherent, which is to say "not going away." If the advocate is able to do this, then she is well-positioned for the third stock issue, solvency.

Solvency refers to the application of the advocate's proposed policy to the stated harm. In more detail, solvency requires the advocate to demonstrate the ways in which the advocate's policy eliminates or mitigates the harm. In other words, solvency requires the advocate to show that his or her policy actually reduces, mitigates, or eliminates the harm. Importantly, the advocate must be detailed and clear at this stage. Policy implementation is famously difficult and convoluted; unforeseen problems and unintended consequences invariably arise whenever we try to fix our problems. Policies are often costly, for example. And in many cases, policies have crippling loopholes within them that give people, organizations, or countries a clandestine means to avoid following the policy. The advocate must then account, to the best of her ability, for these contingencies. Solvency, it turns out, is the most difficult of the stock issues of policy argumentation.

Let us use an elementary example to illustrate the stock issues of policy argumentation. Pretend that Citrus College is considering a campus-wide ban on tobacco consumption. Let us pretend that at the next meeting of the Board of Trustees of Citrus College, the following is proposed: "Citrus College should permanently ban the use of all tobacco products on the campus."

To successfully make the case that tobacco be banned on the campus of Citrus College, those in favor of the proposition need to address the stock issues of policy argumentation. In more detail, the proponents would first need to demonstrate an imminent and significant harm. After all, if students at Citrus College did not consume tobacco to begin with, a ban on tobacco consumption would seem silly. Furthermore, proponents would need to demonstrate that the problem of tobacco consumption is significant, which is to say that the harm is great and/or extensive. To this end, the proponents of the tobacco ban argue the following:

1. Significant tobacco-related litter is found around the campus of Citrus College.
2. Students often smoke near buildings, exposing others to second-hand smoke.
3. The sight of smoking students blights the otherwise beautiful campus.
4. The use of tobacco on campus contradicts the school's efforts to promote healthy lifestyles among its students.

Let us assume that the proponents of the ban are diligent and provide copious examples and reasons as to why these negative consequences are truly imminent and significant. If they do, the Board of Trustees surely must be convinced of the harm of campus tobacco use. But the argument is not yet complete. The proponents must next demonstrate the second stock issue, inherency.

To demonstrate inherency, the proponents of the ban argue that tobacco use on the campus will not dissipate unless action is taken. Moreover, they argue that without the campus-wide ban on tobacco use, students will continue to smoke and thereby continue to litter the campus, expose others to second hand smoke, blight the campus, and curtail efforts to improve the health of the student body on campus. It would be a substantial problem for the proponents of the ban if, in fact, the student body at Citrus College was smoking less and less on campus and that, in fact, litter around campus had been diminishing with each passing year or that complaints of second-hand smoking were decreasing in numbers. The problems associated with tobacco use on campus would not appear inherent if this were the case and, as a result, the opponents of the ban could justly argue that a campus-wide ban was unnecessary. Indeed, the harm appears to be taking care of itself. However, for our purposes here, let us assume that the proponents were able to demonstrate inherency. In other words, let us assume that the proponents of the tobacco ban were able to demonstrate that the imminent and significant harms associated with tobacco use on campus were not likely to go away *without* action. They would next need to demonstrate solvency.

The final stock issue of policy argumentation requires the proponents of the campus-wide ban on tobacco products to show their policy—the campus-wide ban—would, in fact, eliminate or mitigate the harm associated with tobacco use. To do this, the proponents would need to show how the campus-wide ban would eliminate or mitigate:

1. The amount of tobacco-related litter found around the campus of Citrus College.
2. The exposure of second-hand smoke.
3. The blight of smoking students.
4. The challenge to the efforts to improve the health of the student body.

The proponents would also need to show that the campus-wide ban is *feasible,* which is to say possible. The proponents would likely also want to show how the implementation of the campus-wide ban would not result in any significant unintended consequences. For instance, what if a campus-wide ban on tobacco use led students to smoke more in residential areas surrounding the campus? This might aggravate the neighbors and local community members whose tax dollars help to fund Citrus College. What other unintended consequences might a campus-wide ban create? Whatever they might be, the proponents of the ban will want to account for them in their solvency.

If, for the sake of our purposes here, the proponents were able to demonstrate that a ban on tobacco consumption on campus would result in a significant mitigation or an elimination of the harm, and that the ban would be feasible, enforceable, and not harmful, then the ban would seem warranted. Of course, this would require meticulous attention to detail on the part of the proponents. Again, policy argumentation is tricky for precisely this reason: New policies are often accompanied with new challenges. The clever and successful advocate is aware of this and therefore exercises great caution.

As we have done for fact and value argumentation, let us now examine another student essay to show what a more complicated and complete proposition of policy case looks like.

Brief: The Promotion of Drugs and Medication Through Direct-to-Consumer Advertisements Should be Prohibited

by Amanda C. Rives

Key Terms

Prescription drugs/medication: "A drug that can be obtained only by means of a physician's prescription" ("Prescription Drug," 2014, par 1).

Direct-to-consumer advertisements: "The use of mass media—eg, TV, magazines, newspapers, to publicly promote drugs, medical devices or other products which, by law, require a prescription, which targets consumers, with the intent of having a Pt. request the product by name" ("Direct-To-Consumer Advertising," 2002, part 1).

Harm

Arguments

Claim 1: DTC drug advertisements currently weaken the physician–patient relationship, because physicians often feel obliged to prescribe particular, often more expensive, brand-name drugs that patients request.

> Grounds 1: "Physicians felt more pressure to prescribe when the patient requested a specific brand-name drug (31%) than when the patient request was for a prescription in general (16%)" (Huh & Langteau, 2007, p. 155).
>
> Grounds 2: According to Capella, Taylor, Campbell, and Longwell (2009), the cost for brand-name prescription drugs can be broken down into the following categorization: "the manufacturer's price accounts for an estimated 74% of a prescription's retail price, retail pharmacy dispensing fees account for approximately 23%, and wholesaler costs make up the remaining 3%" (p. 147).
>
> Warrant: Based on relevant source information, it can be concluded that physicians felt uncomfortable prescribing the more expensive brand-name drugs compared to the generic drugs.
>
> Backing: Subsequently, when patients asked for a brand-name drug, the physician–patient relationship felt strained.

Significance

Claim 2: Patients are misinformed when side-effects and/or risks are not communicated in their entirety.

> Grounds 1: According to Davis (2007), high-priced DTC advertisements use qualifying language when presenting a particular drug's side-effects. These statements include severity/duration, conditional language, and discontinuation.

> Grounds 2: Studies indicate that qualifying language reduces "individuals' estimates of the likelihood of experiencing specific side-effects, typically side-effects considered more severe" (Davis, 2007, p. 619).

> Grounds 3: online websites "presented side effect information on both the home page and on an internal (interior) page (78.8%), while fewer sites provided side-effect information only on an internal page (17.3%)" (Davis, Cross, Cowley, 2007, p. 33).

> Warrant: Health care and drug costs that go toward the various advertising mediums fail to provide sufficient and accurate information pertaining to the risks associated with a particular medication.

> Backing: A lack of information may result in the perception patients have about fewer side-effects, which might lead to the abuse of drugs, because DTC advertisements fail to provide inclusive risk information.

Inherency

Arguments

Claim 1: Next, inherency is highlighted when DTC drug advertisements encourage prescription drug sales before long-term safety information can be identified; and this ultimately results in a patient's willingness to ask their doctor to prescribe a certain medication, which often leads to unintended consequences like drug abuse.

> Grounds 1: in 2013, the FDA conducted a survey and found that 68% of doctors agreed that prescription drugs were marketed and advertised long before all safety information was collected and tested ("Should Prescription Drugs," 2014).

> Grounds 2: in 2000 and 2001, Merck & Co. promoted Vioxx (a drug intended for arthritis patients), and found that severe cardiovascular risks were later experienced by as many as 140,000 arthritis patients (Tate, 2009).

> Grounds 3: Prescription drug abuse has grown over the last ten years, and is now categorized as one of the largest drug problems the nation faces ("Epidemic," 2011).

> Warrant: Because potential risk and side-effect information is not entirely acknowledged, drug overuse and abuse continues to be an enduring problem.

> Backing: As prescription drug abuse increases, it can be anticipated that this problem will not go away without implemented policy.

Claim 2: DTC drug advertisements have also increased health care and drug costs, and it seems unlikely that these expenses will diminish anytime soon, since demand for these products persists.

> Grounds 1: Health Action International claims, over 40% of the spending in the United States goes toward ten pharmaceutical products, which are mainly new and costly prescription drugs used for chronic long-term illnesses ("Direct-to-Consumer Prescription," 2001).
>
> Grounds 2: Moreover, just in 2008 alone, spending on DTC pharmaceutical advertisements totaled $4.7 billion ("Potential Effects," 2011).
>
> Warrant: This shows DTC advertising has been utilized to increase drug spending on medication for long-term rather than short-term use, and since spending on DTC advertising has substantially increased, it is imperative that policy is created to defer these costs.

Solvency

Arguments

Claim 1: Requiring the FDA list all side-effects and effectiveness rates for a certain drug promotes positive consequences.

> Grounds 1: According to Kees, Bone, Kozup, and Ellen (2008), insisting that the FDA enforce advertised content ensures that a fair balance of information of risks and benefits is presented.
>
> Grounds 2: For instance, Pfizer Inc. and its subsidiary Pharmacia & Upjohn Company Inc. were fined $ 2.3 billion for fraud, because they violated the Food, Drug and Cosmetic Act ("Justice Department," 2009).
>
> Warrant: When the FDA issue fines to pharmaceutical companies who disobey these regulations, there will be a higher compliance and adherence to the rules, because drug manufactures do not want to lose money.
>
> Backing: Hence, with increased regulations made by the FDA, DTC drug advertisement violators can be easily tracked down and fined for noncompliance, which lessens the likelihood for distorted side-effect information.

Claim 2: In order to mitigate the high costs associated with DTC advertising, Congress could initiate a bill that requires the FDA disallow DTC advertising on prescription drugs recently approved for sale, and doctors could recommend generic drugs in place of brand-name drugs.

> Grounds 1: Often times, the latest prescription drugs are promoted the most heavily with DTC advertising, and this raises the risk for adverse side-effects, because various safety concerns have not been fully addressed ("Potential Effects," 2011).
>
> Grounds 2: The Congressional Budget Office claims that consumers save $8 to $10 billion a year when they purchase generic drugs at retail pharmacies ("Generic Drugs," 2013).

Warrant: With the decrease in DTC advertisements, patients will be less familiar with certain brand-name drugs, which make, often less expensive, generic drugs a viable substitute.

Claim 3: Policies that require the implementation of educational programs will decrease the harm of prescription drug abuse.

Grounds 1: Prescription drug monitoring programs (PDMPs) will "track controlled substances prescribed by authorized practitioners and dispensed by pharmacies" ("Epidemic," 2011, p. 5).

Grounds 2: Also, by providing PDMP training programs for practitioners and pharmacy personnel, keeping track of prescribed medication can be easy and efficient ("Epidemic," 2011).

Warrant: This means practitioners and pharmacies will be held accountable for the amount of medication they are allowed to give out, and with the decrease in distributed medication, drug abuse is bound to decline.

Opposition Arguments

Summary: Presumption assumes that DTC drug advertisements encourage patients to seek out medical advice from doctors.

Challenge: Because DTC advertisements enhance product recognition, patients typically ask doctors to prescribe certain medications, which ultimately pressures physicians to grant such requests.

Summary: Presumption also assumes DTC advertisements promote possible treatment information.

Challenge: The argument, however, fails to recognize that side-effect and risk information is typically not communicated in its entirety.

Summary: Lastly, presumption assumes DTC advertising creates revenues for pharmaceutical companies.

Challenge: It, however, falls short in mentioning the increased health care and drug costs associated with DTC advertising.

Works Cited

Capella, M., Taylor, C., Campbell, R., & Longwell, L. (2009). Do pharmaceutical marketing activities raise prices? Evidence from five major therapeutic classes. *Journal of Public Policy & Marketing, 28*(2), 146–161.

Davis, J. (2007). The effect of qualifying language on perceptions of drug appeal, drug experience, and estimates of side-effect incidence in DTC advertising. *Journal of health communication, 12*(7), 607–622.

Davis, J. J., Cross, E., & Crowley, J. (2007). Pharmaceutical websites and the communication of risk information. *Journal of Health Communication, 12*(1), 29–39.

Direct-to-consumer advertising. (2002). *McGraw-Hill Concise Dictionary of Modern Medicine.* Retrieved from http://medical-dictionary.thefreedictionary.com/direct-to-consumer+advertising

Direct-to-consumer prescription drug advertising: The European commission's proposals for legislative change. (2001, December). *Health Action International (HAI-Europe)*.Retrieved from http://www.haiweb.org/campaign/DTCA/BMintzes_en.pdf

Epidemic: Responding to America's prescription drug abuse crisis. (2011) *The White House*. Retrieved from www.whitehouse.gov/sites/default/files/ondcp/issues-content/prescription-drugs/rx_abuse_plan.pdf

Generic drugs: Questions and answers. (2013). *U.S. Food and Drug Administration*. Retrieved from www.fda.gov/Drugs/ResourcesForYou/Consumers/QuestionsAnswers/ucm100100.htm

Huh, J., & Langteau, R. (2007). Presumed influence of direct-to-consumer (dtc) prescription drug advertising on patients. *Journal of Advertising, 36*(3), 151–172.

Justice department announces largest health care fraud settlement in its history. (2009). *The United States Department of Justice*. Retrieved from justice.gov/opa/pr/2009/September/09-civ-900.html

Kees, J., Bone, P., Kozup, J., & Ellen, P. (2008). Barely or fairly balancing drug risks? Content and format effects in direct-to-consumer online prescription drug promotions. *Psychology & Marketing, 25*(7), 675–691.

Prescription drug. (2014). *Merriam-Webster's Online Dictionary*. Retrieved from http://www.merriam-webster.com/dictionary/prescriptiondrug

Potential effects of a ban on direct-to-consumer advertising of new prescription drugs. (2011). *Congressional Budget Office*. Retrieved from www.cbo.gov/sites/default/files/cbofiles/ftpdocs/121xx/doc12164/5-25-prescriptiondrugadvertising.pdf

Should prescription drugs be advertised directly to consumers? (2014, April 16). *ProCon*. Retrieved from http://prescriptiondrugs.procon.org/

Tate, S. (2009). The ethics of direct to consumer marketing of prescription drugs. *Umaine*. Retrieved from http://www.honors.umaine.edu/files/2009/08/2009-tate.pdf

Case: The Promotion of Drugs and Medication Through Direct-to-Consumer Advertisements Should Be Prohibited

by Amanda C. Rives

The promotion of prescription drugs is based on a standard advertising system. According to the Congressional Budget Office, "Advertising for most products is intended to make consumers aware that such a product exists, inform them of its purpose, and, in some cases, persuade them that the advertised product is better than its rivals" ("Potential Effects," 2011, p. 3). This means advertising is used to encourage the distribution and sale of a particular product, and this is done by highlighting favorable aspects. Hence, patients feel more inclined to consult a physician about their health condition "and to ask about the advertised medication as a treatment option" ("Potential Effects," 2011, p. 3). In addition, individuals may become more reliant on a certain prescription drug brand, which may ultimately lead to drug abuse ("Epidemic," 2011). Therefore, it DTC drug advertisements are prohibited, prescription drug problems will likely diminish.

The promotion of drugs and medication through DTC advertisements dates back to the 18th and 19th century when patent medicines were first advertised in newspapers. Stated by Huh, DeLorme, Reid, and An (2010), patent medicines were "drug compounds with colorful names," and newspapers frequently talked about these medicines in deceptive ways (par 3). Furthermore, with the arrival of the 20th century, patent medicine advertisements made up about half a newspaper's advertising revenue, and these ads were not regulated until the Pure Food and Drug Act was passed by Congress in 1906. (Huh et al., 2010). Even then, this had little impact on the misleading advertising practices, because the Pure Food and Drug Act only addressed product labels (Huh et al., 2010).

Before 1962 the Federal Trade Commission (FTC) managed all advertising, and including the promotion of prescription drug marketing. However, that same year, the Kefauver-Harris Amendments transferred ownership from the Federal Trade Commission (FTC) to the Division of Drug Marketing, Advertising, and Communications (DDMAC), which is a subdivision of the Food and Drug Administration (FDA). Until the 1980s, drug and medication DTC advertisements were primarily aimed at doctors, but in 1983, the FDA changed their promotion techniques, and began advertising directly to the general public (Hun et al., 2010).

Since the arrival of the 21st century, DTC drug advertising has become one of the most prominent advertising groups. Stated by Tate (2009), DTC advertising falls into three distinct categories: product claim, help-seeking, and reminder. Product claim advertisements are supposed to include the product's name and what it is used for, help seeking advertisements talk about symptoms for disease and encourage visiting a doctor, and reminder advertisements are used to promote the product's name without referring to its function. Huh et al. (2010) note, because drug manufactures have increased DTC advertisements over recent years, controversy has been expressed by health care experts, legislators, ad specialists, regulatory organizations, and consumer advocates. This indicates that problems still exist with the promotion of drugs and medication through DTC advertisements, which makes future policy essential.

Based on the proposition that the promotion of drugs and medication through direct-to-consumer advertisements should be prohibited, it is imperative that prescription drugs/medication and direct-to-consumer advertisements be defined.

First, prescription drugs/medication can be defined as "a drug that can be obtained only by means of a physician's prescription" ("Prescription Drug," 2014, par 1). This means that patients can only attain a certain dosage of medication with the written approval of a doctor. Consequently, this may hinder the physician–patient relationship, because doctors may feel compelled to prescribe.

Next, direct-to-consumer advertisements use rational and emotional appeals in an attempt to influence and persuade consumer's purchasing decisions (Stange, 2007). DTC advertisements are defined as "The use of mass media—eg, TV, magazines, newspapers, to publicly promote drugs, medical devices or other products which, by law, require a prescription, which targets consumers, with the intent of having a Pt. request the product by name" ("Direct-To-Consumer Advertising," 2002, par 1). What's more, DTC advertisements may be promoted through the Internet, where a majority of sites provide risk information on their home page, but they fail to present inclusive side-effect information on other pages (Davis, Cross, & Crowley, 2007).

By examining both definitions for prescription drugs/medication and direct-to-consumer advertisements, the primary inference can be determined. The promotion of drugs and medication through DTC advertisements will likely result in the misinformation patients receive and lead to strained physician–patient relationships.

The proposition states that the promotion of drugs and medication through direct-to-consumer advertisements should be prohibited. On the other hand, presumption assumes that DTC drug advertisements encourage patients to seek out medical advice from doctors. Because DTC advertisements enhance product recognition, patients typically ask doctors to prescribe certain medications, which ultimately pressures physicians to grant such requests. Presumption also assumes DTC advertisements promote possible treatment information. The argument, however, fails to recognize that side-effect and risk information is typically not communicated in its entirety. Lastly, presumption assumes DTC advertising creates revenues for pharmaceutical companies. It, however, falls short in mentioning the increased health care and drug costs associated with DTC advertising.

The promotion of drugs and medication through DTC advertisements causes harm. This means problems exist in the present nature of things, and it is significant in nature. DTC drug advertisements misinform patients, encourage the sale of prescription drugs before long-term safety information is identified, promote over-medication, make physicians feel pressured into prescribing medication to patients, weaken the relationship between these two entities, and increase health care and drug costs ("Should Prescription Drugs," 2014). With that said, the significance of several disparities will be described at length, then the second stock issue, inherency, will signify that the harm will not go away if left alone.

DTC drug advertisements currently weaken the physician–patient relationship, because physicians often feel obliged to prescribe particular, often more expensive, brand-name drugs that patients request. Studies indicate that "physicians felt more pressure to prescribe when the patient requested a specific brand-name drug (31%) than when the patient request was for a prescription in general (16%)" (Huh & Langteau, 2007, p. 155). According to Capella, Taylor, Campbell, and Longwell (2009), the cost for brand-name prescription drugs can be broken down into the following categorization: "the manufacture's price accounts for an estimated 74% of a prescription's retail price, retail pharmacy dispensing fees account for approximately 23%, and wholesaler costs make up the remaining 3%" (p. 147). Based on relevant source information, it can be concluded that physicians felt uncomfortable prescribing the more expensive brand-name drugs compared to the generic drugs. Subsequently, when patients asked for a brand-name drug, the physician–patient relationship felt strained.

Patients are also misinformed when side-effects and or risks are not communicated in their entirety. According to Davis (2007), high-priced DTC advertisements use qualifying language when presenting a particular drug's side-effects. These statements include severity/duration, conditional language, and discontinuation. Studies indicate that qualifying language reduces "individuals' estimates of the likelihood of experiencing specific side-effects, typically side-effects considered more severe" (Davis, 2007, p. 619). This means that health care and drug costs that go toward the various advertising mediums fail to provide sufficient and accurate information pertaining to the risks associated with a particular medication. For example, online websites "presented side effect information on both the home page and on an internal (interior) page (78.8%), while fewer sites provided side-effect information only on an internal page (17.3%)" (Davis, Cross, et al., 2007, p. 33). Moreover, a lack of information may result in the perception patients have about fewer side-effects, which might lead to the abuse of drugs, because DTC advertisements fail to provide inclusive risk information.

Next, inherency is highlighted when DTC drug advertisements encourage prescription drug sales before long-term safety information can be identified; and this ultimately results in a patient's willingness to ask their doctor to prescribe a certain medication, which often leads to unintended consequences like drug abuse. Hence, in 2013, the FDA conducted a survey and found that 68% of doctors agreed that prescription drugs were marketed and advertised long before all safety information was collected and tested ("Should Prescription Drugs," 2014). Because potential risk and side-effect information is not entirely acknowledged, drug overuse and abuse continues to be an enduring problem. For instance, in 2000 and 2001, Merck & Co. promoted Vioxx (a drug intended for arthritis patients), and found that severe cardiovascular risks were later experienced by as many as 140,000 arthritis patients (Tate, 2009). What's more, prescription drug abuse has grown over the last ten years, and is now categorized as one of the largest drug problems the nation faces ("Epidemic," 2011). As prescription drug abuse increases, it can be anticipated that this problem will not go away without implemented policy.

What's more, DTC drug advertisements have also increased health care and drug costs, and it seems unlikely that these expenses will diminish anytime soon, since demand for these products persists. Health Action International claims that over 40% of the spending in the United States goes toward ten pharmaceutical products, which are mainly new and costly prescription drugs used for chronic long-term illnesses ("Direct-to-Consumer Prescription," 2001). Moreover, just in 2008 alone, spending on DTC pharmaceutical advertisements totaled $4.7 billion ("Potential Effects," 2011). This shows DTC advertising has been utilized to increase drug spending on medication for long-term rather than short-term use, and since spending on DTC advertising has substantially increased, it is imperative that policy is created to defer these costs.

For this reason, solvency or proposed policy solutions are used to create positive or favorable consequences. This means the policy solutions address the disparity, reduce inherency, and are feasible.

Requiring the FDA to list all side-effects and effectiveness rates for a certain drug promotes positive consequences. According to Kees, Bone, Kozup, and Ellen (2008), insisting that the FDA enforce advertised content ensures that a fair balance of information of risks and benefits is presented. When the FDA issues fines to pharmaceutical companies who disobey these regulations, there will be a higher compliance and adherence to the rules, because drug manufacturers do not want to lose money. For instance, Pfizer Inc. and its subsidiary Pharmacia & Upjohn Company Inc. were fined $ 2.3 billion for fraud, because they violated the Food, Drug and Cosmetic Act ("Justice Department," 2009). Hence, with increased regulations made by the FDA, DTC drug advertisement violators can be easily tracked down and fined for noncompliance, which lessens the likelihood for distorted side-effect information.

Also, in order to mitigate the high costs associated with DTC advertising, Congress could initiate a bill that requires the FDA disallow DTC advertising on prescription drugs recently approved for sale, and doctors could recommend generic drugs in place of brand-name drugs. Often times, the latest prescription drugs are promoted the most heavily with DTC advertising, and this raises the risk for adverse side-effects, because various safety concerns have not been fully addressed ("Potential Effects," 2011). With the decrease in DTC advertisements, patients will be less familiar with certain brand-name drugs, which make, often less expensive, generic drugs a viable substitute. The Congressional Budget Office claims that consumers save $8 to $10 billion a year when they purchase generic drugs at retail pharmacies ("Generic Drugs," 2013).

Lastly, policies that require the implementation of educational programs will decrease the harm associated with prescription drug abuse. Prescription drug monitoring programs (PDMPs) will "track controlled substances prescribed by authorized practitioners and dispensed by pharmacies" ("Epidemic," 2011, p. 5). Also, by providing PDMP training programs for practitioners and pharmacy personnel, keeping track of prescribed medication can be easy and efficient ("Epidemic," 2011). This means practitioners and pharmacies will be held accountable for the amount of medication they are allowed to give out, and with the decrease in distributed medication, drug abuse is bound to decline.

References

Capella, M., Taylor, C., Campbell, R., & Longwell, L. (2009). Do pharmaceutical marketing activities raise prices? Evidence from five major therapeutic classes. *Journal of Public Policy & Marketing, 28*(2), 146–161. doi:10.1509/jppm.28.2.146

Davis, J. (2007). The effect of qualifying language on perceptions of drug appeal, drug experience, and estimates of side-effect incidence in DTC advertising. *Journal of health communication, 12*(7), 607–622. doi:10.1080/10810730701615164

Davis, J. J., Cross, E., & Crowley, J. (2007). Pharmaceutical websites and the communication of risk information *Journal of Health Communication, 12*(1), 29–39. doi:10.1080/10810730601091326

Direct-to-consumer advertising. (2002). *McGraw-Hill Concise Dictionary of Modern Medicine*. Retrieved from http://medical-dictionary.thefreedictionary.com/direct-to-consumer+advertising

Direct-to-consumer prescription drug advertising: The European commission's proposals for legislative change. (2001, December). *Health Action International (HAI-Europe)*. Retrieved from http://www.haiweb.org/campaign/DTCA/BMintzes_en.pdf

Epidemic: Responding to America's prescription drug abuse crisis. (2011) *The White House*. Retrieved from www.whitehouse.gov/sites/default/files/ondcp/issues-content/prescription-drugs/rx_abuse_plan.pdf

Generic drugs: Questions and answers. (2013). *U.S. Food and Drug Administration*. Retrieved from www.fda.gov/Drugs/ResourcesForYou/Consumers/QuestionsAnswers/ucm100100.htm

Huh, J., DeLorme, D. E., Reid, L. N., & An, S. (2010, March). Direct-to-consumer prescription-drug advertising: History, regulation, and issues. *Clinical and Health Affairs*. Retrieved from http://www.minnesotamedicine.com/Past-Issues/Past-Issues-2010/March-2010/Clinical-Jisu-March-2010

Huh, J., & Langteau, R. (2007). Presumed influence of direct-to-consumer (dtc) prescription drug advertising on patients. *Journal of Advertising, 36*(3), 151–172.

Justice department announces largest health care fraud settlement in its history. (2009). *The United States Department of Justice.* Retrieved from justice.gov/opa/pr/2009/September/09-civ-900.html

Kees, J., Bone, P., Kozup, J., & Ellen, P. (2008). Barely or fairly balancing drug risks? Content and format effects in direct-to-consumer online prescription drug promotions. *Psychology & Marketing, 25*(7), 675–691.

Potential effects of a ban on direct-to-consumer advertising of new prescription drugs. (2011). *Congressional Budget Office.* Retrieved from www.cbo.gov/sites/default/files/cbofiles/ftpdocs/121xx/doc12164/5-25-prescriptiondrugadvertising.pdf

Prescription drug. (2014). *Merriam-Webster's Online Dictionary.* Retrieved from http://www.merriam-webster.com/dictionary/prescriptiondrug

Prescription drugs: Improvements needed in FDA's oversight of direct-to-consumer advertising. (2006). *United States Government Accountability Office.* Retrieved from http://www.gao.gov/new.items/d0754.pdf

Should prescription drugs be advertised directly to consumers? (2014, April 16). *ProCon.* Retrieved from http://prescriptiondrugs.procon.org/

Stange, K. C. (2007). Time to ban direct-to-consumer prescription drug marketing. *The Annals of Family Medicine, 5*(2), 101–104. doi:10.1370/afm.693

Tate, S. (2009). The ethics of direct to consumer marketing of prescription drugs. *Umaine.* Retrieved from http://www.honors.umaine.edu/files/2009/08/2009-tate.pdf

Flowing

This section will briefly introduce the concept of flowing—a very good way to keep track of the cases presented in each speech and what arguments are made against what portions of the speech. Flowing is also an important technique for judging a round in that it provides a detailed history of the arguments that are advanced during a debate. In short, flowing is a process of taking notes in a debate that assesses each speech as its own column and that emphasizes clash over "chronology." Most notes are taken chronologically, where the first comment is written down at the top of the page, the second comment right beneath the first, and so forth, with the last comment being written down at the end of the page. Flowing is not based on that type of chronological model. Yes, notes on each speech are recorded in order from first to last (see figure 5.1), but the notes on each particular speech are written down based on what argument is being refuted and not *when* the argument is made in the speech. The arguments, however, are written down next to the previous speech's argument that is being refuted.

You will also need to find a way to take notes on each speech in a way that those notes can be compared to each other. The process that works most efficiently for that comparison is flowing. To set up and take a flow, each person involved in the debate should have a series of pieces of paper divided into vertical columns. Each column represents one of the speeches in the debate (for most debates you will need between six and eight columns). Each speech is then summarized into notes that are written down in each column. The trick is to (after the first speech) write the arguments next to the things that are being responded to (instead of simply taking notes from top to bottom). Overall, the flow is intended to show the clash on certain positions (and the lack of clash on other positions).

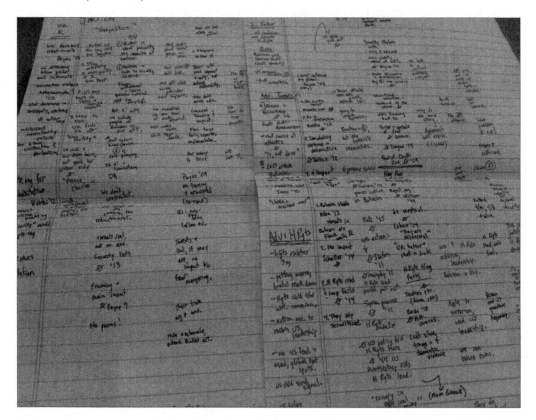

Figure 5.1 Portions of a Policy Debate Flow. K. Kuswa 2015

As with most things, practice makes perfect, so you will want to try flowing a debate and see how it goes. Writing neatly (usually in very small letters to allow for accurate spacing) and coming up with some abbreviations that are specific to the topic at hand will help quite a bit. There are also some ways to reduce the amount of writing you are doing to convey each argument, such as creating acronyms, removing vowels where possible, generating symbols for frequently used concepts, and finding a way to indicate the key elements of evidence that might be introduced (usually getting the year the evidence was published and the author's name on the flow is very helpful).

Here is a sample flow in mathematical terms. This is for a 1 vs. 1 debate, and the possible speech times are listed in the first row. Each letter represents an independent argument. X, Y, and Z are affirmative arguments, and G and H are negative arguments. In an actual debate, things will not be so neat, and arguments will be indirectly compared and contrasted against one another as well. The purpose of providing this chart is to show the basic form of flowing, to represent the clash of independent arguments, and to provide a model for your flows.

Table 5.1 A mathematical flow

1AC SAMPLE SPEECH TIMES 4 min.	1NC 6 min.	2AC 5 min.	2NC 7 min.	1AR 4 min.	1NR 3 min.	2AR 3 min.
X	NOT X	X	NOT X	X	NOT X!	
evidence	evidence		evidence			
Y	NOT Y	Y	NOT Y	Y		Y!!
evidence	evidence	evidence	evidence			evidence
			evidence			
Z	NOT Z	Z	NOT Z	Z	NOT Z!	Z!
evidence				evidence		
evidence						
	G	NOT G	G		G!!	
	evidence	evidence	evidence		evidence	
	H	NOT H	H	NOT H		NOT H!
	evidence	evidence	evidence	evidence		
			evidence			

Some additional items to note here—if an argument is not answered, it is assumed to be true. An argument can be made or answered without evidence (using one's own analysis), but it is usually better to have evidence backing up an argument. This flow may be difficult to interpret, but by the end of this debate, the affirmative is winning Y because Y was unrefuted in the 2nr. The aff is also refuting the negative's "G" argument because the 2NR did not extend G. On the other hand, the negative team is answering X because the 2Ar did not extend X. The negative is also winning G because the affirmative did not respond to G in either the 1ar or the 2ar. Some of the arguments have evidence and some do not, making a difference in the relative strength of the arguments. What becomes most important for judging the debate is the comparison of arguments in the 2nr to those in the 2ar. The flow emphasizes the last two speeches of the debate, such that an argument made early in the debate but not extended in the later speeches will not be taken into account when the judge decides. As a result, the debate above comes down to a strong Y and a contested Z versus a strong G. H does not matter unless it has been turned by the affirmative (a turn can make an opponent's argument your own by proving its opposite). Try flowing an actual debate and then compare your flow to the mathematical version above. Good luck—practice makes perfect.

Chapter Summary

Cases are constructed in order to support or oppose a proposition of fact, value or policy. This chapter detailed this process. First, the advocate or opponent must develop his or her case by describing the significant aspects of the issue. He or she must then detail the pertinent historical context before defining the ambiguous or key terms within the proposition. The advocate or opponent must then address the stock issues. While the case development is the same for fact, value, and policy argumentation, the stock issues are different. Addressing the stock issues is a central aspect of case construction and must be considered by the advocate or opponent with care and precision.

Learning Activities: Chapter Five

1. Read or listen to current events from a news source of your choosing. Find two stories or topics that grab your interest and then create two original propositions that reflect your position on the issues.
2. Create a controversy brief for the following issues:
   a. Gun control.
   b. Government surveillance.
   c. Prescription drugs.
3. Research and create case briefs in support of or in opposition to the following propositions:
   a. Increased social media use decreases academic performance.
   b. Hip-hop music is good art.
   c. All forms of corporal punishment for young children should be outlawed.
4. Place the following "Case for Euthanasia" into a case brief:

The Case for Euthanasia: Physician-Assisted Suicide

The debate surrounding euthanasia, or physician-assisted suicide, has been hotly contested for many years. And rightly so, the debate concerns life and death. Understandably, then, people will have strong opinions on both sides. However, after careful review and consideration of the facts and arguments for and against euthanasia, it is my firm belief that just as people have the right to life, people should have the right to death. I say this for two main reasons: first, legal, physician-assisted euthanasia can end unnecessary suffering and, second, legal, physician-assisted euthanasia affirms individual autonomy.

We should allow legal, physician-assisted euthanasia because people will no longer suffer to the extent that many do now. According to Faye Girsh (2001) of the Final Exit Network, "Americans should enjoy a right guaranteed in the European Declaration of Human Rights—the right not to be forced to suffer" (p. 3). And, indeed, this is what happens in many hospitals and homes around the country. According to the National Medical Association (2014), nearly 50% of family members say that their loved one's suffered more than they should have in their final hours. Worse yet, in an increasing number of cases, people are made to suffer for prolonged periods of time because of advancing medical sciences. It's not uncommon for people to suffer, in pain, for years now because of drugs and technologies that "keep people alive." What is the quality of life in such cases however? Is it not one's own decision to determine the quality of one's life? This brings me to my second argument.

We, as Americans, and as free people embrace the value of self-determination. After all, it is written in our declaration of independence that one has the right to "life, liberty and the pursuit of happiness." Doesn't it follow, then, that if we have liberty, we have autonomy? And does it not follow, then, that autonomy allows for self-determination, especially in regards to the pursuit of happiness? According to the Los Angeles Times (2005), "intensely personal and socially expensive decisions should not be left to governments, judges, or legislators better attuned to highway funding" (p. 4). This sentiment has been echoed by many others. Instead, the decision *when* to end one's life should made by the person herself. What better way to respect the individual and one of country's most sacred and cherished values than to affirm autonomy in all cases.

It is for these two reasons, and many more which I have not covered, that I affirm the position that legal, physician-assisted euthanasia should be made legal. It will end unnecessary suffering and, importantly, it upholds the autonomy of individuals and preserves a core value of this nation, namely self-determination.

5. Which of the stock issues do you think is the most important and why?
6. Which stock issues have the most overlap? Give examples.
7. If you had to assemble a case in favor of US military intervention in Syria, would would the stock issues look like? Give examples of how fact, policy, and value-based arguments would play a role in your case.
8. Now assemble a negative case against the same set of arguments. Where are the biggest weaknesses in the affirmative case and what would be the most likely argument the negative could use to disprove the case? Which side prevails? Do the same thing with the statement: "The US should reduce its confrontational policies with China."
9. Go back through the suggestions for writing a controversy brief. If a brief has a certain *ethos*, *pathos*, and *logos*, which suggestions would be targeting which of the three components of persuasion? Rank the various suggestions by order of importance and make an argument justifying your ranking order.
10. What are three essential pieces of a good overview? How should you go about ordering your arguments in sequence when the arguments seem equally valid—what are some tie-breakers? If one tie-breaker is how recent the evidence in a particular argument is, how would that tie breaker compare to an argument with evidence that comes from more legitimate sources?

CHAPTER 6

Argumentation and the Self

I will try to speak about another aspect of this culture of the self, which concerns the way in which 'cultivating oneself,' 'caring about oneself' gave rise to forms of relationships and to a fashioning of the self as a possible object of knowledge completely different ...

M. Foucault, 2005, p121[1]

Argumentation as Reflection

Foucault always said that it is the task of the social critic to engage in a "history of the present" and map the cartographies of power. That is a mouthful, but complicated times call for complicated thoughts. The idea is that when we think about argumentation, we need to think

about our present context and the way it is organized. Many thinkers and theories can help us understand the ways communication works, but Foucault is especially helpful for linking discourse to power, or the ways arguments circulate influence. Arguments move us.[2]

Michel Foucault is an important theorist for Argumentation to whom we turn for many concepts, but this is not a field that requires memorizing the works of obscure or overly academic theorists.[3] You heard a bit about Stephen Toulmin in Chapter Three, and the Greeks have been following us all the way along, with Plato espousing oratory as pandering (as opposed to the quest for Truth) and Aristotle defining rhetoric as concerned with the determination of the available means of

---

[1] Foucault, M. (2005). *Hermeneutics of the Subject.* New York: Palgrave Macmillan. You need to know where argumentation occurs in public discourse and how it matters. You need to know about argumentation's ties to critical thinking and how critical thinking occurs. You also need to know some of the history of argumentation is order to get a better sense of its value and meaning. We have started on many of those levels; now it is time to merge those dimensions and add a third level: argumentation and "the self."

[2] Many thanks to Elizabeth Lauzon, who assisted with the early research on this chapter for a project on service.

[3] Also see Burchell, G., Gordon, C., & Miller, P. (Eds.). (1991). *The Foucault Effect: Studies in Governmentality.* Chicago: University of Chicago; Gordon, C. (1991). Governmental Rationality: An Introduction. In *The Foucault Effect*; Rose, N., & Miller, P. (1992). Political Power Beyond the State: Problematics of Government. *British Journal Sociology* 43/173, [pp.–pp.]; Foucault, M. (1983). Afterword: The Subject and Power. In *Michel Foucault: Beyond Structuralism and Hermeneutics* 2nd ed. Chicago: Univ. of Chicago Press. Foucault, M. (1990). *History of Sexuality Vol. I* trans. R. Hurley. New York: Vintage.. Foucault, M. (1980). *Power/Knowledge.* C. Gordon (Ed.) New York: Pantheon, 1980.

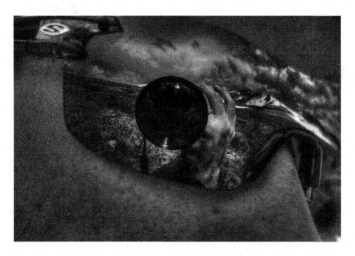

Figure 6.1 What is the Self?

persuasion. When we start talking about modernity, information overload, the age of telecommunications, the technocratic approach to policy, or the ever-shrinking public sphere as it becomes the terministic screen,[4] we have to consider the way argumentation informs who we are as individuals and as a society.

Argumentation has its roots in the ancient art of rhetoric and the practice of debate, as we learned in Chapter One. If you are able to merge the practical pieces of rhetoric (how people communicate) with the purposefulness of debate (how people structure a compelling argument), you will have gone a long way toward understanding argumentation. This chapter goes further into argumentation as "practice" and explores the relationships between argumentation and the self. How do we argue "ourselves" into existence? How do arguments define who we are? How do the notions of "arguing for ourselves," "arguing for others," and "arguing as ourselves" blur together? In other words, is there a type of argumentation that defines us and how we relate to one another? We are going to answer that last question in the affirmative, contending that the self and argumentation are tied up in one another in some complicated and necessary ways. To make sense of these questions and to help you understand what it means to talk about "arguing selfhood," we are going to use an analogy based on the notion of "service." The goal is to show how argumentation serves the self in different ways in different contexts.

Hang on for the ride—this is like the Magic School Bus shrinking down to try to get a better sense of how the human body operates, except our journey is through the human brain and language deployment. We think we can understand how we motivate ourselves and others by looking at the metaphor and meaning between making arguments and providing service. How do arguments serve the self? How does service argue the self?

Introducing Selfhood

You have been introduced to *ethos*, *pathos*, and *logos* and the canons of rhetoric: invention, arrangement, style, memory, and delivery. Now, to bring it all together, we will relate these two schemes and their eight concepts to the self and the example of service. How do we serve? How do we serve ourselves, others, our nation, or humanity? When we serve, what does it tell us about *who* we are and *why* we perform service? This is a multi-layered and powerful example that will shed light on argumentation and why it matters. How does selfhood—the individual—emerge as

[4] Deluca and Peeples (2002). Kevin Deluca and Jennifer Peeples, "From the Public Sphere to the Public Screen" *Critical Studies in Media Communication*, Vol. 19, No. 2, June 2002, pp. 125–151.

a particular person through content, credibility, and compassion? And then, subsequently, how does someone invent, arrange, style, remember, and deliver themselves?

When you make decision each day and go about your life, what makes some experiences mundane and others memorable? When we are at school, at work, at home, how do we extend ourselves and advocate for ourselves and others? How do we express many of our opinions? When we have a dispute, how are things settled? One answer to these questions is through argumentation. We advocate for ourselves and those around us by making arguments. We settle disputes and express opinions through argumentation. We also generate disagreement and locate distinctions and points of clash by engaging in argumentation. It is a process. Even more importantly, it is a process about the self and subjectivity.

It should be no surprise that one of the most significant questions and objects of study across all time is that of the self. Identity, identification, autonomy, individuality, humanism, the subject, subject-positions, and/or subjectivity all operate and constitute the sign of the self. Some of these concepts are more complicated than others, but the good news is that we all have a solid understanding of the main notion here: our own selves. Who are you? Each of us has a sense of who we are and, for the most part, we know ourselves better than anyone else does. We are experts in ourselves. On a more academic level, many scholars have crafted taxonomies or sets of characteristics regarding the self, deploying and critiquing everything from psychological categories,[5] to identity politics,[6] to self-negation.[7] The psyche, one's identity, the absence of the Other, and many other intricate theories of what the self is and how it should be perceived have surfaced over time. These concepts of the self have perplexed and confounded scholars throughout time because, on one hand, everyone generally knows what they experience as a very particular and individual self; but, on the other hand, it is extremely difficult to generalize about others and talk about the self in any universal way. Yet, to learn about argumentation we have to consider the universal self (alongside the individual self) and what it means because these various selves are heavily involved in the reception and generation of arguments.

We believe that argumentation will help create a better understanding of the self based on the importance of advocating the self through argumentation. We argue internally to make certain decisions and ultimately to relate to the world around us. In the same way that "serving society" is a model for how we exist alongside one another, argumentation is a model for what we do and who we are (serving the self). Argumentation is about identification (what and how we identify), and identification is connected to our identities. You may have heard of the phrase "identity politics" in terms of the ways different identities will bond together for the purposes of political strength and advancement. That process relies heavily on argumentation: What arguments make up a given identity and how does an identity assert itself, especially when it becomes necessary to make choices between competing identities? We will pursue questions surrounding *identity* and *argument* in the following chapter, but it is a good dyad to keep in mind as we explore argumentation and the self.

---

[5] Freud, S. (1960). *The Ego and the Id.* Trans. J. Riviere. New York: W. W. Norton; Žižek, S. (2000). *The Ticklish Subject: The Absent Center of Political Ontology.* London: Verso.

[6] Brown, W. (1995). *States of Injury: Power and Freedom in Late Modernity.* Princeton, N.J.: Princeton University Press; Butler, J. (1990). *Gender Trouble: Feminism and the Subversion of Identity.* New York and London: Routledge.

[7] Baudrillard, J. (1994). *The Illusion of the End.* Trans. C. Turner. Stanford: Stanford UP; Modleski, T. (1991). *Feminism without Women: Culture and Criticism in a "Postfeminist" Age.* New York and London: Routledge.

Arguing the Self

To really think deeply about the "self," it is instructive to return to the work of Michel Foucault (pronounced Foo-koh), the French Philosopher who writes about discourse, power and knowledge. In Foucault's series of lectures collected in *The Hermeneutics of the Subject* (2005), he takes on the monumental task of chronicling and mapping the "care of the self" in Western traditions. In short, he contends that the question, "What is one's self?" is simultaneously a proclamation "that one must know oneself."[8] As we have been discovering all the way along with argumentation, asking questions about knowing the self and how we know the self requires context and specificity. Foucault tackles such movements in Greek and Roman life, but also equally vexing configurations of selfhood that circulate through modern and late modern history in the United States. Coming out of two World Wars in the mid part of the last century and now slogging through a global war on terrorism, the United States has experienced countless unique events shaping every aspect of what it means to be an individual, let alone a citizen, in this country. Global conflict with the Soviet Union, the Vietnam War, and the civil rights movement are just the beginnings. So, how do our location and our culture, particularly our perspectives as teachers and students in the United States, influence our understandings of the self and argumentation? Even if we do not have a clear answer to those questions, asking them is an important first step in order to contextualize how a person's temporality, nationality, and historical location influence who they are and what the "self" means in that particularized society.

Figure 6.2 Service Means Information

To help us along, the notion of selfhood has some unique characteristics in this country, especially as we sense the Uncle Sam "I Want You!" sign in the distance (or the past) and we take a turn toward the concept of service. A specific theme running through the ever-changing self in the United States is the trope of service. To map some of the ways the self and service intersect, we will work through a brief history of national, military, religious, and other forms of service in the United States over the past century. Does "national" service tell us something about the self as a member of the nation? How does the nation carry such important significance for individuals? Does the nation make arguments in favor of patriotism and adherence to a national ideology? Does the self make arguments about the importance

---

[8] Foucault continues musing on the theme of the self, arguing that the object of care and the subject of care are both instrumental in the notion of the self-knowing itself: "This is then a methodological question concerning the meaning of what is designated by the reflexive form of the verb 'taking care of oneself'" (2005, p. 52, 53).

of the nation that in turn imbue it with power? Does military service imply a sense of duty and regimen as the self "marches to battle"? Do we argue in militaristic ways to defend the self in the same way that military service represents a commitment to defending the nation? In terms of religious service, when does the self take on a more reflective and spiritual character? How do concerns about helping others in need tie into our own understandings of faith and responsibility? These are difficult questions, but ones that help shed light on these intricate and ever-changing relationships. Ultimately that is what argumentation is about—the flexible and powerful ways we articulate ourselves through language. More specifically, as we think deeply about the service example and "arguing the self through service," it will help us in connecting argumentation and subjectivity. In many of these questions, service could be replaced with argumentation: Does service always accomplish its aims? Does service include positive effects on the service provider? Does "serving oneself" make sense as a way to understand argumentation and the self?

Our overall contention is that service is a significant practice for the governing of the self (How do we make decisions for ourselves?) and a significant marker of the fractured effects of individuality—or, as a better noun to talk about how an individual person communicates, subjectivity. A critical history of the self in the United States runs concurrent with a history of service and the arguments for and against certain kinds of service. This give-and-take, the tug of argumentation, can be seen in attempts to harness service for the government's war on terror. Just assume that making an argument only has an effect on the arguer. Assume that the person who advances the argument is the only one who experiences change and furthers a belief in the argument. Despite those assumptions (which are extremely conservative in terms of argumentation's effects on the world), argumentation still matters because it at least produces some change, some impact on society. What we will find through our assessment of argumentation as service, however, is that argumentation also spills out in many other ways to influence its surroundings. In short, understanding the Self and the Other means understanding how arguments work on the external world around us and the internal world within us.

Thus, from the perspective of "argument as service," even if the only effect of service is upon the self (a proposition many recipients and providers of service would vehemently dispute), than an effect on the self still remains. Caring for the self, especially through argumentation, requires the Other in some capacity, as does any degree of agency. Ultimately, as we are starting to unpack and make ourselves at home, you are probably beginning to realize that this work on the self and the Other is an equation that turns both service and argumentation into particular ways of opening up the possibilities of critical and ethical subjectivity. Let us get more specific and turn to a discussion of national service and the self as a member of the nation.

Service and Argumentation Cultivate the Self

One way to extend this call to bring the self into contemporary life is to assess the intersection between the state and the self. Many arguments and policy disputes involve the nation-state and what is good for the country. Is Policy X the best course for the nation? Will the country benefit from Policy Y? How does a given argument bump up against actions taken by the state or influence held by the government? You cannot talk about most major arguments without discussing the role of government and laws and policies that affect a particular circumstance or situation. Ronald

Figure 6.3 Military Service as a Portal

Greene applies such a method when he links the YMCA's early use of film as a cultural technology to the "governing logics of the liberal state."[9] What that means is that the YMCA was making arguments to its members by showing certain films that supported the state. We agree with Greene in that these changes may portend a "future revolt of the audience," because no group of people will accept an argument completely. As an audience begins to reject given arguments, our path follows those changes as they impact on techniques of the self—the various avenues for expression, participation, and the constitution of the self and others that open up and close down. How can we serve the nation by caring for each other? This is deeply philosophical questioning that implicates the motivations for living and the process of being human. Caring for one's self and others is a project and process bounded by history, culture, and discourse, all of which have taken unique directions in recent times. Throughout history, the public nature of service in the United States has extended and stratified the importance of "what it is to govern well" and has connected the "hierarchies and functions of the soul" to the "question concerning the art of governing."[10]

We are arguing that service and governing mark a substantial intersection between the soul of the individual and the soul of the nation. The actual body runs parallel to the "body politic" or the embodied nation. Paul Light of the Brookings Institution emphasizes the macro-side of government—national policy and the federal government—in his work on public service: "effective governance is impossible if government cannot attract talented citizens to serve at all levels of the hierarchy."[11] The meaning and deployment of service in this country has centered on questions involving motivation or duty. There can be no service unless individuals are somehow compelled to act—to serve. Serve what? Whom? Answering these questions with national pride, President John F. Kennedy emphasized the need for national service when he said on January 20, 1961, "Ask not what your country can do for you. Ask what you can do for your country."[12] This may be one of the most important single quotations in the contemporary American imagination.

---

[9] Greene, R. W. (2005, March). Y Movies: Film and the Modernization of Pastoral Power. *Communication and Critical/ Cultural Studies* v2.n1, 20–26; p. 23.

[10] Ibid. Foucault, 2005, p. 53.

[11] Light, P. C. (1999). *The New Public Service*. Washington D.C.: Brookings Institution Press; p. 2.

[12] For more on Kennedy's remarks in the context of service, see Dionne & Drogosz (2003, p. 1); Light (2003, p. 198); and Wofford (2003, p. 46). Dionne Jr., E.J., & Drogosz, K. M. (2003). United We Serve? The Promise of National Service. In Dionne, Drogosz, & Litan (Eds.), *United We Serve*. Washington D.C.: Brookings Institution Press: pp. 1–10.

Light, P. C. (2003). The volunteering decision: what prompts it? What sustains it? In Dionne, Drogosz, & Litan (Eds.), *United We Serve*. Washington D.C.: Brookings Institution Press: pp. 198–205.

Wofford, H. (2003). Politics of Service. In Dionne, Drogosz, & Litan (Eds.), *United We Serve*. Washington D.C.: Brookings Institution Press: pp. 45–51.

Kennedy's song of service was not a bolt from the blue, however, for service has long been a means of motivating action and inspiring participation.[13]

John F. Kennedy also reminded us, in his Pulitzer Prize-winning book, of the individual responsibility that comes along with democracy:

> For in a democracy, every citizen, regardless of his interest in politics, 'holds office'; every one of us is in a position of responsibility; and, in the final analysis, the kind of government we get depends upon how we fulfill those responsibilities. We, the people, are the boss, and we will get the kind of political leadership, be it good or bad, that we demand and deserve.[14]

The word *service* comes from the Latin *servus*, a concept that informs the English word "slave" and is related to "serf" or "servile."[15] Social arrangements often incorporated the role of the servant in terms of the master—a member of the service. Action can be compelled in a number of ways, the most overt stretching back to master–servant social hierarchies and slavery. Today the notion of service typically rests on actions taken to improve society, actions designed to assist those in need (even though slavery and servitude has not disappeared, it just is discussed in terms of labor politics or structural racism, sexism, and other inequalities, not service). Most modern notions of service include a voluntary component, the conscious decision by an individual to engage in a particular type of service.[16] The various types of service, though, correspond to distinct visions of the self in their respective constructions of progress and responsibility. This is where we see a parallel to argumentation and the example really starts to come alive. Both "ways of arguing" and "ways of serving"—the Way as *la onda*—correspond to different ways of articulating the self. Working for less fortunate others, working for one's self, working for God, or working for the community are all service possibilities. Military service implies the "patriotic self" serving the nation; religious service implies the "virtuous self" extending the soul through good deeds and, in most instances, serving a version of God's word; and community service implies both the "deviant self" being punished through required hours serving the state and the "liberal self" volunteering time, labor, and resources toward the bolstering of the local community.[17] These are all styles and forms of argumentation as well—arguing for the nation, for faith, for the community, for the self. Now it should be coming alive! Yes, we make arguments for ourselves, for our identifications, for our faith, for our family and community, for our nation, and for humanity! These are the same

---

[13] Burk, J. (2001). The Military Obligation of Citizens Since Vietnam. *Parameters, 31* (2), 48–60.

[14] Kennedy, J. F. (1964). *Profiles in Courage.* 1964 Memorial Edition. Foreword by R. F. Kennedy Library of Congress; p. 286. (Original work published 1957.)

[15] Onions, C.T. (1966). "Service," in Oxford Dictionary of English Etymology. New York: Oxford PressOxford English Dictionary (http://www.oed.com/).

[16] Marshall, W., & Magee, M. (2003). Think bigger about citizenship. In Dionne, Drogosz, & Litan (Eds.), *United We Serve.* Washington D.C.: Brookings Institution Press: pp. 72–83; p. 78.
In addition, "Rather than thinking of service as an individual, spontaneous act, service can better be conceived as action that follows from available resources, consisting in closer personal networks and organizational affiliations."
McLellan, J. A., & Youniss, J. (2003). The two systems of youth service: determinants of voluntary and required youth community service. *Journal of Youth and Adolescence, 32* (3), 47–58; p. 56.

[17] While it can be said that working for an employer is service, it is more narrowly defined by the Oxford English Dictionary (http://www.oed.com/) as "a branch of public employment, or a body of public servants, concerned with some particular kind of work or the supply of some particular need."

types of reasons we serve and the causes we support through our service. The metaphor is circling in on itself.

Clearly, many different organizations and institutions provide opportunities for people to participate in community service. These programs are both public and private, including non-profit organizations, religious organizations, and even schools.[18] As you have seen throughout this textbook, the public and the private are significant spheres for argumentation—public and private argumentation stretches from political debate to interpersonal relations. Argumentation is what drives the public and private "spheres" (our personal selves and our social communities), making them both engines of social change and locations of civic discourse. The specifics of

Figure 6.4

"service organizations" tie this analogy together. These organizations seek out means to connect individuals to the community and generate contagious and productive service. The government, for example, offers different programs based on the type of service, the expertise required, the duration of the project, and the willingness of the participants. The YMCA, USA Freedom Corps, and the Salvation Army are well known national service organizations and programs that function to serve the country.[19] As we hone in on the links between service and constructions of the self, we should step back to assess the larger trajectory of service, the mountainous discourses surrounding service, and a history of its manifestations in the United States over the past century. To understand the ways argumentation connects to nationalism, the military, faith, and community, it is valuable to peruse the scope of service through an overlapping map of some of the types of service, including national, military, and religious service.

Serving the Nation as Arguing the Self

Sometimes the best arguments appear as metaphors, and the metaphor between service and argumentation is very useful. One door we are trying to open along this path of inquiry is that of the nation—how does one "serve the nation" and what does that say about the type of self and the type of argumentation that is in play? National service has long been encouraged as a primary way to invigorate political attachments and commitment to the well being of the nation.[20] The

---

[18] Lynn Jr., L. E. (2002). Social services and the state: the public appropriation of private charity. *Social Service Review, 76* (1), 58–82; p. 59.

[19] Perry, J. L., & Thompson, A. M. (2004). *Civic Service: What Difference Does It Make?* Armonk, New York: M. E. Sharpe; p. 39, 47–8.

[20] There are a variety of objectives that can be achieved through service and service projects. In many cases, different objectives are combined to ensure a range of benefits for the participants and the public (Perry & Thomson, 2004,

subject and object of these encouragements is conceived as the "service-citizen"—a key contributor to the energy of the democracy. Service becomes an essential part of being a citizen because it allows for bonding among people while providing crucial public works. Some authors go so far as to connect the emergence of the nation itself to the dynamic between independence and servitude: "Our ancestors were committed to living independent lives, but to survive and thrive they also had to be interdependent."[21] National service, in theory, allows for genuine democracy to emerge because citizens feel connected through their own input and investment, one part of what has been called the "obligation to serve."[22] We have to argue with one another to connect with one another, and the same is true for our investments in the national imagination. The obligation of the citizenry to support the nation has been extended beyond military service and the public sector—it has long been a call to every single individual.[23] Dowd continues: "The result was, in a sense, a nation of servants."

William James, in his essay *The Moral Equivalent of War* (1910),[24] was one of the first people to encourage national service outside of the military. James contended that people could fulfill their civic responsibilities and continue "the tradition of service and devotion" by participating in the war on Nature. During peacetime, citizens could apply the motivations, passions, and morals of war to national service and create a collective community built on pride, honor, and citizenship. A "real war" was not necessary to foster the ideals and motivations of service in the community—national service could create unity without war, and the New Deal fulfilled and extended these ideals.[25] Implementing civic duties and providing jobs were two effects of the Civilian Conservation Corps (CCC) and the National Youth Administration, programs established by the New Deal to offer productive employment opportunities during the Depression. Both programs set precedents and became models for future national service programs.[26] For us, it is important to note how the nation becomes a force and a concept worthy of serving, worthy of adhering to, worthy of arguments for its preservation and expansion.

Of course, non-military national service took a back seat during the World War era as strengthening the armed forces became a priority. National service as citizenship did not become central to the government's agenda again until the 1960s, when Kennedy made his call for service and created the Peace Corps to provide an opportunity for Americans to assist developing countries around the world.[27] These moves continued the trend toward governmental demands on citizens

---

p. 137). It may be chicken or egg, but Perry & Thomson (2004, p. 127) believe that the most important benefactor of most service is the public, despite the positive impacts it may have on the participants.

[21] Dowd, A. W. (2004). Public Service v. Individualism: Is There a Conflict? *Current*, (460), 13–18, p. 17.

[22] Drogosz, K. M. (2003). Citizenship without politics? A critique of pure service. In Dionne, Drogosz, & Litan (Eds.), *United We Serve*. Washington D.C.: Brookings Institution Press: pp. 245–252, p. 252.

[23] "Americans have combated selfishness not with government but with a vast array of what de Tocqueville called associations and free institutions [...] These organizations remind us 'that it is the duty as well as the interest of men to make themselves useful to their fellow creatures.' This is the essence of public service—to be useful to your fellow man (sic.)—despite the smothering embrace of the government, Americans continue to fulfill this duty" Dowd (2004, p. 17).

[24] James, W. (1910). *The Moral Equivalent of War*. Retrieved from http://www.des.emory.edu/mfp/moral.html/

[25] For more commentary on Williams James see Lind (2003, p. 123–4, 130), Marshall & Magee (2003, p. 74), Moskos (1988), and Wofford (2003, p. 46).

[26] Moskos, C. C. (1988). *A Call to Civic Service: National Service for Country and Community*. New York: The Free Press; p. 33–4.

[27] Moskos (1988, p. 49)

Figure 6.5 President Kennedy Greeting Peace Corps Volunteers in 1961

to serve the country.[28] President Johnson used Volunteers in Service to America (VISTA) to support services for the mentally ill, elderly, handicapped, and other deprived groups with the aid of federal grants to local agencies.[29] Since the 1960s, national service has been seen as a civic mission—a space where people come together to do a wide variety of activities in various areas like energy, education, conservation, health, and other public works.[30] Following Johnson, Nixon created ACTION to consolidate service programs and institutionalize volunteer organizations. These efforts were extended by Carter through his contributions to Habitat for Humanity and the Peace Corps. New initiatives continued to augment the theme of service and citizenship: Reagan established The White House Office of Private-Sector Initiatives in 1981 to coordinate partnerships between the government and private service organizations, George H.W. Bush created the "Points of Light Foundation" to connect volunteers with specialized opportunities, and Clinton passed the National and Community Service Trust Act to increase federally sponsored volunteerism through AmeriCorps, Senior Corps, and Learn and Serve America.[31] It should be clear that many Presidents harnessed the idea of national service for particular goals, in the same way we tend to pursue different kinds of arguments to extend ourselves in different ways—as sympathetic, as understanding, as callous, as purposeful, as reflective, as dismissive, etc.

President Obama has gone even further into the appeal to service as synonymous with support for the nation, passing a number of pieces of legislation that prioritize and encourage national service. Obama has expanded existing service programs and developed new initiatives to support more U.S. citizens getting involved. On the White House website (http://www.whitehouse.gov/issues/service), the "service section" outlines some of the President's goals:

---

[28] Light, P. C. (2003). The volunteering decision: what prompts it? What sustains it? In Dionne, Drogosz, & Litan (Eds.), *United We Serve*. Washington D.C.: Brookings Institution Press: pp. 198–205, p. 198.

[29] (Moskos, 1988, p. 53). Despite the importance of national service to the government's agenda, military service remained a primary component of national policy (as it does to this day). For President Johnson, starting the War on Poverty, the Retired and Senior Volunteer Program (RSVP), and the Small Business Administration's Service Corps of Retired Executives (SCORE) did not outpace his focus on encouraging volunteers for the Vietnam War (Light, 2003, p. 199).

[30] Sherraden, M. W. & Eberly, D. J. (1982). Why National Service? In Sherraden & Eberly (Eds.) *National Service: Social, Economic and Military Impacts*. New York: Pergamon Press: pp. 1–20, p. 3.

[31] (Light, 2003, p200). AmeriCorps has recorded that service providers have increased skills such as "communication, interpersonal relations, analytical problem solving, understanding organizational systems and technology" after they have participated in service programs (Perry & Thomson, 2004, p. 56).

President Obama believes that service consists of more than a "one-off" occasion. He believes that civic engagement and service should be a lifelong commitment whether at the school, community, city, state, or national level. This includes community service, government service, and military service. By empowering people at all stages of their lives and at all levels of society to stand up and help solve problems in their own communities, the federal government will encourage sustained civic engagement that will transform those serving, the communities they help, and the nation as a whole.

Think about a few of the general characteristics and controversies emanating from national service. It is important to note the permeable nature of national service and the overlapping scope of categories such as public or community service, but it is equally important to note the distinctions between the related types of service that can translate into policy differences and varying resource allocations. The contagious nature of community service and volunteering in community activities, for example, can be distinguished from civic service and its focus on isolating specific problems and setting goals. National service can be both military and civilian,[32] and civic service typically implies frequent and long-term participation in a formal program where the volunteer is trained to address particular needs in society.[33] All these different types of service mirror the different ways we can engage in argumentation as well. We can argue for promotions, for family welfare, for the good of the community, for the sake of making an argument, to defend a friend or neighbor, or to stand up for a particular cause. In some cases we are coerced or compelled to argue, while in other instances we openly elect to engage in certain arguments as a form of "volunteerism."

While Sherraden and Eberly define national service as periodic effort provided to the community to fulfill civic responsibility,[34] Moskos states that national service occurs when people are involved in service at any level of government.[35] In some instances the government acts directly and in others the services of volunteers are used to fulfill needs that the market and the government cannot provide.[36] Whether or not national service is inclusive of general civic service, most interpretations stress the individual's obligation to perform her civic responsibilities.

The peripheral question here, though, and one that reconnects the care of the self to argumentation, is this: "Should national service at some level be involuntary?" Must we engage in argumentation, or is there a choice to "opt in"? Struggles between being controlled through coercion and exerting agency—the docile self vs. the actualized self—mirror and reflect the question of whether national service should be mandatory. There is an argument that all citizens at a certain age should serve the nation, even if they are given a choice between military or

---

[32] Marshall, W. & Magee, M. (2003). Think bigger about citizenship. In Dionne, Drogosz, & Litan (Eds.), *United We Serve*. Washington D.C.: Brookings Institution Press: pp. 72–83, p. 78–9.

[33] (Perry & Thomson, 2004, p. 40).

[34] Sherraden and Eberly (1982, p. 3).

[35] Moskos (1988, p. 1).

[36] Cooperation continued between the public and private sectors through Kennedy's term and was increased during Johnson's term; he appealed for coordinated efforts from both sides to fight the War on Poverty. Private organizations became dependent on public funds, instead of private charitable donations, in order to do their work. These private organizations became a tool of public policy and supplemented government programs in some instances. Lynn Jr., L. E. (2002). Social services and the state: the public appropriation of private charity. *Social Service Review, 76* (1), 58–82, 67.

civilian service to fulfill their obligations.[37] The other side contends that coercive service programs backfire for lack of motivation and that they do not generate the same attachments to the good of the community.[38] Our aim is not to judge the effects of particular forms of service or to isolate the intent behind service; rather, by displaying how service operates, we hope to connect an active sense of responsibility to "serve" with the productive deployment of argumentation. Toward that end, we contend that most articulations of national service revolve on a cycle of obligation. Public services such as health care and security are provided by the government, private services are provided by charities and non-profit organizations like the Red Cross and the YMCA, and individuals provide services to the government by joining the military or participating in programs like AmeriCorps. We are obligated, by the self, to participate in argumentation just as we are obligated, by the nation, to participate in national service. The idea that argumentation is voluntary is a myth. This is even more of a reason why it is exciting and significant that you are this far along in the text.

The Militaristic Self and Argumentation as Battle

Ironically, it took us a number of chapters and theories, not to mention a multi-layered metaphor between argumentation and service, to get to the standard view of "An argument is a fight. A verbal fight, for sure, but a fight nonetheless." From that perspective, common in vernacular uses of argument, arguing is fighting and it is something to be avoided. Going to war, including volunteering to go to war, has that same connotation. There are reasons to have a military and there are reasons to go to war. There are reasons to learn to argue and times when you just have to disagree and not let go. Military service is a form of national service that compels individuals to prepare for, and enter into, military conflict in the name of the nation-state. Despite its embrace of warfare and all that entails, this form of service is another way for people to fulfill their obligations to society and instill a sense of citizenship. The sense of obligation notwithstanding, the "choice" made by the individual to serve is a practice of the self. Foucault reminds us that "'cultivating oneself,' 'caring about oneself,'" allows for "forms of relationships and a fashioning of the self."[39] Only through the practice of the self can an individual create the self.[40] Joining the military and perhaps dying for the country is an extreme example of the potential effects of the decision—a decision both imposed and enacted—to serve and thus argue for and as the self.

---

[37] Litan, R. E. (2003). Case for universal service. In Dionne, Drogosz, & Litan (Eds.), *United We Serve*. Washington D.C.: Brookings Institution Press: pp. 101–107, p. 102. Litan (2003) explains some of the benefits of mandatory national service including the need for a national service program since Sept. 11. Chapman (2003) is opposed to mandatory national service programs and emphasizes the negative aspects, such as cost, of national service. Chapman, B. (2003). A bad idea whose time has passed: The case against universal service. In Dionne, Drogosz, & Litan (Eds.), *United We Serve*. Washington D.C.: Brookings Institution Press: pp. 108–115.

[38] Chapman (2003, p. 115) also makes the argument that coercive forms of service would destroy its lure and level of respect: "The way to sabotage voluntary service is to coerce it, bureaucratize it, nationalize it, cloak it in political correctness, and pay for it to the point where the 'volunteer' makes out better than the poor soul of the same age who works for a living. Universal service would be civic virtue perverted into a civic vice." As a solution to creating a mandatory service program, Chapman's (2003, p. 115) alternative is to publicize the value of service and develop a structure of positive incentives: "The way to get a nation of volunteers is to showcase voluntary service, praise it, reward it, and revere it."

[39] Foucault (2005, p. 121).

[40] Foucault (2005, p. 125–127).

We have arrived at an important concept for Foucault and one that helps us to understand how arguments operate—how arguments can generate change: biopower. Biopower is evident in the exercise of power over life, a process manifest in this unique form of national service, arguably the most unique, that involves joining the armed forces.[41] Images of the citizen-soldier have defined the "badge of citizenship" throughout United States history, including the desires of minorities and immigrants to prove their worth and attachment

Figure 6.6 Military Marching, Stockholm

to the country to fulfill their citizenship.[42] War typically heightens the sense of obligation to support and provide service to the country, and that has held true for the United States. The American Revolution was fought by volunteer militias that gathered arms and fought for the creation of a new country.[43] In 1792, the Uniform Militia Act required all males ages eighteen to forty-five to enroll in the military. Each state could implement the Act as they saw fit, but it was the first law in the United States that required universal service and fostered the notion of an obligation to serve the nation.[44] Even during the Civil War, the military relied heavily on volunteer soldiers; the draft was only responsible for fifteen percent of those who fought in the war.[45] Certainly the World War era instilled a need to enlist in the military for the benefit of the nation—a view widely held and accepted by the public and buttressed by the concept of a "military family" boasting generations of military service.[46] Shortly thereafter, this military need transcended particular conflicts. The citizen-soldier continued to thrive during the peacetime conscription between the Korean War and the Vietnam War.[47]

Drives for military citizenship ("Uncle Sam Wants *You*"), naturally, generated counter-movements in the same way that regulations on behavior always produce deviance and non-compliance. The Supreme Court declared in *U.S. v. Seeger*[48] that conscientious objector status was legitimate for religious ethics as long as the objector was opposed to all wars. National law still required that

---

[41] Moskos (1988, p. 14).

[42] Burk (2001, p. 55). America is a diverse nation of people from many different ethnic, racial, religious, and socio-economic backgrounds. Service projects have the ability to bring people of different backgrounds together for a common purpose. In the environment of service, a space is created that allows for immersion and an understanding of others (Litan, 2003, p. 104). Examples abound from decades of military service that interaction between people from different backgrounds allows for people to overcome prejudices. Krebs, R. R. (2004). A school for the nation? How military service does not build nations, and how it might. *International Security, 28* (4), 85–124; p. 99. Common experiences that are created by service may establish a foundation on which people can relate to each other.

[43] Skocpol, T. (2003). Will September 11 Revitalize Civic Democracy? In Dionne, Drogosz, & Litan (Eds.), *United We Serve*. Washington D.C.: Brookings Institution Press: pp. 20–32; p. 21.

[44] Moskos (1988, p. 16).

[45] Skocpol (2003, p. 21).

[46] Burk (2001, p. 49).

[47] Moskos, (1988, p. 40).

[48] Burk (2001, p. 51).

any able bodied citizen must perform military duties during a time of emergency.[49] Individuals that selected conscientious objector status were freed from this civic responsibility even though they often had to perform community service. At the end of the Vietnam War in 1973, the draft was revoked and the all-volunteer force (AVF) was established,[50] altering the obligation to serve from conscription to election. While the military provides a space where people can express their "aggressive" or "militaristic" self, it also closes down unique expressions of the self through conformity and obedience to command.[51] Choosing the military path assembles a particular identity—an identity of fullness, autonomy, and empowerment that "becomes all you can become." Yet, as an effect of such choice, the structure of serving also acts to revoke or at least restrict the agency of the self.

This state policing of the self is not only a form of violence against the self, but also a more insidious form of violence than most because it legitimizes itself through the same process. The government practices such "lawful violence" by compelling individuals into servitude and perpetuating structural violence to commit even more unquestioned legitimate violence (a question with a long philosophical history; i.e. the "just" war). This violence can manifest in multiple forms, from the simple struggle, which is physical violence, to coercion and social control by the state.[52] So, what we want to draw from this brief history of military service is the ways that all types of argumentation can be so enveloped in nationalism that they contribute to the wing of the nation-state that practices collective violence—warfare—in the name of security. For argumentation, this is the troubling arena of incendiary speech, rhetoric as violence, the oppression of threats and threat-based arguments, and all the incantations of hate speech and group exclusion. Patriotism can take many forms, as can argumentation. The crusades may have involved military conquest and plunder, but they began with a rhetoric of "Us vs. Them" and an argument that certain populations were "heathen," and thus lesser or inferior. Such arguments of exclusion and dehumanization are often a prelude to or even synonymous with violent extermination and warfare. Speaking of the crusades, the contradictory notions of serving faith as care for the Other or coercive conversion of the Other is a fascinating way to understand the assimilation and appropriation inherent in argumentation. The "confession" is simply the understanding that the self is contextualized by larger structures of judgment and righteousness.

Religious Extensions of the Self: Serving Faith

The government is not the only institution that requires service; many religious institutions either request or require service from their members in order to fulfill a moral obligation to God and to others. These institutions and individuals are not only serving God, for they can also

---

[49] Burk (2001, pp. 50–51).
[50] Moskos (1988, p. 43, 45).
[51] Governmentality focuses on the "problematization" of our lives through forms of conduct. Dean, M. (1996). Foucault, government and the enfolding of authority. In Barry, Osborne, & Rose (Eds.), *Foucault and Political Reason*. Chicago: The University of Chicago Press: pp. 209–229, p217. This form of control over conduct is an example of how the government uses the technologies of domination to impact and control the self. "This contact between the technologies of domination of others and those of the self I call governmentality." Foucault (1988, p. 19).
[52] Deleuze, G., & Guattari, F. (1987). *Thousand Plateaus: Capitalism and Schizophrenia*. Minnesota: University of Minnesota Press, pp. 447–8.

indirectly serve the government. Robert Wuthnow, Professor of Sociology and director of the Center for the Study of Religion at Princeton University, notes that church-goers tend to branch out beyond a specific faith or denomination to participate in other service programs that may not have religious affiliations. It is clear that religion plays a major role in terms of time and resources in the provision of service to the community.[53] Social and personal commitments run through all of these attachments and loyalties.

Even though it is acceptable for Christians to fulfill their calling by joining the military, people of faith often turn to other forms of service to perform their civic duties and commit to the community. Volunteers endure the "moral, physical and spiritual burden of service" in order to provide for the needs of others and carry out the "self-sacrificial Christian calling."[54] Surveys demonstrate that in the United States religious participation is connected to civic service and that church-goers are inclined to participate in civic engagement because religious teachings promote helping others and include lessons on being responsible citizens.[55] Thus, a strong correlation exists between church attendance and volunteerism in religious organizations that provide social services.[56] For example, the YMCA (Young Men's Christian Association) deals with problems associated with industrialization, urbanization, immigration, and welfare.[57] Religious institutions consider acts of service to be "self-sacrificial," but what exactly is the self-sacrificing about participating in service? Is it time, money, autonomy? People participate in service activities partially because institutions place a moral obligation upon them to help others. On the other hand, the imposition of morals on an individual "curtails ... autonomy" and is oppressive.[58]

Former President George W. Bush called for faith-based organizations in the past to increase their involvement in national service to help assuage social problems. Initially, private organizations were dependent on donations to survive, but over time local and state governments began to contribute

Figure 6.7 Buddha

[53] Wuthnow, R. (2003). The Impact of Religious Involvement on Civic Life. In Dionne, Drogosz, & Litan (Eds.), *United We Serve*. Washington D.C.: Brookings Institution Press: p. 222–237; p. 231, pp. 223–4)

[54] Cook, M. L. (2001). Soldiering: Can Christians serve in the armed forces? *Christian Century, 118* (20), 22–25; p. 22, 24–5.

[55] Wuthnow (2003, p. 223–4)

[56] Wuthnow (2003, p. 229)

[57] Greene (2005, p. 22)

[58] Newman, S. (2003). Stirner and Foucault: toward a post-Kantian freedom. *Postmodern Culture. 13* (2); 10.

funds to these private organizations to do charity work.[59] The link between the government and the "private voluntary sector" had been created. To care for a nation that was rapidly falling apart during the Great Depression, President Roosevelt created the New Deal. Even though the federal government began to play a major role in the public welfare system post-New Deal, it did not completely prevent dependency on private sector organizations to provide services.[60] By the end of World War II, most social services were being provided by private institutions and organizations, not the government,[61] and the importance of faith-based organizations involved in providing welfare in collaboration with the government decreased with time.[62] Of course, in theory, private providers of service that were associated with government welfare could not have any religious affiliation, as the U.S. Constitution implies that any service provided by the government must be secular.[63]

This separation changed in 1996 when former President Clinton signed the Personal Responsibility and Work Opportunity Reconciliation Act, altering the public welfare system to allow for faith-based organizations to provide services to the poor. Faith-based organizations were allowed to work collaboratively with the government through the Charitable Choice section. This section permitted the government to take a neutral position towards religion yet still allowed for faith-based organizations to provide welfare, as long as the resources were allocated for secular and public welfare.[64] This legitimate blurring of the line was confirmed by Allen Dowd:

> The line between public service and the private sector—indeed, between government and nongovernment service—is rapidly blurring, as faith based organizations and corporations partner with federal, state, and local governments to provide goods and services that once were the sole responsibility of the government.[65]

This is a big moment in the metaphor and in the comparison to argumentation because it means that the cultivation of the self does not occur in segmented parts, but that connections to spirituality—primarily emotional—can either take on secular dimensions or can blur into other conceptions of the self that are more practical, or about more immediate living conditions. What is happening to the new "blurred self" as the private self and the public self become one and the same, partially through the operations of a service nation? In some ways the self is empowered through the ability to enter the public sphere in order to improve the private sphere. At that moment, however, the uniqueness of the self is lost, lost to the machinations of a governing structure that makes agency a subject-object choice between service and welfare. The trope of service in the United States, thus, requires a turn back to some of the abstract questions concerning the care of the self.

---

[59] Lynn Jr., L. E. (2002). Social services and the state: the public appropriation of private charity. *Social Service Review,* 76 (1), 58–82; p. 60. For more information see Carlson-Thies (2001, p. 110).
[60] Carlson-Thies, S. (2001). Charitable Choice: Bringing Religion Back Into American Welfare. *Journal of Policy History,* 13 (1), pp109–132; p. 112.
[61] Lynn (2002, p. 61).
[62] Carlson-Thies (2001, p. 111).
[63] Carlson-Thies (2001, p. 114).
[64] Carlson-Thies (2001, p. 117–121).
[65] Dowd, A. W. (2004). Public Service v. Individualism: Is There a Conflict? *Current,* (460), 13–18; p. 18.

Arguing Service, Serving Argument

Our argument about service and the self is motivated by two related observations. First, talking about how argument "works" is easier when it is compared and related to how service works. In other words, the ways service has a definite but often unpredictable effect on the people or the organization "being served" exist alongside the way service has a noticeable impact on the person or groups doing the service. Both of these equations are complicated enough to warrant looking at specific examples. Specific service and specific types of argumentation can make sense of this complexity by talking about national, military, community, or religious forms of service.

Second, the standard reasons for why service can be productive for the "servers" themselves—the service providers—have yet to be reconciled with broader criticisms of the autonomous subject. Argumentation contributes to this uncertainty in many ways, especially by lending more ammunition to the "critiques of the self," but this is precisely why we have to connect argumentation back to subjectivity. That is the core of the chapter. Let us lay it out.

1. Service (soft) *For* Nation	Soft	External	Effect on provider: Nationalism
2. Service (hard) *For* Military	Hard	External	Effect on provider: Order & Violence
3. Service (either) *For* Religion	Hard or Soft	Internal	Effect on provider: Conviction

All three of these charts show how larger institutions or ideologies deploy the energies of the individual for other ends. The individual, then, is not discrete, but is simply an effect of argumentation and the way it "serves certain selves." Thus, without reconciliation between agency and the self through argumentation (and one may never fully emerge), the agency available to individuals in the United States through service becomes so complete, so universalized and un-tethered, that it opens itself up to external domination and loses the ability to position itself as an integral component in a care of the self that affords partial empowerment to the contemporary self. Let us move through each portion of this argument in turn. Certainly the aims of service can be criticized from a variety of angles, but those criticisms rarely challenge the effects on the self that result from service—effects that can emerge regardless of the type of service. We use "national-

ism" in this first observation by exposing the ways service as a whole opens up the soft underbelly of citizenship to the disciplinary techniques of the liberal state. Arguing for something to replace the self is a mode of subjectivity. That objectification of the self is also a passivity that releases the self to the authority of a larger structure or institution.

No matter which form of service one chooses to

Figure 6.8 Cultivate the Self

analyze, a common thread in all of them includes a certain obligation to participate, an obligation both imposed by external sources and generated internally through an individual's sense of responsibility. The rules and norms by which we conduct self-governance comprise these "modes of obligation." The constant presence of others around the self also helps to determine the obligations adopted by the self. And, adding a further set of variables, there may be multiple obligations to competing regimes or institutions that the self must fulfill.[66] Implied obligations motivate people to perform acts of service. The obligation, however, does not have to have one source; the obligation can be created by a deity, by the state, by both, by neither. Military and national service construct and enforce a moral obligation to the state, whereas religious service imposes a moral obligation to the deity.

Collaborative governmental and religious service often enhances the imposition on individuals to serve these supposedly universal morals. Greene notes the combination of these techniques in the development of links between the YMCA and the welfare state:

> The conservative memory of the progressive era recalls the YMCAs as an example of a successful faith-based welfare service to argue that their re-birth can replace the legacy of modern liberalism's reliance on 'welfare-statism.' Today, a neo-liberal state is replacing a modern one by deploying faith-based organizations to generate new pastoral relationships free from market and cultural distortions blamed on the welfare state.[67]

Service relies heavily on the process of governing, providing a mechanism by which the welfare of the state can exert and strengthen itself. Government, then, must be conceptualized as both a form of individual conduct in the singular and as a collective that modifies and crafts the conduct of other individuals.[68] Government works to exercise power through individuals in order to affect the ways they behave—a technique of domination stemming from techniques of the self. Military service, popular psychology, and newspapers provide just a few examples of how the government, through socialization, exerts authority over the self and works to construct a particular self-image.[69] In the same way that the government can deploy certain images of society to expand its influence,[70] the obligation to serve can also be crafted by the government. The government is able to direct the behavior of the populace through the obligations of citizenship in the broadest sense.

Even though liberalism is designed to limit the power of the state by emphasizing rights, these freedoms often manifest as techniques of the self that allow the state to expand its authority over the governed. In order to cultivate relationships between the government and the

---

[66] Dean (1996, p. 224).

[67] Green (2005, p. 32)

[68] Burchell, G. (1996). Liberal Government and Techniques of the Self. In Barry, Osborne, & Rose (Eds.), *Foucault and Political Reason* (pp. 19–36). Chicago: The University of Chicago Press; p. 19.

[69] Dean (1996, p. 217). Military service, psychology, and newspapers all attempt to impact the way a person thinks. Military service entails discipline and order. A person's behavior is affected by this inherent ridge structure of military service that operates under the control of the government. Psychology also influences the way in which a person thinks about situations and the behavior of others. Newspapers are a form of media that controls information given to the public, allowing the government to limit and control what is provided to the public. These are indirect and discrete forms of control.

[70] Burchell (1996, p. 27).

governed, policies often offer opportunities for individuals to resolve societal problems. This process of "responsibilitization" creates new forms of power over the individual.[71] The integration of neo-liberalism into the techniques of the self through the freedom of choice allows for new strands to grow between the government and the self through ethics and politics.[72] This is our main point—that the way we govern ourselves is through argumentation, the way that we serve the world around us is how governing connects to specific individuals. To argue is to govern. It bears repeating because it means that what you are learning in this textbook is also the root of politics and government. To argue is to govern. To serve is to govern and to argue is to serve the self. Just as we all grow and change, techniques of government continuously evolve and find new ways to exert their power, engaging in malevolent and benign relations to expand authority over the conduct of the governed. Mitchell Dean provides the example of Community Action Programs in the U.S. during the War on Poverty as a way in which the state "empowered" citizens by having them join government-run programs.[73] Service becomes another mechanism for the integration of techniques of the government with techniques of self in order to establish and legitimize control. Control can be productive or constraining, but it is control.

Consequently, toward the end of this Chapter, we would like to discuss the notion of "government" as contrasted to the notion of "freedom." Both are extremely important to any theory of argumentation and what we are after here. That is, both government and freedom are the effects of argumentation and often the goals as well. Arguing and enacting certain arguments is exactly what government is designed to do. We govern through policy, and policy is formulated and implemented based on a series of arguments. These arguments, in many instances, are part of a government's underlying ideology, such as liberal democracy or centralized autocracy, etc. Democracy prides itself on its connection to freedom and the belief that individuals have the freedom to choose. That commitment to freedom is built on the argument that there are basic rights that belong to individuals who are upstanding members of society. The standards for what constitutes the individuality necessary to fully participate in a democracy are often arbitrary or can privilege inequality in some way or another, but they have as aspiration to expand and offer freedom. Freedom allows argumentation and is the effect of argumentation. Let us see how this plays out.

This integration of the technologies of the self allows for the government to manipulate the promises of self-government and identity. Dean explains how the government uses the situation of unemployment to instruct individuals how to behave and become self-governed. Through state programs, allowances, the notion of citizenship, self-esteem, and other ways of "resisting" dependency on the state, the self learns how to govern its own actions by "enfolding" control of the government within the self's independence, also known as Foucault's "enslaved sovereign."[74] Self-actualization is an inherent goal of service even though a stable and unified identity does not exist.[75] On both personal and societal levels there have always been desires to define and

---

[71] Burchell (1996, p. 29).

[72] Truth and existence act as a foundation for the relationship between the self and the government. As the relationship expands, the government uses these tools to control the self and modify its actions; however, if and when the self were to re-examine these events, actions, and behaviors, the tools can then become turned against the government and can be used to create new selves, changing the relationship between the governed and the government.

[73] Mitchell Dean (1996, p. 211).

[74] Dean (1996, p. 221).

[75] Dean (1996, p. 214).

create self-identity, a quest that service facilitates. Serving the needs of the city gave the Romans the label of *philopatris*, "lovers of the city," while Catholics are known as *philoptochos*, "lovers of the poor."[76] We continue to give individuals names or identities based on their actions and what they contribute to society (philanthropists).

We believe that our identity is shaped by the choices that we make; therefore, nothing is more prized in our nation than the freedom of choice—we are "expected" to make choices that fulfill our responsibilities and improve our lives.[77] Freedom of choice does not exist. It only appears as if we have freedoms because there are always options, supporting the argument that freedoms, in addition to generating the possibility of a transcendent care of the self, are also used as a technique of the government. When people use their freedoms to engage in responsible actions, such as service, the government is still exerting subtle control over conduct.[78] How does this process occur, and how does it help explain the way the self might exercise its own agency by denying the/it self? Is there a purely "self-sacrificing self?"

One of the results of service as defended by Perry and Thomson is an elevated sense of self-esteem in the participant after providing for others.[79] Self-esteem can be a way to govern the self, for Barbara Cruikshank contends that individuals can fulfill the responsibilities of citizenship by engaging in solutions to social problems, simultaneously achieving a high sense of self-esteem. Service, through "responsibilitization," provides a way to become involved in solutions to social problems, converting self-esteem into self-governance. "We owe it to society" because our service can address social ills and create a "true democracy."[80] Since people want to improve their self-images and the conditions of society, self-esteem through service offers a ready-made solution. Personal narratives of success and failure then generate additional self-esteem and ensure further motivation for others to include service in their lives.[81] Optimistically, self-esteem can help to build a foundation on which democracy can flourish as people realize their obligations to their selves and to others.[82] On the other hand, the effects of service do not always translate into the ideal, let alone functional, conditions for democracy. Such contradictions require a theoretical merging of the oppressive mechanisms of the state with the empowering threads between self-esteem and a thriving democracy. This is a clear manifestation of the point: argumentation can exert control and thus limit peoples' freedoms, but it can also expose controls that are not justified and thus expand peoples' opportunities.

---

[76] Dean (1996, p. 216).

[77] Dean (1996, p. 211).

[78] Burchell (1996, p. 26).

[79] Perry & Thomson (2004, p. 62).

[80] Cruikshank, B. (1996). Revolutions within: Self-government and self-esteem. In Barry, Osborne, & Rose (Eds.), *Foucault and Political Reason*. Chicago: The University of Chicago Press: pp. 231–251, p. 232. "For de Tocqueville, a fundamental reality of democracy is that its citizens, as free and equal participants in the *demos*, are, in the end, 'powerless if they do not learn voluntarily to help one another.' The capacity for joint action, what he calls the 'science of association,' is what represents the hope for 'civilization itself.'" Perry & Thomson (2004, p. 145).

[81] Cruikshank (1996, p. 233–4).

[82] Cruikshank (1996, p. 233–5). After participating in service, people feel good about what they have done and the help that they have provided to others. No matter which service program a person is involved in, and no matter what age he or she is, the participant often experiences a heightened sense of self-esteem (Perry & Thomson, 2004, p. 62–63). There is a sense of satisfaction and self-worth that people feel after contributing to their communities.

Stultitia and Student as Argument

This merger also needs a more complex description of how the effects of service on the self can entrench *stultitia* so that we do not assume all dangerous manipulations of service derive from external sources. In other words, how do we think about a person who does not argue, does not listen to arguments, does not participate in argumentation? "This mental restless, this irresolution is basically what we call *stultitia. Stultitia* here is something that is not settled on anything and not satisfied by anything."[83] *Stultitia* is characterized by the *stultus*, which is a person that does not care for him or herself; it engages in the opposite of the practices of the self. The *stultus* does not have free will and is subjected to representations presented to her externally, which are usually internalized. These stultified selves do not actively take a role in their lives and they do not take part in engaging with the past to establish commitment. In other words, the *stultus* changes her viewpoint frequently—with each new representation presented to her, she changes her old ideas and internalizes these new ones, making them a part of the newly constructed self. These subject-positions never have a steady viewpoint and always rely on the external to guide them. As Foucault explains: "It means willing without what it is that one wills to being determined by this or that event, this or that representation, this or that inclination." Moreover, "... *stultitia* is that will that is, as it were, limited, relative, fragmented, and unsettled."[84]

The self can participate in its own oppression, and there is no better argument to buttress this point than Pierre Schlag's criticism of normative thought. Normative thought, a set of values enveloping the rhetoric of service, provokes the questions: "What should we do?" "What should we say?" "Where should we go?"[85] Schlag contends that morality itself has been constructed by normative thought and carries no inherently valuable meaning that can foster change.[86] Notions such as responsibility, obligation, and service have the ability to manipulate one's self-image and prompt performances that strive to solve the problem.[87] Normative discourse removes the self's ability to be free because even the institutions designed to protect our freedoms become a tool of normative thought, further prescribing the actions of the self.[88] When we choose that we "should" do something, we (unknowingly) replace our autonomy with normativity and/or vice-versa. Normativity manipulates rhetoric to create the self-image of an autonomous being.[89]

Let us bring this home to you as students. Let us relate these influences to the ways schools make particular arguments in favor of a certain type of "studious and docile" self. In schools, normative thought seeps in through the different programs offered to students to provide for the "community." Currently an increase in participation in certain types of service is being required for students to receive their diplomas, even to the point where students must have a certain number of community service hours to graduate.[90] The goal of these requirements is to encourage

---

[83] Foucault (2005, p. 130–33).

[84] Foucault (2005, p. 130–33).

[85] Schlag, P. (1990a). Normative and nowhere to go. *The Stanford Law Review, 43* (167).

[86] Schlag, P. (1990b). *Le Hors De Texte, C'est Moi*: The Politics of Form and the Domestication of Deconstruction. *Cardozo Law Review, 11* (1631).

[87] Schlag, P.. (1991). Symposium: The Critique of Normativity: Article: Normativity and the Politics of Form. *University of Pennsylvania Law Review, 139* (801).

[88] Schlag (1990a).

[89] Schlag (1990b).

[90] Magarrey, M., & Francis, R. (2005). Student learning and student academic success. *Academic Exchange, 9* (3), 245–248; p. 245.

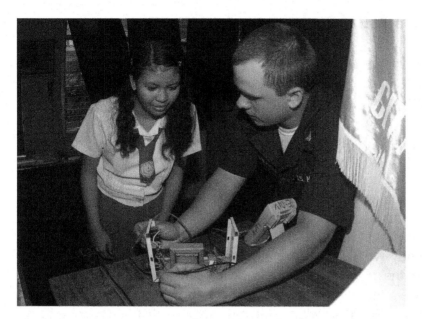

students to participate in the community and provide service early in their lives so that such behavior becomes ingrained as a habit. This is a very positive development in some ways but also something to scrutinize, as it contributes to a certain type of student. This engagement in community service is called service learning, the quintessential example of a benevolent and productive form of enhancing the community, perhaps even

Figure 6.9 Breaking *Stultitia*

the opposite of military service on the spectrum of civic "construction" vs. "destruction." On the other hand, no form of service is always productive just as no form of service is entirely vacuous; rather, all service moves in multiple directions in multiple contexts. Regardless of its intent, then, service learning seeks to further inscribe morals and obligations into the youth of the nation, promoting the integration of normative thought and self-governance.

Corresponding to the inward and outward selves of the student, at least two different types of service learning have been identified. The first type simply asks students to participate in community service and interact in the community. The second type, also called "academic service learning," occurs when the community service provided by the students is tied to the school's curriculum.[91] Advocates of service learning contend that the requirement of service for graduation benefits the community while the students are educated about civic responsibilities. The significance of service that benefits others becomes visible to the students and they learn the functions of government. The process can help create a better understanding of what is required of a citizen.[92] Skills and values, such as effective problem solving and cooperation with others, are developed through these service programs.[93] Students can then apply what they have learned in the academic setting to the outside world and develop an awareness of what is expected from them as individuals in society.

Even though and because service learning has a major impact on constructions of responsibility and citizenship, it becomes another example of how obligations can operate to modify the behavior of the self through governmentality and self-governance. Around the nation schools are

---

[91] Magarrey & Francis (2005, p. 246).
[92] Other references that provide information on how service is a form of education on citizenship and government structure are Magarrey & Francis (2005, p245) and McLellan, J.A., & Youniss, J. (2003). The two systems of youth service: determinants of voluntary and required youth community service. *Journal of Youth and Adolescence, 32* (3), 47–58; p. 47.
[93] Magarrey & Francis (2005, p. 245).

implementing service learning programs because of the valuable civic education it provides.[94] Even students in higher education programs, for example, said they became more aware of civic responsibilities due to their involvement in service learning projects.[95] Service learning demonstrates how the government integrates its techniques with the techniques of the self through the construction of a need to fulfill an obligation to society. For example, teaching oriented service programs such as Teachers Corp and Teach for America provide their participants the skills needed in order to teach others. Other findings show that academic skills increase among students who are engaged in service learning programs.[96]

Now we have returned full circle to the observation that service is a form of subjectivity, and it works in the same ways that argumentation does: through advocacy and change. The message being advocated and the change being pursued are not automatically good. Service learning is similar to military service in that it offers individual empowerment, but it has good and bad sides. To provide the limited agency that is available through service, that service must be coupled with a challenge to the biopolitical norms of an oppressive governing structure both of the self and of the nation. The concept of service carries an implicit sense of equality as well, a universal call to serve. The call to serve is a human instinct to fulfill one's ability to help others. The possibility "to serve," then, is a means of interpolating human agency and cultivating the self. Dowd relates the stakes of these possibilities:

> The challenge today, as in Jefferson's and Madison's day, as in Kennedy's, is to strike a balance ... without expanding the size and scope of government any further. A step in that direction is to recognize that anyone can participate in public service.[97]

The step can lead to many paths, both the insidious invitation to an oppressive state and the process of participating in the care of the self.

For the Greeks, one way to approach the practice of the self was "to be concerned with oneself." According to Foucault, Socrates posited three crucial components in the engagement of this practice of the self: First, she must not abandon her mission; second, there shall be no reward (she acts out of benevolence); and, third, her tasks must be useful to the city in a way that goes beyond military service.[98] Later, Foucault outlines what is necessary in order to cultivate the self, including interacting with the Other. Service fulfills these categories—it is a mission that must be completed, in most cases no reward is garnered other than gratitude and raised self-esteem, and service is beneficial to the community in a way that extends beyond the bounds of military service.[99] Service may actually be a practice of the self.

---

[94] McLellan & Youniss (2003, p. 47).

[95] Light, P. C. (2003). The volunteering decision: what prompts it? What sustains it? In Dionne, Drogosz, & Litan (Eds.), *United We Serve*. Washington D.C.: Brookings Institution Press: pp. 198–205; p. 202.

[96] Perry & Thomson (2004, p. 55).

[97] Dowd, A. W. (2004). Public Service v. Individualism: Is There a Conflict? *Current*, (460), 13–18; p. 13.

[98] Foucault, M. (1983). Afterward: The Subject and Power. *Michel Foucault: Beyond Structuralism and Hermeneutics* 2nd ed. Chicago: Univ. of Chicago Press:, p. 213. Also, Foucault (1988, p. 21).

[99] Foucault (2005, p. 127–9). Criticism and an awareness of the history of service may help negotiate the pitfalls of normalization and the total loss of agency. Genealogy acts as an alternative in that the process of "reproblematization" (Burchell, 1996, p. 31). It allows historians to deconstruct what they "know" and look at historical events differently or otherwise. This alters not only the individual but the relationships that the individual has with others and the government. It allows for a disrupting of the norm and a questioning of truth and existence as individuals are able to

> By entering into the activity of shaping our own subjectivity, each of us can potentially thwart, challenge, or at least question the ways in which we have been made [...] the spread of the technologies of the self will result in so many newly resistant points.[100]

The "ethics of intellectual work"[101] is a technique of the self that is created by various interpretations of history and events that directly or indirectly involve individuals. Given the omnipresent duality of service and its connection to practices of the self, it becomes incumbent to weave together the motivations of service and the self with the conditions defining the current era in the United States.

Even before September 11, 2001, this country was predisposed to a nationalism that would define the "Other." Whether it was Native Americans, the British, the Germans, the Soviets, or the terrorists, the United States had an Us–Them mentality. The Global War on Terrorism has merely revived the desire to serve the United States in a time of need and reestablished service as a critical part of being a citizen. Well over a decade ago, as the towers fell and part of the Pentagon went up in flames, the tragedy forced Americans to turn to family and friends to cope with the catastrophe.[102] People were inspired to contribute to their communities because they felt compelled to help those affected by this disaster. Some donated money and blood while others provided homes and worked on rescue teams. An increased level of civic engagement even continued for months and years after the attacks and expanded again after Hurricane Katrina. Americans are moved by the needs of others and contributed generously to September 11 funds.[103] Following September 11, multiple calls were made by then President Bush asking Americans to be more active and participate in national service. He created the USA Freedom Corps to organize the national service programs, to make them more available to the public, and to effectively increase homeland security.[104] In the State of the Union Address in 2002, Bush called for more individuals to join the Peace Corps or AmeriCorps and give 4,000 hours of their time to civic engagement.[105]

---

explore the relations between the government and the governed. A genealogical praxis allows for the recognition of the relationships between truth and existence and how both are tools of governmentality.

> Reality that has been is still available to us through memory [...] memory is the mode of being of that which no longer is [...] it therefore makes possible a real sovereignty over ourselves, and we can always wander in our memory. Foucault (2005, p. 468).

[100] Ransom (1997, p. 152).

[101] Burchell (1996, p. 30).

[102] Putnam, R. D. (2003). Bowling together. In Dionne, Drogosz, & Litan (Eds.), *United We Serve*. Washington D.C.: Brookings Institution Press: pp. 13–19; p. 13.

[103] Skocpol (2003, p. 20, 30).

[104] For more information on the creation of programs immediately following September 11 see: Dionne Jr., E.J. & Drogosz, K. M. (2003). United We Serve? The Promise of National Service. In Dionne, Drogosz, & Litan (Eds.), *United We Serve*. Washington D.C.; Brookings Institution Press: pp. 1–10; p. 3.
Wofford, H. (2003). Politics of Service. In Dionne, Drogosz, & Litan (Eds.), *United We Serve*. Washington D.C.: Brookings Institution Press: pp. 45–51.
Bridgeland, J. M., Goldsmith, S., & Lenkowsky, L. (2003). Service and the Bush Administration's Civic Agenda. In Dionne, Drogosz, & Litan (Eds.), *United We Serve* (pp. 52–59; p. 55). Washington D.C.: Brookings Institution Press. For more information on Americans joining service programs see Dionne & Drogosz (2003, p. 3), Skocpol (2003, p. 26), Moskos (2003, p. 40), Wofford (2003, p. 51), and Bridgeland, Goldsmith, & Lenkowsky (2003, p. 55).
For more information on the creation of the USA Freedom Corps see Moskos (2003, p. 40) and Bridgeland, Goldsmith, & Lenkowsky (2003, p. 52).

[105] Wofford (2003, p51).

After his endorsement and appeal for service, applications for the Peace Corps and other civilian service programs dramatically increased.[106] National unity was inspired by these horrendous attacks: "Though one good reason for adopting universal service now is to respond to military and homeland threat, universal service makes sense in other ways in this time of national peril."[107] Despite increased involvement in civilian service programs, recruitment for the military remained constant after September 11.[108] A possible cause for this stagnant recruitment rate, even after a national crisis, could be a result of multiple factors—the risk of assignment in Iraq or Afghanistan, the President's focus on the civilian sector, a planned draw-down in forces, or better opportunities elsewhere. The call to play an active role in national service prevails despite our feelings of reluctance. The only question is whether a balance can be reached between the government's tendency to harness the immense energies of service to wage the war on terrorism (border patrol, citizen surveillance) and the cultivation of self-empowerment as well as the possibilities for a democracy based on social justice and compassion.

Serving the Self as Arguing the Self

Even though service is a technique of the self and allows for the agency of the individual, it has become apparent that this technique of self has been inverted. It is also a tool by which the government can subtly control the conduct of individuals and ensure the survival of the state. The opportunities provided by the President's call to service offer a sense of "empowerment," but they also risk an abandonment of autonomy by the self as unquestioned faith in the nation justifies service *against* the Other, not *with* or *for* others. There seems to be no escape from this cycle of service that propels and haunts our nation. The cycle links techniques of the self with the perpetuation of the state in the same way interpellation connects subjectivity to interactions with institutions through discourse. Ideology must, to maintain itself, exert influence on a very specific and personal level. All "lures to serve," on the other hand, do not automatically suppress individual agency. It may be possible, by critically examining the trope of service and its relationship with and to the self, to expose and resist how the government corrupts the techniques of the self in order to solidify its power.

Figure 6.10 Speaking the Self

We started with questions involving the self and caring for the self. To answer and explore these questions in today's United States, the notion of argumentation as service must be considered in all of its manifestations. We have noted that service entails an obligation, but one with a multitude of allegiances.

[106] Skocpol (2003, p. 29).
[107] Litan (2003, p. 103).
[108] Moskos (2003, p. 33).

Serving the self may be a primary or peripheral consequence of serving the nation, serving the church, serving a sense of humanity, serving a more specific cause, or serving to fulfill debt, guilt, or responsibility. Whether the expected effects on the participant are the primary or the peripheral motivations to serve, the underlying contention still holds: service is an indispensable part of exercising self-agency, but the ways that service changes the world (or the self) are not always good or bad; indeed, service can exacerbate the most horrific human behavior as well as ward against cruelty with an unlimited spark of compassion. The same can be said for argumentation, as words of advocacy can be used by dictators and democrats alike.

Learning Activities: Chapter Six

1. Define "self" in three different ways. Which is the best definition and why? Do the same thing with service and argumentation.
2. If a "drone-like" self, or a person just going through the motions, is considered to be in a state of *stultitia*, what would that state of inertia mean for service? Can a person engage in service and not actually care about helping an external person or institution?
3. Compare religious, national, and communal arguments to one another? What are some examples where those perspectives might clash? How does that influence the analogy between service and argumentation?
4. List two ways that service and argumentation represent the self. Does it make more sense to talk about how a particular person "argues" for oneself or "serves" oneself?
5. What is the role of the self and the role of argumentation for critical thinking? Go back to the concept of critical thinking and weave it into the ways the self can improve. Provide some examples of critical thinking that involve service.
6. Any history buffs in the room? Tell the group about an historical event—it could be anything. How is the historical account advancing an argument. What is the claim, warrant, and grounds of that history? Does it make sense to talk about history as argumentation? If so, how does the contemporary history of service compare to what it means to be an American today versus forty years ago (or twenty years ago)?
7. Reflect on what you have learned through the course of this book. Is your reflection actually an argument about the personal meaning the book has imparted? If so, what do you think you will still remember about the book in the next year, in the next five years?
8. Going into the last chapter, can you think of ways that society has changed based on a certain argument? How do social movements create change?
9. Give examples of five social movements (such as PETA). What arguments are being made by each group and how successful are those arguments?

Figure Credits

Fig. 6.1: Copyright © Zach Dischner (CC by 2.0) at https://commons.wikimedia.org/wiki/File:Mirror_Mirror_(6024014126).jpg.

Fig. 6.2: Hobart Jackson, "Historic Interior View, 2nd Floor Teller Window," https://commons.wikimedia.org. Copyright in the Public Domain.

Fig. 6.3: Copyright © Mattes (CC BY-SA 3.0) at https://commons.wikimedia.org/wiki/File:Suvarnabhumi_International_Airport_-_Domestic_entrance_2.JPG.

Fig. 6.4: Copyright © AAYMCA (CC BY-SA 3.0) at https://commons.wikimedia.org/wiki/File:S2C_logo_100mm_150dpi.jpg.

Fig. 6.5: Abbie Rowe, "Kennedy Greeting Peace Corps Volunteers," https://commons.wikimedia.org/wiki/File:Kennedy_greeting_Peace_Corps_volunteers,_1961.jpg. Copyright in the Public Domain.

Fig. 6.6: Copyright © UKgeofan (CC BY-SA 3.0) at https://commons.wikimedia.org/wiki/File:Stockholm_palace_guards_marching.JPG.

Fig. 6.7: Copyright © Rohini (CC BY-SA 3.0) at https://commons.wikimedia.org/wiki/File:Budhha_statue.JPG.

Fig. 6.8: Herr Stahlhoefer, "Arroz (Field)," https://commons.wikimedia.org/wiki/File:Arroz_102.jpg. Copyright in the Public Domain.

Fig. 6.9: Mass Communication Specialist 1st Class Geronimo Aquino, "Student," https://commons.wikimedia.org. Copyright in the Public Domain.

Fig. 6.10: Copyright © Lanesutton (CC BY-SA 3.0) at https://commons.wikimedia.org/wiki/File:Sutton_at_MegaTweetup.jpg.

CHAPTER 7

Argumentation, Race, and Identity

Having just taken the journey through the self and argumentation, using the concept of "service" as our link to argumentation, it is now time to follow a path from the self and subjectivity toward how we identify ourselves. We want to be able to link our sense of *who we are* to our understandings of arguments constituting others who are like us and others who are not. The operations of lived reality through the identification of ourselves in argumentation is a complicated way to define identity, but it works. Identity is rhetorical, particularly in the sense that materiality (our bodies) must be framed and articulated in order to take shape and interact. That is a major proposition—that our identities are rhetorical. We believe that such a proposition can be demonstrated by connecting the study of argumentation to the formation, concentration, and endurance of identity.

The idea of identity itself packs a wallop, let alone the ways individuals borrow, adapt, and change culture and society to create various subject positions. We contend in this chapter that the process of identification happens, in part, through argumentation. Thus, if we are careful, we should be able to outline the kinds of characteristics that make up a given individual and the ways those characteristics form and dissolve. The way to do this is to focus on how argumentation shapes, or *constitutes,* different subject-positions, or "positionalities." To add depth to this hypothesis, we will focus on the concept of race—what is it, how does it manifest itself, and what is the role of argumentation in the process? We will get to the notion of race, however, by slowly making our way through the thicket of identification and the multiplicity of group identities that define particular people in particular places at particular times. The three themes to keep in mind are individual identity, group formation, and the circulation of difference. We will work through those themes and more in a number of ways, starting with some general definitions and then moving more directly into race and argumentation with a case study on "whiteness."

Keep in mind that we could center Chapter Seven on any of a few dozen major identity configurations, but our intention is not to simply line up and describe the standard list of traits (race, gender, class, etc.). No, the goal here is to show how all of these dynamics connect back to the ways we argue ourselves. In

Figure 7.1 It's Important to Learn About Our Identities

other words, to "claim" to represent a various identity has an eerie connection to Toulmin's notion of "claim" as the thesis or purpose of an argument. Both senses of "claim" rely on a type of rationalization, perception, or understanding (warrant), and both claims depend on the accumulation of evidence. Arguments about how a certain identity matches up to a particular person have to be judged and accepted, and then the articulation of who that person is becomes mapped and marked by the arguments that are generated or followed by that subject at a given time. Talk about being specific! We will make this call for specificity less complicated through some examples along the way, but the goal is to demonstrate, simply, that identity is argued.

What is Identity?

What is identity? This is a tough but extremely important question. One way to think about answering it would be to go through some of the earlier taxonomies presented in this book and add some angles to the question. If we look at *ethos, pathos,* and *logos,* the question can be thought of as a way to define a person's inherent characteristics in three overlapping ways: as a means of establishing credibility, as a way of relating to others, and as a means of exhibiting certain beliefs about society. That is a helpful exercise, in that it shows how an individual develops a sense of self, extends that self in interactions with other people, and expresses support or disapproval of how society is organized and how we are governed. It gets a bit tricky, though, in that a person is never simply one stagnant identity, and these different positions are in constant flux and competition, even within one individual. It almost becomes necessary to take a snapshot of a very specific event in order to freeze the ever-moving flow of context and engage in critical analysis. Who is *this* person at *this* time and in *this* place?

Another useful way to break down identity is to run it through the matrix of the canons of rhetoric introduced in Chapter One: invention, arrangement, style, memory, and delivery.

Canon	Identity-based inquiry	Argumentation
Invention	How does an identity come about or originate? How does an identity emerge?	Argumentation begins with opposition and distinction, the elaboration of a problem.
Arrangement	When two competing identities clash, which one prevails and why? Is one side of the binary always privileged?	Argumentation requires ordering and prioritizing. When two things conflict, what prevails?
Style	How does a given identity keep its core, but adorn various differences?	Argumentation has an aesthetic, and if the medium is the message, the expression of an argument is the identity.
Memory	How does identity become instinct or ritualized and what is remembered and repeated?	Duration and exposure matter because arguments are bound by time. When is an argument a temporary gesture and when is it essential?
Delivery	How is identity rehearsed, performed, and mimicked?	Arguing identity = identification. Performing the self is forming subjectivity.

This chart raises more questions than it provides answers, highlighting the point that identity is complicated and intertwined with layers and layers of other variables, which makes the list of variables that compose a given individual virtually infinite. At a very minimum, we are talking about race, sex, gender, orientation, class, physical and mental ability, indigeneity, nationality, religion, age, region, and ethnicity, as well as social signifiers such as education, occupation, degree of incarceration, political ideology, and so forth. Thus, instead of talking about all of these different axes as if they fit into the same-sized boxes with any degree of permanence, we want to concentrate on argumentation and race, noting that all of the other markers of subjectivity do not vanish, and race cannot be (and should not be) generalized as a category or completely removed from a context of multisectionality.

Multisectionality will be defined and discussed shortly, but we must linger on the notion of identity a bit longer to fully extract the position that we take on different identities through argumentation—"identifying" is a rhetorical process in which the currency of the transaction is a shifting set of indicators and materialities that define a person.

Figure 7.2 Humans Racing

Identity: The operations of lived reality through the identification of ourselves in and through argumentation.

There is a tautology there in terms of defining identity using identification, but the point is to make it an active process and to put agency in the ways that positions are disputed or assimilated and how those struggles translate into subjectivities that cluster together. The short of it is that we need to know how disagreements and norms are created and settled as a precursor to considerations of what makes up interlocking groups of people. The ways people define themselves and others, in addition to the way those same people are defined *by* others, becomes an engagement with argumentation.

Arguing Race

From here, it makes sense to run that intersection through the praxis and concept of race. Race offers both an example of how identity is argued and an example of a more significant aspect of society that enacts itself through and despite argumentation. From the perspective of argumentation and critical thought, this is a good place to briefly introduce two philosophical concepts that help exemplify race as an example of both "argued identity" and a structural precondition to argumentation. In rough ways, these two descriptions of race represent epistemology and ontology. Race epistemology refers to how we come to know and understand race; race ontology refers to the notion of race itself—its presocial meaning, or race without mediation and appropriation. Race epistemology and race ontology are set up as opposite ends of a spectrum, but that division is not meant to encompass the multitude of ways to think and write about race. In many ways, race epistemology relies on an ontological sense of race that is being "uncovered" or revealed, hinting at a race ontology. Likewise, putting race at a sort of sterile distance from human perception in order to rely on race ontology will still come at the question with a particular gaze—that of the academic or otherwise. Thus, race ontology is just another type of learning about race, which means that it is also race epistemology. Even race ontology implies knowledge production *about* race. So, do not be turned off by the theoretical words. Because race is complicated, one way to start the conversation is to talk about how we know race (race epistemology) and what race is (race ontology).

Race is paramount, omnipresent, and inevitable. Like time, it is an inescapable site of being and becoming, a moment of collective and individual awareness, an ever-changing mechanism for inclusion and exclusion, and an entrance into the lived experiences of our multi- and intersectionality. There is intense emotion in something that cannot be put down; there is compassion in every expression of race and every attempt to communicate it. Denying race means suffocation, drowning, and the artificial separation of liberal "postracial" progress and extreme racial violence. Sometimes censorship (or worse) can hide behind calls for reconciliation. When we add the idea that race generates and relies on arguments to the equation, the connections become clearer. The way that a racial formation can operate in a particular context—say, contemporary American life—represents a massive social force using discourse to enact itself. A telling example is the complexity of the racial binary in the United Sates which rests on whiteness and blackness. White privilege and the race labeled in the US as white, European, or Anglo is just one example of how race argues. Whiteness tries, often successfully, to make itself invisible, even to the point that is considers itself the absence of race. That argument breaks down under scrutiny, but it still has a tremendous effect in that other races are forced to emulate or compare themselves to whiteness in order to achieve cultural capital or social currency.

We can see the ways whiteness attempts to project and solidify itself as the norm and the race to aspire to in the term "model minority." This is a problematic phrase that must be criticized for assuming that the "good minorities" are those who strive to work hard and copy the "white" values of a Puritan ethic. Even the debates over what groups make up this "model" category show how whiteness puts itself at the center and works by dividing and diminishing other groups. Every argument has a counterargument; it is just a matter of embracing a critical approach and beginning to see argumentation as a form of citizenship that seeks better answers, more evidence, sound reasoning, and claims that find value in some notion of social justice. Race arguments are even more significant in this context, however, because they become (implied) justifications for certain policies and ways to differentiate people—distinctions that also promote exclusion and racial hierarchy. Those exclusionary arguments can be challenged, but it is important to recognize the sophistication of something like institutional racism and to be able to continuously research and learn about the world in order to generate effective responses, allegiances, and criticisms. This happens whether we are talking about the flag on the South Carolina capital or far more subtle forces such as the job market and the educational structure. When assessing identities and what these categories mean, in this sense argumentation is a necessary way to explain how, why, when, and where people connect with each other and relate to, or recoil from, themselves and others.

The differences are argumentative, but certainly life-altering. The difference between #BlackLivesMatter and #AllLivesMatter is the difference between seeing the necessary emergence of a new movement for racial justice in the protests surrounding Michael Brown and Freddie Gray or, by contrast, dismissing mobilization based on events in Ferguson, Missouri and Baltimore, Maryland in the beginning of 2015 as contained responses to individual instances of police brutality. One perspective argues that this is a movement bringing together various rebellions to fight against structural racism that is killing young black people through police practices and imprisoning a massively disproportionate number of others. The opposing perspective sees these events as generally unconnected to race and simply individual examples of justified policing that has been caught on tape. Both perspectives build their arguments through traveling tropes—terms that pack meanings together in an ideological formation. Thus, the perspective that race is being criminalized contends that to say that "all lives matter" is to ignore a war on black people that has not subsided, only changed form. What was the plantation is now the prison industrial context or the underserviced inner city. Argumentation, in a broad sense, governs the effects of the discourses about the role of race in this country.

A Case Study: Decentering Whiteness

To understand the ways that race becomes an argumentation strategy propping up something like white privilege, we need to reconsider and reconceive of the color "white" in the context of race—we can think of a "white" person as occupying a particular racial structure whether that person supports or rejects the manifestations of the structure. This kind of scholarship proliferated in the 1990s, and it is not our desire to repeat this work[1]; rather, it is our attempt to add the importance and framework of argumentation. The editors of a 1997 collection of essays called *Off White* cite Toni Morrison (1987) and W.E.B. Du Bois (1969) as their intellectual base, positioning the book as an attempt to "place 'whiteness' front and center … in order to subject it to the kind of scrutiny that rouses it off of unmarked space." [2]

We could show how argumentation is used to critique institutional and structural manifestations of whiteness for hundreds of pages (without even making a dent in the potential array of criticism). We could begin with the Washington Monument and the White House and move through multinational corporations and the global balance of power, mapping how whiteness operates on a variety of levels to privilege a certain capitalist, heterosexual, male, and bourgeois ideal of society and civilization. On the other hand, it may be more fruitful to begin by narrowing the focus. The discursive and disciplinary

Figure 7.3

formations of whiteness are most evident on a local or micropolitical plane. Opposition and transgression are also most possible through specificity and concrete examples of complicit practices. Thomas Nakayama and Robert Krizek assist us here with the outline of six manifestations of whiteness.[3]

Strategy	Manifestation
1) associating whiteness with social influence	*"I'm well off financially because of my whiteness."*
2) considering whiteness as the "default" race	*"Well, I'm white because I'm not anything else."*
3) accepting a naturalized or scientific definition for whiteness	*"I'm white because of my skin color—it is a simple and objective trait."*

---

1 Collections began to really hit the shelves in the '90s, including *Displacing Whiteness* (1997), *White Trash* (1997), *Off White* (1997), and *Whiteness: A Critical Reader* (1997). These volumes are only the tip of the whiteness berg. Richard Delgado of *Critical Race Studies* fame has edited a volume called *Critical Whiteness Studies.* Other similar work abounds. *Whiteness: A Critical Reader.* ed. Mike Hill. New York: NYU, 1997; *Displacing Whiteness: Essays in Social and Cultural Criticism.* (ed.) Ruth Frankenburg. North Carolina: Duke UP, 1997; *Off White: Readings on Race, Power, and Society.* (eds.) Fine, Weis, Powell & Mun Wong. New York: Routledge, 1997; and *White Trash: Race and Class in America.* (eds) Matt Wray & Annalee Newitz. New York: Routledge, 1997.

2   *Off White*, Fine, et. al., 1997, p. viii. Morrison, Toni. *Beloved.* New York: Penguin Books, 1987; Du Bois, W.E.B. *The Souls of Black Folk.* New York: Signet, 1969.

3   Nakayama, Thomas K. & Krizek, Robert L. "Whiteness: A Strategic Rhetoric," *Quarterly Journal of Speech 81* (1995): 291–309.

Strategy	Manifestation
4) confusing whiteness for an American identity	*"What do you mean, 'What's my race?' I'm an American—of course I'm white."*
5) refusing to recognize any race or ethnicity at all	*"I'm not any color or ethnicity. That stuff doesn't matter."*
6) attaching whiteness to European roots	*"White means I am descended from European white people."*

What can we learn from this table? When something is trying hard to maintain control while remaining invisible, where would it manifest itself? Where can we apply the "decentering visibility" that critical whiteness demands? This table shows that even though racial categories are contingent, relative, shifting, and permeable; they are set up to provide more choice and flexibility for certain groups compared to others. Racial relativism (interchangeability) is built on hierarchies; as Nakayama and Krizek contend, "the social location of 'whiteness' is perceived as if it had a normative essence."[4] *Despite* the actuality of a multitude of shifting racial differences, whiteness often remains the unspoken standard—the litmus test with which society judges and treats the Other. It is precisely the illusive nature of whiteness that demands an engaged theory of argumentation. By connecting identity and materiality to certain strategies of articulation, whiteness studies can open new possibilities for critique that challenge racial hierarchy.

To make the center visible, though, a risky practice of isolating or pinpointing the center has to be a part of the strategy. This is risky because of the danger of reifying the dominant structure by illuminating it. Mike Hill notes the fact that some arguments can buttress their opposites by informing the reactionaries or highlighting the terms of the struggle: "oppositionality itself may sometimes function in order to maintain the status quo."[5] Take a close look at the arguments advanced here by Homi Bhabha:

> The move away from the singularities of 'class' or 'gender' as primary conceptual and organizational categories, has resulted in an awareness of the subject positions—of race, gender, generation, institutional location, geopolitical locale, sexual orientation—that inhabit any claim to identity in the modern world. What is theoretically innovative, and politically crucial, is the need to think beyond narratives of originary and initial subjectivities and to focus on those moments or processes that are produced in the articulation of cultural differences. (p.1)[6]

Homi Bhabha takes the lead from theorists of a "fluctuating" notion of culture, such as Stuart Hall or Walter Benjamin, to hone in on the "in-between." Bhabha expands on the space between and beyond rhetoric and materiality through "a third space of enunciations."[7] His argument is that subjectivities (subject positions) have diversified and fragmented in our era of late capitalism.

---

4   Nakayama and Krizek, (1995, p. 293)
5   Hill, Mike. "Vipers in Shangri-la: Whiteness, Writing, and Other Ordinary Terrors." in *Whiteness: A Critical Reader.* (ed.) Mike Hill, New York: NYU Press, 1997: pp. 1–12; p5.
6   Bhabha, Homi K. *Location of Culture.* New York: Routledge, 1994, p1.
7   Bhabha, 1994, p48.

As a result, new strategies of self-hood and identity are necessary to think about the effects of cultural difference.

We have to take into account the other dimensions of identity—in this case, economic class—that will invariably play a role. In addition to class-based and nation-based explanations for race, any other single identity characteristic is too narrow in scope to account for the pervasive nature of race in the political, economic, and social fabric of the country.[8] In the United States, a "loosely" or in(di)visibly aligned racial majority uses the narrative of the demise of slavery, the reconstruction of the South, and the civil rights movement to appease white guilt and pave the way for white privilege as the hidden consequence of colorblindness and a multicultural norm that supposedly transcends race. It is lucky to obtain whiteness. Whiteness, of course, means more than just race, propelling us toward a consideration of multisectionality.

Figure 7.4 Black Lives Matter

Multisectionality

You may be familiar with the term "intersectionality" as a description of how identities are actually made up of a number of intersecting traits and group associations. Multisectionality agrees with that premise but goes a step further by noting that identity is not just about crossing or intersecting; it can also and simultaneously be about discrete categories repelling each other or joining up in clusters. Race is not simply about differing physical appearances, social customs, religious practice, family heritage, language, or affiliation, but all of those markers can play a role. In the case of whiteness in the United States and throughout North and South America, we have noted that race takes on a settler narrative that allows supporters and structures of white privilege to connect race to arguments about the superiority of certain nationalities and races over others. Labeled as white hierarchy, privilege, or supremacy, this configuration creates a pyramid of racial identities, with whiteness at the top. This racial superiority and white privilege

---

8   Two classic authors on the subject, Omi & Winant, concur:

> There is a continuous attempt to think of race as an essence, as something fixed, concrete, and objective … The effort must be made to understand race as an unstable and decentered complex of social meanings constantly being transformed by political struggle. With this in mind, let us propose a definition: race is a concept which signifies and symbolizes social conflicts and interests by referring to different types of human bodies.

Omi, Michael & Winant, Howard. *Racial Formation in the United States: From the 1960s to the 1990s, 2nd ed.* New York: Routledge, 1994, p55.

is the same insidious configuration that led to the purposeful assassination of black churchgoers in Charleston, South Carolina. Linking whiteness to neocolonialism is just the starting point of a multisectional approach emphasizing argumentation.

To reinforce this point, multisectionality occurs *within* a particular identity as well. In other words, we know that whiteness represents a race, as contradictory and diverse as any other and as tied to specific contexts as any other. Whiteness can both merge with, and diverge from, other races. In the United States, its connections to colonialism and imperialism are certainly visible across history, but those types of pejorative connections are frequently de-linked from larger considerations of whiteness as a race. Thus, critical whiteness becomes a supplement to a radical antiracist stance that seeks to decenter and color white privilege, but it also becomes a position that can critique other identity binaries and forms of oppression. For those with access to its yoke of privilege, when whiteness is not visible as a source of fear or insecurity, not associated with the legacy of slavery, and not evident or overt on a daily basis, it often becomes the silent back-drop that quietly defines progress and civilization from an Anglo-Saxon starting point perfected through the resources of white Christianity united with American exceptionalism and economic globalization. For example, the view that "white trash" is an aberration and that white nobility is the norm contributes to the sanitization, purification, and social authority of whiteness. The unconscious possession of whiteness as a currency reserved to a particular group has oppressive effects on Blacks, Latinos, and the entire race constellation. The white serial killer, the white atomic bomb, the white meth lab, the white tendency toward militarism and extermination are not visible as "white" and typically not associated with the (white) American majority. Despite the generalizations and the risks of essentialism, there is a context and a history here worth exploring.

Many practitioners of critical whiteness studies admit that such work will not solve racism, it will not reverse the effects of discrimination, and it will not eliminate the need to open spaces for marginalized voices. Racial utopia is not being promised, even if it were feasible. What critical whiteness does strive for, at its very best, is to help make the center visible. By advancing an argument of recognition and exposure, such critical thought can help to challenge the hegemony of the dominant class by emphasizing an unfixed perspective of the "everyday." A critique of white privilege can help to conceive of "white" as less than "in(di)vis-ible." In addition to the notions of nationality and European colonialism, another good example of how multisectionality can reinforce whiteness is in the area of gender and feminism. Anita Hill's challenge to the appointment of Supreme Court Justice Clarence Thomas is a case in point. What Michael Staub does in his analysis of the Hill–Thomas hearings is not to supplant the diverse narratives of Hill and Thomas, but to add a critique of the "shades" of gender and whiteness norms claimed by the senators conducting the questioning. Staub gestures to the multiplicities of how racism works:

> But in all this crucial attention to the complexities of African American lives, the issue of whiteness—and the particularities of the white senators' (mis)management of the hear-ings—has gone out of focus … I suggest that looking at how whiteness functioned in the Hill–Thomas hearings helps illuminate a number of broader developments, among them the tensions within contemporary American whiteness, the changing shape of

American racism, and the consolidation of a sophisticated and highly successful right-wing assault on both leftism and liberalism.[9]

Staub shows that an evaluation of whiteness can lend insight into specific instances of racial oppression and other identity hierarchies within the public sphere.[10] Race is indispensable to the formation of whiteness as a discourse, but other forms of identity and identification are also at play. The same is also the reality for Chicana women who live on the borderland between the United States and Mexico—race is indispensable, but so is being a woman and living on the border.

As whiteness becomes visible, so too do systems of patriarchy, capitalism, neocolonialism, and other structures—structures that reinforce a dichotomy of superiority and inferiority. Race, gender, class, sex, age, religion, physical and mental condition, nationality, and all the other components of identity are caught up in a complex process. Identity swirls through a cycle of centering and decentering, of marking and unmarking, and of including and excluding. Lisa Flores writes about the ways rhetoric contributes to life on *la frontera* for Chicanas, and she posits that making efforts to reclaim marginalized identities requires discursive struggles about what "centering" really means, how we treat difference, and the creation of a home through empowering argumentation. This is where multisectionality broadens into a very active call for contextualized equality—a radical equality that starts from the grassroots and argues in defense of a local standpoint: people living and interacting in a specific place.

> ... a discursive space can be opened through a rhetoric of difference which allows a marginalized group to reverse existing and external definitions and to create their own definitions. The creation of one's identity which relies upon the material conditions of the people is more likely to reflect the culture of the people, rather than the dominant culture of the empowered. Such a process is necessary for those groups who experience the decentering associated with a lack of space of their own, as it is a means through which the oppressed can move themselves from the periphery to their own center. For Chicana feminists, who carry the baggage of their border existence and who often find themselves straddling different cultures, creating a home is essential.[11]

Chicana feminists struggle against white privilege alongside many other groups, but the multidimensional reality and impact of what these women are confronting on a day-to-day basis is a more poignant argument about the need for argumentative shelter within one's own identity. If it is a matter of survival, the calculus of starting with one's own social location and building a home becomes all the more urgent. Even for identities that are excluded within a larger set of

---

9   Staub, Michael E. "The Whitest I: On Reading the Hill—Thomas Transcripts," *Whiteness: A Critical Reader*. Ed. Mike Hill. New York: NYU, 1997; p49.

10   When added to Clarence Thomas' "boot-straps" narrative, the whiteness of the legislative system can be seen as forming an alliance with the "antiracists" to suppress the voice of a woman. Yes, the woman, Anita Hill, is also black, but her gender became the emphasized trait. Her gender was the primary point of opposition because of the nature of the claim (sexual harassment) and because the senators and Clarence Thomas (the defendant/s) were all male. These hearings demonstrate the interlocking systems of dominance that circulate around whiteness.

11   Lisa Flores (1996). "Creating Discursive Space through a Rhetoric of Difference: Chicana Feminists Craft a Homeland," *Quarterly Journal of Speech*, v82, n2, May, pp142–56; 142–3.

marginalized people, it is possible to create a discursive space of empowerment. The more groups begin to define themselves, the less they are defined by outside. This is exactly the way that arguments about identity can stave off the metadiscourses that would objectify and exclude those same identities.

Figure 7.5 Migrant Family Workers

> Chicana feminists and other marginalized groups who find that their politics put them at odds with their own culture are pushed to the margins of the margin. The creation of discursive space means that the margins are transformed into the center of a new society, and the disempowered find power. Within the writings of Chicana feminists, we find the processual move from carving one's space, to creating a homeland, and finally to establishing bonds with others, and in this process, the move from other-defined to self-defined is illustrated … As we become aware of the different ways in which women use the resources available to them to construct their identity, we can continue to build feminist theory that opens space and provides voice for women.[12]

Multisectionality encourages this kind of resistance through articulation, a purposeful assertion of one's identity in an active refusal of stereotypes of rigid hierarchies. Argumentation as a way to implement criticism of white privilege helps accomplish these discursive carvings. As Nakayama & Krizek insist, the aim is to "position the discursive space of 'white'" and recognize that whiteness manages to remain relatively unarticulated while it wields so much influence: "It affects the everyday fabric of our lives but resists, sometimes violently, any extensive characterization that would allow for a mapping of its contours."[13]

A Return to Critical Thought

Race and the example of white privilege show how all-encompassing the process of identification really is. Many scholars find it so significant that they describe it as "interpellation" in an attempt to really capture the spirit of what happens at the moment identity is argued. Chris Sinha, for example, focuses on the *appeal* at the root of interpellation. The Latin *appellare* means "to call upon," but it also has connotations of "assigning, designating, or naming." Likewise, the French *pellere* speaks to a drive or a pulse, associating "appellant" with verbs such as "accost, address, appeal to, or impeach."[14] In a linear framework, the appeal would occur *after* the address and

---

12   Flores (1996), p.143.
13   Nakayama & Krizek, 1995, p. 291. They seek to deploy "a nominalist rhetoric; that is, by naming whiteness, we displace its centrality and reveal its invisible position" (Nakayama & Krizek, 1995, p. 292).
14   Onions, C.T. (1966). "Appeal," in *Oxford Dictionary of English Etymology*. New York: Oxford Press; p44.

before the "naming" and the "name." This linearity (the address, moving to the appeal, moving to the naming, moving to the name ...) only begins to touch the complexity of interpellation theory.

> (S)teps in argumentation can and should be seen, not merely as steps in 'problem solving', but also (and at the same time) as strategic performative—appellative acts which can be conceived as tactical maneuvers in an overall discursive 'war of position'. A crucial function of (pre-supposed) norms in argumentation, in this interpretation, lies in mapping the terrain of this conflict and employing it to the speaker's advantage. The speaker's advantage is secured, not so much through frontal attacks on the positions of the adversary, as by means of subtle enticements, seductions, and invitations to entrapment. [15]

This speech–act theory may be too centered on persuasion and therefore risks ignoring the "imaginary" and its ideological materialism. In short, a speaker and an audience are both isolated prior to the workings of interpellation in this work.

As support in our discussion of race, Sinha stresses "the importance of 'appeal' in argumentative discourse," but he still conceives of the audience as a microcosm of a larger community, leading to an overemphasis on the ways ideological persuasion acts as "a discursive form which seeks to secure the consent of an audience to a proposition."[16] Sinha may claim that he avoids "speaker-centered" critiques because the argument is supplied by the audience, not by the speaker, but the self and the Other are still distinct, floating in a magical ether awaiting interpellation. As Raymond Williams adds, the processes of articulation and identification, as well as the concomitant roles of linkage and representation, must be considered as components within a:

> ... saturation of the whole process ... of lived identities and relationships.... It is a whole body of practices and expectations, over the whole of living: our senses and assignments of energy, our shaping perceptions of ourselves and our world. It is a lived system of meanings and values—constitutive and constituting—which as they are experienced as practices appear as reciprocally confirming.[17]

Certain groups at particular moments and in particular places will rely on representation to signify meaning, advancement, or empowerment. It is that turn to representation that hails to argumentation because a given identity has to be projected outward and occupied. Henry Louis Gates Jr. (1988) talks about the importance of such processes of "signifyin(g)" to the black community in America: "The employment of figurative rhetorical strategies that repeat and imitate elements of dominant culture ... enables blacks to respond indirectly to an exclusionary white culture."[18] Although movement within this representational sphere is materially restricted, such restrictions allow or necessitate local acts of resistance, moments of insubordination that mark a refusal of the dominant logics of representation.

---

15   Sinha, Chris (1989). "Appealing Rhetorics: Ideology and Argumentation," in R. Maier (ed.) *Norms in Argumentation.* Providence, RI: Foris Publications, pp179–195; 191.

16   Sinha (1989, p190; p179)

17   Williams, Raymond. 1977. Marxism and Literature. Oxford: Oxford University Press; p110.

18   Coombe, Rosemary. 1997. "The Demonic Place of the 'Not There': Trademark Rumors in the Postindustrial Imaginary." in *Culture, Power, Place: Explorations in Critical Anthropology.* (ed.) Gupta & Ferguson. Durham: Duke University. (pp 249–277); p263.

We could not conclude this chapter any better than by remembering the words of Edward Said in his "Afterward" to *Orientalism*:

Figure 7.6

The construction of identity—for identity, whether of Orient or Occident, France or Britain, while obviously a repository of distinct collective experiences, is finally a construction—involves establishing opposites and "others" whose actuality is always subject to the continuous interpretation and re-interpretation of their differences from "us." Each age and society re-creates its "Others." Far from a static thing then, identity of self or of "other" is a much worked-over historical, social, intellectual, and political process that takes place as a contest involving individuals and institutions in all societies. Debates today about "Frenchness" and "Englishness" in France and Britain respectively, or about Islam in countries such as Egypt and Pakistan, are part of that same interpretive process which involves the identities of different "others," whether they be outsiders and refugees, or apostates and infidels. It should be obvious in all cases that these processes are not mental exercises but urgent social contests involving such concrete political issues as immigration laws, the legislation of personal conduct, the constitution of orthodoxy, the legitimization of violence and/or insurrection, the character and content of education, and the direction of foreign policy, which very often has to do with the designation of official enemies. In short, the construction of identity is bound up with the disposition of power and powerlessness in each society, and is therefore anything but mere academic wool-gathering. What makes all these fluid and extraordinarily rich actualities difficult to accept is that most people resist the underlying notion: that human identity is not only not natural and stable, but constructed, and occasionally even invented out-right.[19]

Learning Activities: Chapter Seven

1. Define "race" in three different ways. Which is the best definition and why? Do the same thing with whiteness and identity.
2. How does geography determine the meanings of race? Research what race means in four different parts of the world and compare and contrast those regions. Do you have explanations for the differences?

---

19   Edward Said. (1995). Orientalism. London, Penguin Press, p.301.

3. Make the argument that race is a more important social indicator than another category and defend that position with three different examples. Now find three counterexamples. Which set of examples is more persuasive and why?

4. What does it mean to make arguments in favor of white privilege? How might those arguments play a role in society, and are there ways to counteract such effects?

5. 5Within the concept of "whiteness," how does nationality, religion, and ethnicity factor into the equation?

6. Research #BlackLivesMatter and report back to the group. What arguments are being made through this hashtag?

7. Identification occurs all the time—go through some examples of where you have identified with a certain characteristic or trait and explain them. What labels would you put on your own identity? Are there labels you would like to change, and how might you do that? Are there labels you cannot change? What does this say about the concept of "visibility"?

8. What aspects of race can be isolated and to what degree? Start with language and culture.

9. Provide a contemporary history of whiteness in the United States in terms of the growth of the prison industrial complex or another state structure. What are the key arguments you need to make?

10. Why is is a "distraction strategy" to talk about events like the shooting in Charleston as a gun control issue before emphasizing the racial dimensions?

Figure Credits

CHAPTER 8

Argumentation, Social Movements, and the Public Sphere

It is time to broaden our scope and re-assess the ground we have covered. We have attempted to provide you with a very solid foundation in Argumentation as a platform for some deeper and more complicated questions surrounding critical theory, advocacy, advanced reasoning, debate, and subjectivity. We will try to merge these various strands of thought and practical guidelines into a conclusion about "social movements," a concept that will bring a lot of this work together. The "social" is not as important as the idea of a communicating community or a governing structure that unifies groups of people living in the same nation. Likewise, the "movement" is not as important as the concept of "political change," both in theory and in reality—the ways in which norms and policies come together to define a people and an era. Thus, in many ways, the notion of "social movement" is one of the best ways to describe how arguments work and why.

Social Movements

In the introductory Chapter, we relied on the examples of Zack Kopplin and his political battles against the Louisiana Science Education Act as well as the rise of the Tea Party. Both of those examples, even though you may not have realized it at the time, provide a perfect set-up for this chapter on social movements and the last section of the book. Why? Because they represent the power of social movements to make change through argumentation. It is argument that gives social movements the currency to stand up against powerful interests and make a difference. The political effects of a given movement may be conservation or liberal, reactionary or progressive, cautious or reckless, but they always operate and grow through the deployment of various arguments. Indeed, we will contend in this chapter that social movements are built on arguments, and respond to, as well as generate, arguments as a primary mechanism for change.

The Tea Party has added a set of arguments to the social sphere that has "changed the debate," so to speak, but they also began to fall flat on questions of credibility and compassion. If we think of the "fiscal restraint" position as the *logos* of the Tea Party, than the strength of that content has slowly faded away as the Tea Party's perceived sympathy for everyday Americans has been exposed as shallow. Through arguments about *ethos*, the legitimacy and credibility of the Tea Party's backers have fallen apart; arguments have highlighted their support for corporate influence, which has prevailed over the democratic principles they claim to uphold. This left the Tea Party without *ethos* and *pathos*, opening the door to a response in the form of Occupy Wall Street (#Occupy). The story of these two movements in the context of argumentation will lead us to a better understanding of social movements and how argumentation contributes to social change.

It becomes more and more difficult to assess the strength of a particular social movement outside the currency such a movement gains (or steals) from the media. The embedded nature of a number of recent social movements raises the question of how opposed to the system they really are, whether on the right or the left. To pursue this fruitful link between rhetoric and social movements it makes sense to continue our comparison of two of the more recent movements representing two wildly divergent groups in this country: the Tea Party and the Occupy movement. What would the Tea Party have been without Fox News? What would the Occupy Wall Street movement (#Occupy) have been without twitter and other forms of social media? Then again, how influential were these movements and how did they go about effectuating change? Most importantly, what do they tell us about argumentation? It may make more sense to talk about them as social arguments rather than movements. As critics of rhetoric and scholars of communication, we ask whether there are threshold moments in particular movements that allow those movements to go beyond outsider status in the media and express their own arrival, effectively propelling the social.

More specifically, what does it mean when these movements must announce their own importance from the very megaphones they denounce? Does our conclusion boil down to a version of McLuhan's "the medium is the message?" Because both the Tea Party and the Occupy Wall Street movements ostensibly challenged corporate media, even if from different angles, can we learn from the changes created when social movements "cross the aisle" and proclaim their own importance? Ushered in by the fiscal tug-of-war over bailouts and the proper level of austerity, this debate became a heated sounding board for the extremes on both sides of the political spectrum, a culminating location of controversy that generated policy platforms as well as political subjectivities. The pendulum for these movements swings back and forth, and we can see each reflected in contemporary manifestations of political ideology—the Tea Party still influences the Republican Party and #OWS-pushing politicians like Bernie Sanders and the liberal wing of the Democratic Party.

The Mad Hatter? Revisiting the Tea Party

In the 2010 midterm elections, the Republicans won their largest majority in 62 years—242–192, in substantial part thanks to the Tea Party provoking a significant enthusiasm gap. The make-up of the new House consisted, in part, of politicians such as Allen West (R-FL), who wrapped themselves in the Tea Party and took reckless positions on issues such as the increase in the debt ceiling, effectively toying with a U.S. default on its debts and contributing directly to a downgrading of the U.S. credit rating. The new Republican majority made John Boehner the Speaker of House, changing the debate in Washington, D.C. by obstructing all legislation proposed by the White House and creating a disturbance aligned against progressive reform. We will see how 2014 reinforces these earlier tendencies given Republican control of the Senate alongside the

House. Speaker Boehner himself characterized the 2010 moment: "We've changed the debate here ... We're not talking about spending more money."[1] Current Speaker Paul Ryan may continue the obstructionist trend, although enough bipartisanship emerged to pass a budget. The bottom line here is that social movements and political ideologies rub each other's backs in mutually reinforcing ways. The fluid between these groups is essentially a set of arguments.

On the other hand, while playing a significant role in electoral politics, particularly in the 2010 midterm elections, the Tea Party movement cannot be reduced to an extended arm of the Republican Party.[2] The cultural origin of the fervent sentiments expressed in many Tea Party rallies is a "sweeping cultural anxiety in predominantly white, middle-class sectors of the nation about social change ... the gradual march of America moving toward a non-white majority so abruptly punctuated for many by the sudden arrival of a non-white president in 2008."[3] Obama seemed to be the primary focus of this social disturbance that had emerged in response to his election. A July Gallup Poll found that:

> ... nothing energized them more than their discomfort with Barack Obama, which for many morphed into the notion that he is fundamentally un-American. The numbers back up what I heard at places like the Knob Creek Machine Gun Shoot. Today, for example, 52 percent of all Republicans believe that Obama definitely or probably "sympathizes with the goals of Islamic fundamentalists who want to impose Islamic law around the world."[4]

There is a race element to the Tea Party's ideology, a piece of the puzzle that cannot be ignored and an aspect that turns the country toward an even more polarizing conversation. In other words, the debate began to shift based on a degree of "baiting" and a dangerously nostalgic notion of what "America" should be in the first place. The University of Washington's Matt Barreto found that, "The data tells us this opposition and frustration with government is going hand in hand with a frustration and opposition to racial and ethnic minorities and gays and lesbians."[5] As a result, when we talk about the Tea Party changing society, it is not just an emphasis on a bloated government and overspending, it is also a conservative reaction to political advances by non-white groups and the perception of "too much" difference and multiculturalism in society. The members of the Tea Party were feeling alienated, and they were going to act in kind. It is not a big step to connect many of these sentiments to the 2016 "Make America Great Again" campaign and Trump's insistence on stoking fears of terrorism, immigrants, and minorities as a whole.

---

[1] Lightman, D. (2011, November 4). Boehner: 'We've changed the debate.' *McClatchy Newspapers*. Retrieved from http://www.dispatch.com/content/stories/national_world/2011/11/04/boehner-weve-changed-the-debate.html

[2] Drum, K. (September/October, 2010). Tea Party: Old whine in new bottles, *Mother Jones*. Retrieved from http://www.motherjones.com/politics/2010/08/history-of-the-tea-party?page=3

[3] Bunch, W. & Schoen, D. (2010, September 12). The Tea Party's true power. *The Daily Beast*. Retrieved from http://www.thedailybeast.com/articles/2010/09/13/tea-partys-true-power-will-bunch-and-douglas-schoen-debate.html

[4] Berman, R. (2010, July 5). Gallup: Tea Party's top concerns are debt, size of government. *The Hill*. Retrieved from http://thehill.com/blogs/blog-briefing-room/news/107193-gallup-tea-partys-top-concerns-are-debt-size-of-government

[5] Garber, A. (2010, June 1). Tea Party views toward minorities. *The Seattle Times*. Retrieved from http://seattletimes.com/html/politicsnorthwest/2012005031_new_poll_looks_at_tea_party_vi.html

Figure 8.1

The roots of the Tea Party's passion should not be described as unique or new. Instead, this movement has tapped deeply into the powerful strain of middle-class cultural conservatism that has been a force in America since the 1960s, the psychic place that historian Rick Perlstein has labeled "Nixonland." For example, Tea Party advocate Glenn Beck has attempted to "reclaim the civil rights movement," although reclaiming might be a generous way to describe a destructive whitening and abandonment of decades of social progress. The image of the Tea Party movement as a spontaneous rescue of American values featured a conspicuously missing element from these snapshots of an ostensibly grassroots and populist uprising: Tea Party moves to "save society" were simply signs of a positive return on investment by the three major funders, Rupert Murdoch and Charles and David Koch.

In short, the Tea Party movement did not represent a spontaneous outpouring of public sentiment. The movement has been exposed as simply AstroTurf, complete with fake grass (roots) events, manufactured by the usual suspects. Indeed, a key role was being played by Freedom Works, the organization run by Richard Armey, the former House majority leader, and supported by the usual group of right-wing billionaires. And Tea Party events were, of course, being promoted heavily by Fox News.[6] The peak of this movement has waned, it seems, but the effects were pronounced and the landscape has been altered. It is from here we turn to the counter-counter response that took place: Occupy Wall Street.

Serving Tea to Occupy the Harbor

The Occupy Wall Street protests have often been framed as a reaction to the rise of the Tea Party.[7] As such, the Tea Party "rallies" framed a set of questions and proffered their answer to what a national debate over government economic policy ought to be asking and answering. The Occupy Wall Street protests responded to this argument by addressing the inequality of the overall framing. Nobel laureate and *New York Times* columnist Paul Krugman invested hope in the Occupy Wall Street movement to not just respond to the Tea Party's position on austerity, but

---

[6] Krugman, P. (2011, October, 21). Trying to Unwarp the Debate. *The Conscience of a Liberal*. Retrieved from http://krugman.blogs.nytimes.com/2011/10/21/trying-to-unwarp-the-debate/

[7] Acosta, J. (2011, October 6). Occupy Wall Street: The Tea Party of the left? *CNN*. Retrieved from http://articles.cnn.com/2011-10-06/politics/tea.party.left_1_tea-party-express-chairman-amy-kremer-political-movement?_s=PM:POLITICS

Shaw, J. (2011, October 26). Occupy Wall Street Is No Tea Party. The Heritage Foundation. Retrieved from blog.heritage.org/2011/10/26/occupy-wall-street-is-no-tea-party/

to, "Unwarp it."[8] Before the emergence of the Occupy Wall Street protests, the public discussion over economic policy had been dominated by a group Ari Berman termed the "austerity class" of economic watchdogs.[9] This referred to an "an allegedly centrist coalition of politicians, wonks and pundits who are considered indisputably wise custodians of U.S. economic policy." Through various forms of pressure and support from the conservative media, this group successfully defined the parameters of responsible economic policy by pushing their message through congressional hearings and sympathetic journalists, even if their sense of austerity was not aligned with public opinion or reputable public policy research. Having effectively sidelined dissident Keynesian voices from the public debate about economic policy, the austerity class achieved what UC Berkeley economist J. Bradford DeLong termed an "intellectual hegemony over the course of the debate in Washington, from 2009 until today."[10] One influential group armed with a particular social vision and an argument to achieve it, can exert enormous influence even when the policies are antithetical to the public good.

This monopoly on defining the public economic argument explains the mystery of how "in the midst of a massive unemployment crisis—when it's painfully obvious that not enough jobs are being created and the public overwhelmingly wants policy-makers to focus on creating them—the deficit emerge[d] as the most pressing issue in the country."[11] In an interview with Keith Olbermann on *Current TV,* Krugman described the pre-Occupy Wall Street national economic debate:

> ... before this started, we were basically having an insane national discussion. Here we were with 14 million people unemployed, and with the government able to borrow at the lowest interest rates in history and with enormous increase in inequality ... And yet—what were we talking about? Deficits, austerity ... doing something for the vast majority of Americans was completely ruled out of the discussion.[12]

The national economic debate was held hostage by the austerity class, who profited greatly from status quo policies. It is into this captive debate that Occupy Wall Street intervened and changed the conversation by shifting focus and priorities. Contrasting the influence of the Occupy movement with his own limits as a public intellectual, Krugman worked hard to hail the impact of Occupy Wall Street and show how the group began to influence our sense of justice:

> I tried to write about it, other people have tried to write about—but somehow, that was not making a dent in the conversation. And then a group of people started camping out in Zuccotti Park, and all of a sudden the conversation has changed significantly towards being about the right things. It's kind of a miracle.[13]

---

[8] Paul Krugman (October 21, 2011).

[9] Berman, A. (2011, November 7). How the austerity class rules Washington. *The Nation.* Retrieved from http://www. thenation.com/article/164073/how-austerity-class-rules-washington#axzz2WbXfQJBM

[10] A. Berman (2011).

[11] A. Berman (2011).

[12] Olbermann, K. (2011, October 21). Interview with Paul Krugman. Complete transcript of the October 21, 2011, edition of 'Countdown with Keith Olbermann.' *Current TV.* Retrieved from http://www.countdownlibrary.com/2011_10_21_archive.html

[13] Olbermann (2011).

Figure 8.2 The Rise of the 99%

The actual shock here is thus a reversal back to the "real" issues, away from the interest of the rentier class back to the 99%, away from pseudo-wonks warning of the dangers of debts and deficits back to credible economic researchers who unsuccessfully tried to steer the conversation back to the massive unemployment rate and persistent inequality. Rhetorically what we are most interested in observing is how #OWS has posited a much needed argumentative corrective. This is argumentation, critical theory, and advanced reasoning all emerging in the advocacy of the Occupy movement, in that they raised the issue of unfair wealth distribution to the level of national and international consciousness by arguing, "Enough!" We want to observe that move as a way to defend a sense of argumentation as empowerment and active citizenship.

Occupy the Debate

Debate is at least academically understood as "fundamentally cooperative rather than competitive" because it is "primarily a method for collective decision making."[14] However, the way debate is typically framed in the context of a national conversation about politics is to deploy the term as a rhetorical trope emphasizing competing frames. Ultimately debate is about the implementation of argumentation as well as the process by which we can test and determine everything from logic to identity. Competition is important, and delineating two sides (the right and the left) becomes significant for the competition itself, almost a pre-requisite to the turn taking of constructives and rebuttals in a formal debate. Gordon Mitchell and Joe Bellon go back and forth on the merits of a competitive focus within the pedagogy of debate, but the question of using "role-play"[15] vs. structural policy debate[16] in the classroom is a different one than the war of words that surrounded the Tea Party and still surrounds the remnants of the Occupy Movement. For these social movements, debate is a competition between rival ideologies that have distinct visions for the role of the government and the ideal shape of the American polity. Compared to an academic debate or a collegiate forensic event where the same question of public policy can be illuminated from many

[14] Zarefsky, D. (2001). Debate. In Thomas O. Sloane (Ed.), Encyclopedia of rhetoric (pp. 191–197). Oxford: Oxford University Press; pp. 193–4.

[15] Mitchell, G. (2000, Winter). Simulated Public Argument as a Pedagogical Play on Worlds. *Argumentation and Advocacy* 36, 134–150.

[16] Bellon, Joe (2000). A Research-Based Justification for Debate Across the Curriculum. *Argumentation and Advocacy* 36 (2000), 161–175.

different angles, effectively fostering deliberation, the news cycle itself can only reward one topic as the lead story, one primary economic indicator as the most important statistic.

For both the Tea Party and the Occupy Wall Street movement, then, advocating their "argument" refers to a shift in the topics and criteria for evaluating the debate. The Tea Party-dominated Congress defined the debate by discussing and legislating spending cuts as opposed to funding government programs or alleviating unemployment. Occupy Wall Street and its supporters defined the debate by "unwarping it," which is to say that they shifted the topic from balanced budgets and deficits to the unemployment rate that depressed the economy and left tens of millions of Americans without a paycheck.

As a result, we see a national debate over the topic of the debate itself: Are we focused on distributing wealth to those in poverty or are we focused on reducing the size of government? These are significant questions. Moreover, these paths compete and find currency in a number of issues that will continue to see more of the light of day as the election cycle continues. In some ways the election mirrored the issues raised by the Tea Party and Occupy Wall Street, but in other ways there is a much deeper dynamic falling in place after the novelty and response to Septempber 11 in the form of the Global War on Terror. Now we have a Global War on globalization itself, with a massive conflict between the rich and poor—the 1% and the 99%—taking shape. Occupy has touched off—or tapped into—another response to the Tea Party movement that asks about the proper intersection between social policy, economics, and the responsibilities and obligations of government. This is where the communicative force of social movements just may offer an alternative to a future controlled by corporate power and the exploitation of global labor. This sentiment did not start with Bernie Sanders.

> Yet it was the Occupy movement—initiated by a handful in a small park near Wall Street—that captured mainstream media with its message of "We are the 99%." The movement has now successfully defended people's homes against eviction, marched and rallied in defense of city services, called for the cancellation of a trillion dollars' worth of student debt and supported workers' struggles ranging from the locked-out Sotheby workers in New York City to the Longview struggle. To be sure, there have been tensions in the alliances that formed between Occupiers and the unions, and of course the resistance itself is uneven. Anti-immigrant, anti-women's reproductive rights and anti-union legislation such as Indiana's right-to-work-for-less bill continue to be passed. Politicians continue to rant against the rights and dignity of poor people, working people, gays and lesbians, immigrants and women. Employers continue their aggressive tactics, including locking out workers. Unions have continued to sell the need for concessions to their members, and members have reluctantly gone along. Resistance has not stopped the attack. Yet the new-found energy is amazing. We are beginning to fight and realize that turning around a country based on inequality and injustice is not an easy task. It's too easy to believe we aren't having much of an impact. Two months before the scheduled G8 meeting in Chicago, President Obama announced the meeting would be transferred to Camp David.[17]

---

[17] Aaron, M., Davis, W., Feeley, D., Finkel, D. & Wainer, K. (2012, May). The Politics of Austerity, Occupy and the 2012 Elections. *Solidarity*. Retrieved from http://www.washingtonpost.com/wp-dyn/content/article/2010/09/12/AR2010091201425.html

Occupy Wall Street and the Tea Party cannot be understood outside of their mediation as "most, and the most important discussions, take place via "screens."[18] The protests are public events intended for mediation on public screens, demonstrating their support visually through massive crowds on the Washington Mall or in Zuccotti Park, mediated through television. In contemporary American media, MSNBC and Fox News are two 24-hour cable news channels particularly drawn to political narratives favoring the two major political parties. It should thus not surprise us that Fox News effectively promoted Tea Party rallies by providing free advertisement space on their news shows in addition to their very favorable coverage. Writing on television, DeLuca and Peeples describe the current cable news environment as a medium that "places a premium on images over words, emotions over rationality, speed over reflection, distraction over deliberation, slogans over arguments."[19]

With regard to the initial Occupy Wall Street protests, *The New York Times*, along with every other North American news publication save the *Toronto Star* and a Manhattan free newspaper, chose not to report on the protests.[20] Paul Krugman, in his NYT column, opined that credit ought to go to the protesters for making the protests "too big to ignore."[21] Only after 700 protesters were arrested on the Brooklyn Bridge was media attention directed toward the protest movement.[22] As the movement gained mass media and social media attention, protests spread virally across major American cities, giving the movement momentum to legitimately claim to have influenced the debate.

Since the Tea Party protests received institutional support from the beginning of the movement, as well as favorable news coverage from the biggest cable news network (Fox News), it is difficult to assess how the movement would have fared had it not been given immediate legitimacy. From 2009 until the midterm elections the Tea Party movement governed the political calculus in Republican primary debates by rewarding ever more radical policies while rejecting establishment Republicans, for instance electing Christine O'Donnell over former Governor Michael Castle for the Republican candidate for Senate in Maryland. For both movements, reporting on them as significant becomes a self-fulfilling prophecy as the movements achieve the currency they seek—either in primary elections or on the shape of the national debate on economic policy— through their validation on news channels and social media. Social movements and mass media then cooperatively conceptualize a national debate as a political calculus based on an attention economy. In a cable news age sharply divided along partisan lines, we witnessed directly opposed social movements that competed for political viability through their ability to define public screens. What does all this mean in terms of argumentation? It is series of case studies showing how the very operation of society in the broadest of terms is a relationship between competing arguments.

---

[18] DeLuca, K. & Peeples, J. (2002). From public sphere to public screen: Democracy, activism, and the "violence" of Seattle. *Critical Studies in Mass Communication, 19*, 125–51; p. 131.

[19] Deluca and Peeples (2002, p. 133).

[20] Olbermann (2011).

[21] Krugman (2011).

[22] Sledge, M. (2011, October 2). Occupy Wall Street protesters remain defiant after Brooklyn Bridge arrests. *The Huffington Post*. Retrieved from http://www.huffingtonpost.com/2011/10/02/occupy-wall-street-protest-arrests_n_991423.html

Concluding Toward the Public Sphere

The ways these movements—whether the Tea Party or Occupy Wall Street—used arguments to advance their agendas is the same way the individual asserts identity through argumentation that "serves" the self. Backing up even further, the building blocks of these more sophisticated clusters of arguments are found within the terminology of formal debate and the theories postulated by Stephen Toulmin. We can then take those building blocks and go full circle into history by assessing the views the Greeks propagated regarding education, citizenship, and the Roman-inspired notion of "a good person speaking well." This meta-sense of argumentation is the genesis and maturation of thought and advocacy on a macro and micro level.

Go back to some of our triads. An argument requires a claim, grounds, and reasoning (i.e., a warrant). A good argument needs to tie those three components to effective communication as a speaker, to the audience, and through the message, affectionately known as *ethos*, *pathos*, and *logos*. Does your argument surface with credibility, does it contain compassion, and is its content sound?

DATA/EVIDENCE = Logos <Content> "The Matter"

CLAIM/THESIS = Ethos <Credibility> "The Source/Speaker/Author"

WARRANT/REASONING = Pathos <Compassion> "Connection to the Audience"

If those triads can be answered, we look to contextualize these arguments by creating a case that demonstrates facts, values, and policies. The nature of argumentation, alongside the practical questions involving how to create the platform for arguments and how to generate arguments for or against a given proposition, is simply a swarming array of suggestions and advice on how argumentation works—but such predictions can only go so far. We have to travel deeper into the self, subjectivity, and service before we can take the conception of an individual arguing herself into being in the same way that a change in society or a social movement might argue itself into being. That dumps us off in a giant field of argumentation and a feeling of being both in a war zone and a natural garden at the same time—with only our capacity for critical deliberation to determine which is which. In other words, can we say a few things about argumentation and "the public" before it is all said and done?

The big question we have arrived at is essentially the one we encountered in Chapter Five when discussing the relationship between argumentation and the self. As one serves the self in various models (military, national, religious, etc.), one argues a certain subjectivity. In more direct terms, arguments create selfhood. We know, however, that arguments do a lot more than reflect back on the self. Many arguments operate on a much larger level and are advancing policy for an entire nation or large collection of people. That is the relationship we have returned to in the conclusion of the book: How does argumentation connect to the public sphere and what responsibilities does each have for the other?

Habermas and the Public Sphere

Alongside Foucault, this is also a figure you will encounter in future interactions you have with argumentation and debate: Jürgen Habermas. Habermas was born in Germany and heavily influenced by a group of Philosophers (The Frankfurt School) who were grappling with some of the deeper questions surrounding fascism and the struggle over democracy in most modern nations. We approach Habermas with a particular concern for argumentation; he interests us because of how careful and optimistic he is with words like argument, discussion, debate, deliberation, communication, and dialogue. Most of his work about how the public can nurture a more robust democracy emphasizes these same words and concepts that are very much descriptive of the field of argumentation. This is no more evident than in the connection between argumentation and the public sphere, more specifically between "rational-critical debate" and the *Structural Transformation of the Public Sphere*.[23] In section 18, Habermas makes a pivotal distinction between a "Culture-Debating" and a "Culture-Consuming Public." We hope to analyze this separation between argumentation and consumption at the center of Habermas's work on the public sphere because this will help us to center the question of agency in arguments. Are we simply passive obedient clones of the system when we adhere to certain arguments, or is argumentation itself an alternative to a consumptive and complacent existence?

If we can demonstrate—even partially—that argumentation can be the way out of an overly pre-determined reality full of uncritical consumerism and general disengagement, then this book will have been worth its weight in gold. You are realizing that argumentation is the best tool for effective and meaningful social change. The key to participating in the world instead of letting the world construct who you are, is to engage in the practice of argumentation. Indeed, argumentation may be a method in and of itself in that it encourages an active and questioning perspective rooted in a specific position's deployment of *ethos*, *pathos*, and *logos* to build

Figure 8.3 Habermas in Munich, 2007

a claim, surround it with evidence, and establish the links between the two. Can argumentation reclaim the public sphere as a solution to an alienated and uninterested citizenship? Let us take a quick look at Habermas's public sphere project, particularly his history of structural and institutional change within society. From there we can conclude with the Habermasian notion of argumentation, or what he calls a "rational-critical debate of private people in the salons, clubs, and reading societies."[24]

Contextualizing the Public Sphere Project

Sometimes you just have to dive into an important book. Habermas's *Structural Transformation of the Public Sphere* (*STPS*) (1962) is just such a book. What is Habermas describing in *STPS*? Is this transformation appropriately explained through a historical method that traces social structures?

---

[23] Habermas, J. (1989). *The Structural Transformation of the Public Sphere: An Inquiry into a Category of Bourgeois Society*. Trans. T. Burger. Cambridge, Mass: MIT Press (Original work published 1962), p. 170. Hereafter *STPS*.
[24] Habermas (*STPS*), p. 160.

Written in 1962, its scope begins during feudalism in Europe and extends over five hundred years into the mid-1900s. Habermas studied under Adorno and Horkheimer of the Frankfurt School, who instilled in him a suspicion of mass media, the culture industries, and state-sponsored nationalism. What we would like to borrow from Habermas, however, is the way he holds on to an enlightened "kernel of hope" as he isolates a brief period in history where citizens were able to freely express their opinions as human beings. This is not to say that communication is the solution to violence—often it is the prelude—but it is to say that human progress and government has to rely on a vigorous form of accepted argumentation—the justifications for power—whether authoritarian or democratic in nature. We need to pay attention to the fact that many private people, according to Habermas, constitute themselves as a public sphere through rational and democratic deliberation unrestricted by the state. For Habermas, we must continue to strive toward this model of universal democracy built on communicative action—a free and open marketplace of discussion (opinion).

In more specific terms, Habermas shows how the principles and procedures of the bourgeois established themselves in the private realm. As that private system of exchange developed self-awareness it transformed into a critically engaged public. This public did not offer space for women or other disenfranchised groups, a major problem that we address, but it did contain the seeds of a universally accessible public sphere. Habermas elaborates:

> The public sphere in the world of letters was replaced by the pseudo-public or sham-private world of culture consumption. At that time, when private people were conscious of their double role as *bourgeois* and *homme* and simultaneously asserted the essential identity of property owner with "human being," they owed this self-image to the fact that a public sphere evolved from the very heart of the private sphere itself. Although, in regard to its function, it was only preliminary to a public sphere in the political realm, nevertheless this public sphere in the world of letters itself already had the kind of "political" character by virtue of which it was removed from the sphere of social reproduction. Bourgeois culture was not mere ideology. The rational-critical debate of private people in the salons, clubs, and reading societies was not directly subject to the cycle of production and consumption, that is, to the dictates of life's necessities. Even in its merely literary form (or self-elucidation of the novel experiences of subjectivity) it possessed instead a "political character in the Greek sense of being emancipated from the constraints of survival requirements. It was for these reasons alone the idea that later degenerated into mere ideology (namely: humanity) could develop at all.[25]

This passage is too critical to leave floating in the text. The sleight of hand that Habermas describes throughout *STPS*, as well as his general theme of the refeudalization of the public sphere, are both evident in the above paragraph. Habermas states that the evolution of the "public" through the world of letters was replaced by "culture consumption." The replacement occurred in many ways across England, France, Germany, Russia, and the rest of Europe, with the general assumption that all of these nations began to formulate certain "rules" or customs that now govern the public terrain. These rules have their origins in some type of private setting, particularly the bourgeois

---

[25] Habermas (*STPS*), p. 160.

family. Habermas writes that this "public" made up of private individuals began to engage public authorities themselves "in a debate over the general rules governing relations in the basically privatized but publicly relevant sphere of commodity exchange and social labor."[26] Yes! Exactly! That is a mouthful, but it is worth chewing on because the flavor is absolutely terrific. Here's why: This is a description of how a public sphere and a private sphere clashed through various ideas—written and spoken arguments—in order to create a state that offered protection but also threatened the free and neutral exchange of opinions at the same time. In other words, the way the public has become the place where individuals interact with the government as well as the border of the private sphere is a story of the clash of argumentation. Politics relies on discourse. Political change occurs through the clash of arguments on the edge of the public and the private. This is the ultimate link between critical theory and distinct notions of the state.

Reinforcing all of this, Habermas argues that the public and the private will tend to blur together and encompass other institutions, but the notion of a "world of letters" does rest on a fairly rigid distinction between the two arenas. The public, at least in principle, initially dealt with opinions of people outside of the state. Moreover, the ability to express such an opinion in public had aspirations of being available to everyone. Habermas writes: "The public sphere of civil society stood or fell with the principle of universal access."[27] The public, though, did not thrive outside of institutional relations for long. Precisely because of the ideal of universal access, the newly constituted public had to turn toward the state for protection and legitimacy. These two poles—private individuals coming together to express and deliberate important social issues on equal footing with their peers, and institutions creating and obtaining legislative authority—find themselves in a constant and frenzied tug-of-war. This is precisely our point.

> *The building blocks of society—both the elements that make an individual unique and the threads the tie together the public and the private through the state—are the same building blocks at the heart of debate and argumentation: evidence, reasoning, and a theme.*

If you add in *ethos, pathos,* and *logos,* combine it with the canon of invention, arrangement, delivery, style, and memory, and then package the whole constellation of argument's tropes with the stock issues and the genres of argument coming out of formalized debate, you will be sitting on the most explanatory and important descriptions and taxonomies in human thought.

Let us follow this logic and see if Habermas might help us substantiate such a bold claim! Soon after Habermas introduces the "bourgeois idea of the law-based state," he elaborates on the tug-of-war between publicness and governing authority. This is where argumentation really comes to the surface. "Although construed as 'power,' legislation was supposed to be the result not of a political will, but of rational agreement."[28] A strong argument arises here that political will and rational agreement are indistinguishable.[29] Michael Kelly outlines the stakes of this

---

[26] Habermas (*STPS*), p. 27.
[27] Habermas (*STPS*), p. 85.
[28] Habermas (*STPS*), p. 82.
[29] Foucault, for example, understands power "by something other than the states of domination. The relationships of power have an extremely wide extension in human relations." Foucault, M. The Ethic of Care for the Self as a Practice of Freedom. In Bernauer & Rasmussen (Eds.), *The Final Foucault*. Cambridge, Massachusetts: MIT Press, 1991: p. 3.

critique in his book, *Critique and Power*: "To answer this question is to take a position on the ways in which power affects the presuppositions and consequences of the practice of critique." On the other hand, Habermas has made the significant observation that law-making and the "will of the people" operate against and alongside each other. From here, the sleight-of-hand that is essential to the transformation of the public sphere becomes evident. Following his quotation from section 18, Habermas proceeds to reiterate the dual roles of *bourgeois* and *homme*. More specifically, he is concerned about the conflation of bourgeois citizen" with human being (*homme*).

It is here, though, that argumentation and the notion of rational-critical debate assert themselves. The bourgeois elite were able to conceive of themselves as speaking for (or as) humanity as a whole because they were able to "tap into" the democratic potential of argumentation and communication. This sounds anti-democratic (which it was because only a limited number of people had access to this form of argumentation, but it opened a door to how a more democratic society might emerge). In a direct way, the salons and literary clubs were a doorway to democratic citizenship because they were the sites of debate. Like the marketplaces before them, these public settings linked the populace to governing authority through critical discussion. These locations of debate faded away, however, as the media and the liberal welfare state succeeding in co-opting the public sphere. The last section in STPS, "A Sociological Attempt at Clarification," places rational-critical debate at the center of the present-day controversy over consumption vs. democracy, disengagement vs. argumentation.[30] Habermas writes about the contemporary existence of official proclamations and certain publicist organs "that cultivate rational debate." The crisis, though, is that these sources of rational debate are presented to the public instead of generated by the public. Habermas contends: "Although these quasi-official opinions can be addressed to a wide public, they do not fulfill the requirements of a public process of rational-critical debate according to the liberal model." He continues: "The communicative network of a public made up of rationally debating private citizens has collapsed."[31] We have hope, however, partially through the messages of this textbook, that such a collapse is short-lived and can be rectified.

Outgrowing the Public Sphere: Debate in America

Given that we started the text with the examples of creationism in Louisiana being resisted by Zack Kopplin and Obama's Presidency being resisted by the Tea Party, it is only fitting that we would turn toward an example that extends the messages of the first chapter and speaks to the question being posed by Habermas: competitive debate. Can debate offer a better model for the public sphere? Can the study of argumentation re-center the practice of debate as essential to a more participatory and egalitarian democracy?

A multitude of similar questions naturally arise at the conclusion of *STPS*: Has the practice of rational-critical debate completely collapsed? Are there remnants of such practices? If so,

---

[30] Habermas includes two short sections in his concluding chapter on public opinion. Given earlier connections between opinion (doxa), rhetoric, and speaking (Isocrates), it is fitting that this last chapter characterizes public opinion as the site where the life world finds itself being colonized by the systems world. The citizens are no longer participating in or creating public opinion; rather, the populace consumes public opinion. Thus, "political consensus formation" is based on a public opinion that is essentially fiction (display and manipulation). Habermas (*STPS*), p. 247.

[31] Habermas (*STPS*), p. 247.

where are they most clearly manifest? Is the Habermasian framework sufficient for a careful consideration of argumentation's potential? And, finally, how does training come into the picture in relation to argumentation and citizenship? Written back in 1905 by Baker & Huntington, *Principles of Argumentation* revolves around the idea that "good argumentation rests ultimately on the ability to think for oneself."[32] That is a crucial statement for us and one that we could easily end the text repeating: "[G]ood argumentation rests ultimately on the ability to think for oneself." How can thinking critically be encouraged and improved? Argumentation and debate may have the answer. Remember, certain principles can assist in the practice of argumentation, a practice that does not differ substantially from collegiate debate in the U.S. and throughout the world. Collegiate debate today centers on research, style, critical analysis, and a number of other aspects of argumentation theory. This puts the theory of argumentation in the exact same conversations that were taking place concerning competitive debate and intercollegiate debate leagues. For example, Baker and Huntington worked through the nature of argumentation, analysis, evidence, brief-drawing, presentation, and debating in their book:

> On the other hand, in the ten years since the *Principles of Argumentation* appeared, it has become steadily clearer that the principles of analysis needed restating for greater ac-curacy and simplicity; that the difficult subject of evidence, especially refutation, should be given fuller treatment; that the material in the chapter on brief-drawing could be simplified and clarified by rearrangement and a different emphasis; that persuasion needed much more detailed exposition; and that, perhaps the most marked need of all, the importance of rhetoric in argumentation should be given insistent emphasis.[33]

Their work admits that persuasion (or "presentation") is critical to the "success" of an argu-ment, but they still insist on a clear demarcation between the substance of an argument and the way it is sold. The key for Baker and Huntington is that argumentation is not "contentiousness." Argument takes place with the assumption that "opinions can change."[34] Debate, which they label the "most rigid form of argumentation," is a discussion that progresses toward a conclusion and follows a pre-determined sequence of speeches. On the other hand, debate is also oral (spoken) for Baker and Huntington and thus highly governed by persuasion and the ability of a speech to "influence its audience."[35] All of this is consistent with the messages we have been emphasizing throughout the textbook: that argumentation is flexible and cannot be rigidly defined, that the way individuals and society enact change is partially through argumentation, and that the details of how arguments function are important for understanding how to create, defend, and adapt a given argument.

Returning to the Greeks: Argumentation Comes Full Circle

This view of debate—that it operates within argumentation theory and depends on an influence model of persuasion—gestures back to Gorgias and Isocrates. Through argumentation, debate

---

[32] Baker, G., & Huntington, H. (1905). *The Principles of Argumentation*. New York: Ginn; p. vi.
[33] Baker & Huntington (1905, p. vi).
[34] Baker & Huntington (1905, p. 2).
[35] Baker & Huntington (1905, p. 398).

locates itself in "rhetoric as art." For Huntington and Baker, debate is an art form that parallels refined painting or sculpting. "Severe training" is necessary, for oral argumentation "is a difficult art, to be mastered only through persistent, conscientious practice of its principles."[36] Isocrates says in his *Antidosis*: "From what is left, I would say that those who are wise are those who are able by opinion (*doxa*) to hit upon what is for the most part the best course of action."[37] For Isocrates, human knowledge is limited in that we can never know, with certainty, what is "right." Instead of pursuing the futile quest for "pure knowledge," it is better to negotiate life through eloquence and articulation. In other words, the ability to speak well becomes the "surest sign of sound understanding."[38] Some distinctions need to be reinforced here, though, between argumentation as a means to achieve truth and argumentation as a practice of subjectivity. Isocrates turns to "speaking well" because he believes that ideals are non-existent, or at least not attainable. For him, truth is contingent, leaving the maintenance of reason and meaning to "speech." In other words, Isocrates is trying to combine rhetoric, ethics, and political action into a practice of training that bridges the division between the public and the private.[39] This is argumentation!

Isocrates's defense of speech (speakers speaking well) helps us build on the public sphere logics supporting Habermas's theory of communication. The public sphere logic would not admit that all ideals are illusions. Habermas, for instance, sees universal hope in the public sphere as it existed prior to colonization by the welfare state and the consumption mode set in motion by capitalism and the media. Indeed, Habermas may reserve rhetoric to private life during the Middle Ages, but his nostalgia does not temper his optimism for communicative action in general. Moving away from the cynical roots of his Frankfurt School predecessors, he sees potential for successful democracy in the Enlightenment. He admits, obviously, that the Enlightenment carried the seeds of fascism, but he characterizes the downfall of reason as an effect of instrumental reasoning. Critical reasoning, by contrast, emphasizes a dynamic unity between the subject and the object, but it also strives to resurrect reason. Regardless of how accurate the distinction between instrumental reason and critical theory is, this is the way Habermas is able to hold on to the Enlightenment without embracing fascism. Interestingly, Laura Crowell published a book the year after *STPS* entitled *Discussion: Method of Democracy*.[40] One of her chapters is called "Organizing for an Enlightenment Discussion," and her goal is to set forth guidelines for discussion as a method of democracy. Her task is one severely needed in Habermas's early work, and her position on training shows just how difficult such theory can be. She draws a line between "problem-solving" discussion and "enlightenment" discussion, arguing that individuals must be able to isolate and overcome a problem before they will be ready for "exploratory" dialogue. This distinction may make training easier, but it fails to justify why solving problems (policy) is a different process than more "open" discussions. In other words, it is significant that Habermas omits his conception of how society should produce citizens capable of critical-rational debate.

---

[36] Baker & Huntington (1905, p. 422).
[37] Conley, T. (1990). *Rhetoric in the European Tradition*. Longman; p. 18.
[38] Conley (1990), p. 18.
[39] Conley (1990), p. 18.
[40] Crowell, L. (1963). *Discussion: Method of Democracy*. Chicago: Scott, Foresman & Co.; p. 155.

Argumentation as Critical Deliberation

So much weight is placed on the opposition between instrumental reason and critical deliberation that it is practically essential to mention how to encourage one and not the other. The goals of such training are varied and complex, making it clear that Habermas needs to unpack his phrase "rational-critical debate." The training notion appears throughout scholarship concerning argumentation and debate. A. Craig Baird devotes a portion of his work on argumentation theory to debate and pedagogy.[41] Baird answers the question "Why debate?" by outlining five aims:

> (Debate) aims chiefly to (1) educate you for active and responsible participation in democratic government, (2) assure you more efficiency in your occupation or profession, (3) strengthen your self-confidence and enable you to make more satisfactory social adjustments, (4) provide you with defenses against "bad" propaganda, and (5) widen your general influence in social movements.[42]

Other scholars follow the same vein.[43] Halbert Gulley writes: "discussion is one of the fundamental processes of decision-making in a democratic society."[44] William Behl tackles debate and discussion as methods of argument. He also strives for democracy through communication, contending that "the most common tools for expressing our ideas are discussion and debate."[45] Here again, however, terms demand clarification. Behl opts for a narrow definition of debate, distinguishing between formal and informal debates that involve "a controversy between two or more persons who are committed, by choice or assignment, to a given side of a proposition."[46] The pre-existence of the speakers, the audience, and the proposition are all problematic in a constitutive theory of rhetoric,[47] but Behl is at least specifying his terms and outlining a method for training. Whether debate refers to a formal match or informal dialogue, the process of preparing and practicing must enter the equation if argumentation is to assist in the production of an expressive citizenry.

From Here, We Go Where?
Roaming Forth Through Argumentation

Finally, the foray into argumentation in debate poses two problems for Habermas that we can borrow:

1. Given that rational-critical debate is crucial to the possibility of democratic freedom for everyone, debate itself needs to be placed on the map. Debate can occur formally, informally,

---

[41] Baird, A. C. (1950). *Argumentation, Discussion, and Debate.* New York: McGraw Hill.
[42] Baird (1950, p. 4).
[43] See: Shurter, E. (1917). *How to Debate.* New York: Harper; Winans, J., & Utterback, W. (1930). *Argumentation.* New York: Century Co.; and, Stone, A. & Garrison. S. (1916). *Essentials of Argument.* New York: Holt Co.
[44] Gulley, H. (1960). *Discussion, Conference, and Group Process.* New York: Holt-Dryden; p. v.
[45] Behl, W. (1953). *Discussion and Debate: An Introduction to Argument.* New York: Ronald Press; p. iii.
[46] Behl (1953, p. 241).
[47] Volumes could be written in this footnote alone. For now, let is suffice to say that constitutive rhetoric questions the stagnant and autonomous subject by conceiving of individuals as effects (constituted) by the knowledge/power of discourse.

in writing, or through speech. The effects of debate range from fascism to freedom. As practiced, it has the potential to transform violence into productive social change; or, on the other hand, it can draw in the emotions to such a degree that the "sting" of argument motivates oppression and suffering. Simply, debate and rational-critical discussion can follow competing trajectories. When the concept broadens to include discussion, dialogue, speech, language, communication or any other expression, the "kernel of hope" loses its meaning.

2. Bracketing the first issue of "what is debate?" Habermas faces another equally troubling problem. The second problem concerns three elements: training, expansion of the forum, and the inseparability of knowledge and power. We focused primarily on training and argumentation theory, but, together, these three elements critique Habermas's answer to the question: How can we progress or reform? If we assume that Habermas does inform us what form of rational-critical debate is desirable, we still do not know which structures or which methods of education provide the best path to that type of argumentation. There may not even be a "best" path. We also do not know how to promote equality in the forum, let alone universal access. Issues of access go beyond "identity politics" or group inclusion because they place doubt on the entire public sphere project. It might not be enough to include a women's (counter) public sphere like Nancy Fraser does or admit to a "plebian" public sphere like Habermas does thirty years later.[48] These counter-publics still privilege homogenous conceptions of identity and still privilege Habermas's vague notion of who gets to sit down at the argumentation table.

In sum, none of these solutions are perfect, and it would be troubling if they were. Making an argument, just like engaging in critical thought and reasoning through a proposition, is always messy, never complete, and often contradictory in parts. That is ok—we must be more content with the inevitability of uncertainty and contingency. What we can rely on in times of doubt or competing conceptions of the way society should be headed, is that argumentation is the key to advocacy, and if we are able to participate in argumentation with a sense of critical thought and concern for the community as well as the individuals that make up the community, we will find this often forgotten field of argumentation and debate to be the most important component of who we are and who we want to be.

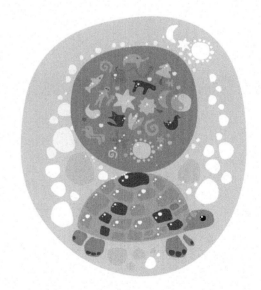

Figure 8.4 It's One Turtle on the Way Down

[48] Fraser, N. (1992). Rethinking the Public Sphere. In Calhoun (Ed.), *Habermas and the Public Sphere*. Cambridge: MIT; pp. 109–142. Also, Habermas, J. (1992). Further Reflections on the Public Sphere. In Calhoun (Ed.), *Habermas and the Public Sphere*. Cambridge: MIT.

Melissa Deem provides a critique of a feminist counterpublic by making the argument that "the public" may privilege male communication styles by labeling women as "complainers" or inherently embodied. Feminism itself is too diverse to tack it on to the project, let alone sex, race, religion, class, age, and the rest of the "counterpublics" that would have to fit into the bourgeois big tent.

Ultimately, that is why argumentation is at the core of critical thinking, the clash of reasons, and critical rhetoric. This text has traveled through the nature of argument, the study of argument, and the structure of argument as an initial path toward two different trajectories: the first a practical one through two chapters discussing how to research, build and negate a case; the second philosophical trajectory examined subjectivity in the context of argumentation and then revisited the public sphere as a way to understand argumentation. As all of these angles come together, you will find you have done far more than engage the field of argumentation—you have also started an in-depth exploration of critical thinking, debate, and the clash of reasoned decision-making.

Figure Credits